Laetitia,
   with best wishes
        Carol...

The autobiographical poems of Gregory of Nazianzus, fourth-century Father of the Greek Church, are remarkable not only for a highly individual picture of the Byzantine world but also for moments that are intimate, passionate and moving. This book contains Greek text and facing English translation of a selection from his one hundred or so surviving poems. Gregory is best known for the five orations he gave in Constantinople but, *De Vita Sua* apart, his poems can only be read in a nineteenth-century Greek edition and have never before been translated into English. The selected poems highlight Gregory's spiritual outlook and also his poetics; Gregory shows his expertise in a variety of metres and literary dialects, deriving from his knowledge of classical Greek literature. The substantial introduction provides biographical information against which to set the poems, focusing particularly on the years which Gregory spent in Constantinople.

**Cambridge Medieval Classics 6**

Gregory of Nazianzus, autobiographical poems

# Cambridge Medieval Classics

*General editor*
PETER DRONKE, FBA
*Professor of Medieval Latin Literature, University of Cambridge*

This series is designed to provide bilingual editions of medieval Latin and Greek works of prose, poetry, and drama dating from the period c. 350 – c. 1350. The original texts are offered on left-hand pages, with facing-page versions in lively modern English, newly translated for the series. There are introductions, and explanatory and textual notes.

The Cambridge Medieval Classics series allows access, often for the first time, to outstanding writing of the Middle Ages, with an emphasis on texts that are representative of key literary traditions and which offer penetrating insights into the culture of medieval Europe. Medieval politics, society, humour, and religion are all represented in the range of editions produced here. Students and scholars of the literature, thought, and history of the Middle Ages, as well as more general readers (including those with no knowledge of Latin or Greek) will be attracted by this unique opportunity to read vivid texts of wide interest from the years between the decline of the Roman empire and the rise of vernacular writing.

*Opening titles*

1. Nine Medieval Latin Plays, translated and edited by PETER DRONKE
2. Hugh Primas and the Archpoet, translated and edited by FLEUR ADCOCK
3. Johannes de Hauvilla, *Architrenius*, translated and edited by WINTHROP WETHERBEE
4. Dante, *Monarchia*, translated and edited by PRUDENCE JAMES
5. Dante, *De Vulgari Eloquentia*, translated and edited by STEVEN BOTTERILL
6. Gregory of Nazianzus, Autobiographical Poems, translated and edited by CAROLINNE WHITE

*Other titles in preparation*

Prodromic Poems, translated and edited by MARGARET ALEXIOU and MICHAEL HENDY
Adelard of Bath, *Quaestiones Naturales* and *De Eodem et Diverso*, translated and edited by CHARLES BURNETT
*Digenis Akritas*, translated and edited by ELIZABETH JEFFREYS
Nigel of Longchamp, *Speculum Stultorum*, translated and edited by JILL MANN
Dhuoda, *Liber Manualis*, translated and edited by MARCELLE THIÉBAUX
Peter Abelard, The Theological and Polemical Letters, translated and edited by JAN ZIOLKOWKSI

# Gregory of Nazianzus
## *Autobiographical poems*

TRANSLATED AND EDITED BY
### CAROLINNE WHITE
*University of Oxford*

Published by the Press Syndicate of the University of Cambridge
The Pitt Building, Trumpington Street, Cambridge CB2 1RP
40 West 20th Street, New York, NY 10011-4211, USA
10 Stamford Road, Oakleigh, Melbourne 3166, Australia

© Cambridge University Press 1996

First published 1996

Printed in Great Britain at the University Press, Cambridge

*A catalogue record for this book is available from the British Library*

*Library of Congress cataloguing in publication data*
Gregory, of Nazianzus, Saint.
[Poems. English and Greek. Selections]
Gregory of Nazianzus, autobiographical poems /
translated and edited by Carolinne White.
   p.   cm. – (Cambridge medieval classics: 6)
English and Greek.
ISBN 0 521 47281 4
1. Gregory, of Nazianzus, Saint – Translations into English.
2. Christian poetry, Greek – Translations into English.
3. Christian saints – Turkey – Biography – Poetry.
4. Gregory, of Nazianzus, Saint – Poetry.
5. Authors, Greek – Biography– Poetry.
6. Christian biography – Poetry.
7. Autobiography – Poetry.
I. White, Carolinne.  II. Title.  III. Series.
PA3998.G73A28  1996
881'.01–dc20  96–7338  CIP

ISBN 0 521 47281 4 hardback

# Contents

| | |
|---|---|
| *Abbreviations and bibliographical note* | *page* viii |
| *Introduction* | xi |
| **The poems** | |
| To his own verses (II 1.39) | 1 |
| Concerning his own life (II 1.11) | 11 |
| Complaint concerning his own calamities (II 1.19) | 155 |
| On silence at the time of fasting (II 1.34) | 165 |
| Epitaph and synopsis of his life (II 1.92) | 183 |

# Abbreviations and bibliographical note

PG    J.-P.Migne's *Patrologia Graeca*
CSEL  *Corpus Scriptorum Ecclesiasticorum Latinorum*

The text of the *De Vita Sua* is taken from the edition of Christoph Jungck (Heidelberg, 1974), while the other poems are taken from volume 37 of Migne's *Patrologia Graeca* (Paris, 1857). A few minor emendations to these texts have been made for this edition; these are noted at the foot of the pages where they occur.

The following is a selection of works in which various aspects of the life and writings of Gregory are discussed:

Beuckmann, U. *Gregor von Nazianz: Gegen die Habsucht*. Einleitung und Kommentar (Studien zur Geschichte und Kultur des Altertums. NF, 2. Forschungen zu Gregor von Nazianz, 6), (Paderborn etc., 1988).

Dagron, G. *Naissance d'une capitale: Constantinople et ses institutions de 330 à 451* (Paris, 1974).

Fleury, E. *Saint Grégoire et son temps* (Paris, 1930).

Gallay, P. *La vie de S. Grégoire* (Paris, 1943).

Misch, G. *A History of Autobiography in Antiquity*, part II (London, 1950), pp. 600–24.

Moreschini, C. (ed.) *Gregory of Nazianzus: Poemata Arcana*, with translation and commentary by D. A. Sykes (Oxford, 1996).

Oberhaus, M. *Gregor von Nazianz: Gegen den Zorn.* Einleitung und Kommentar (Studien zur Geschichte und Kultur des Altertums. NF, 2. Forschungen zu Gregor von Nazianz, 8), (Paderborn etc., 1991).

Otis, B. 'The Throne and the Mountain', *Classical Journal* 56 (1961), 146–65.

Pellegrino, M. *La poesia di S. Gregorio Nazianzeno* (Milan, 1932).
Ritter, A. M. *Das Konzil von Konstantinopel und sein Symbol* (Göttingen, 1966).
Ruether, R. *Gregory of Nazianzus, Rhetor and Philosopher* (Oxford, 1969).
White, C. *Christian Friendship of the Fourth Century* (Cambridge, 1992), ch. 4.
Wyss, B. 'Gregor von Nazianz, ein griechisch-christlicher Dichter des 4. Jahrhunderts', *Museum Helveticum* 6 (1949), 177–210.

# Introduction

## Gregory of Nazianzus: a biographical outline

Gregory of Nazianzus was one of the three leading orthodox Christians in the Greek church of the fourth century: like his friend Basil of Caesarea and Basil's brother Gregory of Nyssa, Gregory was a native of Cappadocia, in what is now eastern Turkey, and the three of them are therefore often referred to as the Cappadocian Fathers. Gregory of Nazianzus himself is also known as Gregory the Theologian in the Eastern church, largely on the strength of the five theological orations which he gave in Constantinople[1] and which stand out among his forty-four extant orations for their detailed and precise discussion, based on principles laid down at the Council of Nicaea in 325, of Trinitarian doctrine – of the relationship between Father, Son and Holy Spirit. The importance of his orations is shown by the fact that during the Middle Ages they were translated into Latin,[2] Syriac, Coptic, Georgian, Armenian, Slavonic and Arabic. Gregory enjoyed high prestige because of his outstanding rhetorical talents: he and John Chrysostom are generally considered the greatest Christian orators in the late antique Greek world[3] and Gregory has been referred to as the Christian Demosthenes. His virtue in this field lay in his ability to communicate clearly,

---

[1] *Orations* 27–31.
[2] Jerome's one-time friend Rufinus chose to translate the following nine of Gregory's orations: nos. 2, 6, 16, 17, 26, 27 (the first of the five theological orations), 38, 39 and 41, in which form they became available to readers throughout the west. (See *PG* 36 or *CSEL* 46.1 for an edition of these translations.)
[3] On Gregory's place in the history of rhetoric, see G. A. Kennedy, *Greek Rhetoric under the Christian Emperors* (Princeton, 1983).

relying more on evocative images than on dialectic. Gregory's literary achievements extended also to thousands of lines of verse, of which certain of the autobiographical poems are the most famous, in particular the long poem *De Vita Sua* translated in this volume. However, Gregory was not only a theologian and a man of letters: throughout his life he longed to be able to lead a life of ascetic contemplation, for he believed that only a pure mind, one freed from earthly concerns, can perceive God. Yet he was not permitted to pursue this life as he wished: time and again he was drawn back into the world of ecclesiastical duties and politics, being both ordained as priest and consecrated bishop against his will. However, although he always felt unfit for such responsibilities, he achieved much even in this sphere. He was greatly respected for his work in uniting the church and in defending orthodox doctrine at a time when the Christian church, which had only recently, under the emperor Constantine, become the privileged religion, was in danger of shattering on the reefs of numerous schisms and heresies. Despite all the doubts, tensions and contradictions threatening to cripple Gregory's sensitive nature, his was a significant and lasting achievement in the theological, spiritual and literary fields.

Although we know more about Gregory from his orations, letters and poetry than about anyone in antiquity apart perhaps from Cicero and Augustine, there still remain some fundamental confusions regarding Gregory's biographical data. It seems he was born on an estate called Arianzus in the vicinity of the town of Nazianzus, where his father Gregory was bishop. Although Ruether says that Nazianzus was apparently 'a flourishing city',[4] this seems to contradict the picture of the place given by Gregory.[5] There is also some uncertainty over where exactly in Cappadocia Nazianzus lay. Further doubt attaches to the date of Gregory's birth: the Byzantine encyclopaedia known as the Suidas implies that he was born in 301, but it is now agreed that a much later date is likely, probably around 329 or 330. More

[4] R. Ruether, *Gregory of Nazianzus: Rhetor and Philosopher* (Oxford, 1969), p. 18 n. 3.
[5] Cf. *Oration* 19.11, 33.6.

complicated but perhaps less hard to resolve is the question of Gregory's status as bishop. Although he is always known as Gregory of Nazianzus and he is sometimes said to have been bishop of Nazianzus,[6] this designation does not refer, as with most fourth-century bishops, to the place where he held his episcopacy. He was never officially made bishop of Nazianzus but merely assisted his father there, taking over from him unofficially after the elder Gregory's death in 374 until he could persuade the authorities to appoint another in his place. Rather, he was consecrated bishop of Sasima in 372, but he never agreed to take up the position. This was why he felt able to accept the archbishopric of Constantinople in 381 when urged to do so by the emperor Theodosius. Nevertheless his enemies accused him of rejecting his bride, Sasima, and lusting after another, Constantinople, insinuating that ambition was his motivation, which Gregory vehemently denies. In the event, Gregory was consecrated at Constantinople in May 381 but resigned in June of the same year. His career as bishop was in fact severely blighted by his unwillingness to exercise high office in all three places, Sasima, Nazianzus and Constantinople.

But before we examine the course of events at Constantinople which led to his resignation and retirement and which provide the subject matter for so many of his writings, in particular the poem *De Vita Sua*, we must offer an outline of Gregory's earlier life prior to the dramatic happenings in the capital of the Eastern empire in which he was involved during the years 379–81. Whatever his exact date of birth, we do know that Gregory was born to well-off Christian parents. His father had not been raised as a Christian but was converted after his marriage to Nonna, a dedicated believer. Both parents clearly had an enormously strong influence on their eldest son – one might almost say, too strong

---

[6] Jerome, for example, describes Gregory as bishop first of Sasima and then of Nazianzus (*De Viris Illustribus* 117). Gregory however denies this explicitly in *Ep.* 182 to Gregory of Nyssa, written in 383, after he had given up episcopal duties at Nazianzus. In this letter he claims, 'It is a fact well known to everyone that I was made bishop not of Nazianzus but of Sasima, although for some time, out of regard for my father and for those who begged me to do so, I agreed to be in charge of the church at Nazianzus as a visitor.'

an influence: in his adult life Gregory was constantly torn between his duty to his parents, to his father's strong will, and his longing to throw off that yoke and lead a life of contemplation and solitude to which he felt himself more suited. Despite the tensions between pagan and Christian at this period, his parents' Christian commitment did not prevent them giving their son an excellent education along traditional pagan lines: at Nazianzus, Caesarea in Cappadocia, Caesarea in Palestine, Alexandria and Athens, Gregory spent many years studying Greek literature, rhetoric and philosophy.[7] It was during the years at Athens that his deep friendship with Basil, whom he had first met at Caesarea, developed, a friendship which was to last, despite its vicissitudes, until Basil's death in 379. Beside Gregory's parents, Basil was the strongest influence in Gregory's life: the two men shared and provided mutual support for a view of Christian life laying supreme emphasis on the contemplative life, which they regarded as the truly philosophical life. In his poem *De Vita Sua* and in his funeral oration on Basil (*Oration* 43) Gregory gives a vivid picture of the inspiration he felt in Basil's company, though he does not conceal his bitterness at what he felt to be Basil's later betrayal of their relationship and their shared ideals.[8] When Basil and Gregory returned from their studies in Athens, Basil initially retired to a life of solitude while Gregory went back home to Nazianzus. Although he longed to join Basil, he was only able to do so for short periods:[9] pulling him in the opposite direction were his commitment to his ageing parents and the feeling that withdrawal from human society was not proper for a Christian. Gregory found it hard to reconcile the arguments for the contemplative life of solitude (which had become so popular among dedicated Christians during the

---

[7] It was while at Athens, Rufinus tells us (in his letter to Apronianus which prefaces his translation of nine of Gregory's orations), that Gregory was visited in his sleep by two lovely young ladies, Wisdom and Chastity, who asked if they could move in with him as he had prepared his home so well for them. (Cf. Aldhelm, *Prosa de virginitate* 27.)

[8] See further C. White, *Christian Friendship in the Fourth Century* (Cambridge, 1992), pp. 61–70.

[9] Gregory, *Epistles* 1, 2, 4–6.

fourth century)[10] and those for the active life, fulfilling Christ's commandment to love one's neighbour. It was an internal conflict which was to harass Gregory throughout his life and render him often incapable of decisions as to what course that life should take. This left him vulnerable to the decisions of others, with far-reaching personal consequences. Firstly, at the end of 361 or the beginning of 362, Gregory the elder forced his son to be ordained at Nazianzus against his will. The younger Gregory felt himself unworthy of the priesthood[11] and feared that it would interfere with his commitment to the monastic life. This time, as so often, the pressure exerted on Gregory caused him to run away: he fled to Basil's retreat near Neocaesarea in Pontus. This was only for a while as fear of, and concern for, his father soon made him feel he ought to return to Nazianzus. Here he began work as a priest at Easter 362. For the next ten years he supported his father but also continued as Basil's close friend despite their separation. He encouraged Basil, who had also been ordained against his will, and then helped his father in working for Basil's election as Bishop of Caesarea.[12] This marked a change in the friends' relationship, for Gregory came to feel that with Basil's elevation to the episcopate in 370, the equality necessary to their friendship was lost and that Basil had betrayed their commitment to the philosophical life.

Their relations were to deteriorate even further, however, for in 372 Gregory found himself elevated to the episcopate against his will, as a result of what he saw as Basil's political machinations. The emperor Valens had suddenly divided the province of Cappadocia in two with one half centred on Caesarea and the other on Tyana. Anthimus, the Arian bishop of Tyana, had then claimed that Tyana was now the ecclesiastical capital instead of Caesarea. In order to counter this claim and maintain the power of his own church Basil felt forced to create a number of new bishoprics, installing his brother Gregory at Nyssa and appointing his friend Gregory to Sasima, a small uncivilised settlement

[10] See e.g. D. Chitty, *The Desert a City* (London, 1966).
[11] See Gregory, *Oration* 2 on the duties and difficulties of the priesthood.
[12] See Gregory, *Epistles* 41–6.

which was nevertheless of strategic importance to Basil.[13] Although it seems that Basil, with the support of Gregory's father, managed to persuade Gregory at first that his elevation was in a good cause,[14] Gregory later expressed his bitterness at the way he had been manipulated.[15] Rather than going to Sasima after his consecration at Easter 372, Gregory fled to the mountains, for not only was Sasima beneath his dignity, he felt, but it was now in the hands of Anthimus. After a while the elder Gregory managed to persuade his son at least to return to Nazianzus, if not to take up his position at Sasima. This, however, was the last time the father got his way; in 374 he died, followed not long after by Gregory's mother. For about a year after their deaths Gregory accepted the task of running the church at Nazianzus, while trying to persuade the other bishops of the province to appoint an official successor to his father. Unsuccessful in persuading them, Gregory once again felt the need to slip away from his unwelcome responsibilities, this time fleeing to Seleucia[16] where he spent about three years in a monastic existence. But Gregory was not to be allowed to continue in this peaceful existence and once again he was dragged back into a position of responsibility, this time at Constantinople.

## Constantinople 379–381

Why was Gregory invited to leave Seleucia and make the long journey right across the country to Constantinople? He himself says that a group of bishops[17] asked him to go and take charge of the small number of Christians there who still adhered

---

[13] See Gregory, *De Vita Sua* 439–62 for a description of Sasima as seen through his eyes.
[14] In his *Oration* 10 Gregory appears resigned to acceptance of the episcopate, speaking of how he felt he had to respect the demands of friendship and old age: in other words, he felt compelled by Basil and his father to submit against his will.
[15] See Gregory's *Oration* 9 and *Epistles* 48 and 49. Unfortunately Basil's letters to Gregory from this period are not extant.
[16] See *De Vita Sua* 536–50; Seleucia (now Silifke) was a town in Cilicia, near Tarsus.
[17] *Poem* II.1.12.81–2 (PG 37.1172).

to the faith as defined at Nicaea. It may seem strange that they chose him, since he had already proved that he was unsuited to leadership or ecclesiastical politics, but he had also shown that he was both an excellent orator and a man of peace,[18] as well as a firm supporter of the orthodox (i.e. Nicene) cause, and a close friend of Basil, who was the prime champion of this cause until his death at the beginning of 379. The invitation to Gregory may have come already in 378, but it was not until after Basil's death that Gregory agreed to go, feeling perhaps that it was his duty now to take over Basil's mantle in the struggle for the survival of orthodox Christian belief.

That struggle had reached a critical stage: in fact Gregory's arrival was to coincide with the beginning of the disestablishment of Arianism at Constantinople and in neighbouring cities. Because of the ascendancy of the Arian heresy in the Eastern church (an ascendancy strengthened by the fact that a succession of emperors after Constantine had been committed Arians), for some forty years there had apparently been no orthodox Nicene bishop of Constantinople, except for a few short periods when the Nicene party had attempted to install a bishop of their own alongside the Arian incumbent. On the whole, after the death of bishop Alexander in 338, the Nicene congregation had been unable to support an orthodox bishop, and by 379 there were apparently few Nicenes left in the capital of the Eastern empire.[19] Those whom the Nicene supporters regarded as heretical, groups of Christians holding a broad spectrum of heterodox beliefs from Arian through to Homoiousian[20] and all denying that the Son was of one substance with the Father, had definitely been in control. When Gregory arrived in Constantinople in the

---

[18] *Oration* 36.3.
[19] *Oration* 36.6 and 42.2.
[20] Arians claimed that the Son of God was created by the Father and was not therefore God by nature; to combat this belief the members of the Council of Nicaea in 325, including Athanasius (who became bishop of Alexandria in 328 and was to prove himself one of the strongest defenders of the orthodox position in the following decades) had used the term 'homoousios' (of the same substance) to describe the relation between Father and Son. Some opponents of Arianism preferred to use the term 'homoiousios' (of like substance) because they felt it left more room for distinctions in the Godhead.

spring of 379 he found there was not even a church free for him to use for the Nicene congregation; instead he had to convert a room adjoining the house where he was staying with relatives, naming this improvised chapel the Anastasia, i.e. the church of the Resurrection.

However, after the Arian emperor Valens died at the battle of Adrianople in 378, fighting against the increasingly menacing barbarians pushing down on the Roman empire from the east and north, the situation gradually changed. From the Nicene point of view it was fortunate that Valens' successor was the orthodox Theodosius. He was a strong leader and a man of vision who was able to work with his western colleague, the young Gratian, for the firm establishment of the Nicene faith and the uprooting of Arian doctrine, which at that time posed the greatest threat to the unity of the church. When Theodosius took up office on 19 January 379 he had already decided to take seriously his imperial duty to act as head of the church. This meant working for a more radical settlement of the Arian problem than Gratian had yet attempted with his edict of toleration, reversing Valens' policy of persecution of non-Arians. A year later, at the beginning of 380, Theodosius published an edict announcing that all must accept the Nicene faith and confess that the three persons of the Trinity, Father, Son and Holy Spirit, were one God and of equal majesty.[21] In November 380 he entered Constantinople after a successful campaign against the barbarians and immediately expelled the Arian bishop Demophilus.[22] He intended to replace him with Gregory of Nazianzus, whom he escorted, with great pomp and circumstance as well as an armed guard, into the church of the Apostles, now no longer to be used by the Arian congregation.[23] Gregory, however, declined to be made bishop of Constantinople, insisting that the matter needed to be discussed by the members of the Council which was being planned for the following year. Although Gregory defended

---

[21] J. Stevenson (ed.), *Creeds, Councils and Controversies*, revised edition (SPCK London, 1989), no. 112.
[22] See Socrates, *Historia Ecclesiastica* V.7, Sozomen, *Historia Ecclesiastica* VII.5.
[23] See Gregory's description of his entry into this church which forms the highpoint of the *De Vita Sua* (lines 1305–95).

himself against a charge of abandoning Sasima and aiming at a more prestigious position as bishop of Constantinople,[24] he did recognise that Canon 15 of the Council of Nicaea technically prevented him transferring from one bishopric to another.

During Gregory's eighteen-month stay at Constantinople, before the entry of the emperor into the city and his public recognition of Gregory's achievements, Gregory had certainly managed to build up the congregation of Nicene adherents. The historian Theodoret sums up Gregory's achievement thus: he opposed the Arian heresy, imbued God's people with the gospel teachings, called back those sheep which had strayed from the flock and led them away from harmful spiritual sustenance, thus increasing the number of his flock.[25] Another admirer of Gregory's work in Constantinople was Jerome, who was staying in the city after his departure from Antioch. Jerome refers to Gregory several times in his writings,[26] notably as his 'teacher' who explained the Scriptures to him, just as Jerome was later to become a scriptural adviser to a circle of aristocratic Christian women, while he worked for Pope Damasus in Rome.

However this time had not been without its problems: Gregory had also made many enemies along the way, not only among the heretics – whom he was unable to dislodge from their position of predominance – but also within the Nicene party.[27]

## Maximus the Cynic

One of the most unpleasant and lengthy episodes in which Gregory was involved began with the arrival at Constantinople,

---

[24] *Oration* 36 is a bitter and ironic piece of self-defence, written shortly after the events of November 380.
[25] Theodoret, *Historia Ecclesiastica* v.8.
[26] Jerome, *De Viris Illustribus* 117; *Adversus Jovinianum* I.13; *Apologia adversus Rufinum* I.13, 30; *Commentary on Ephesians* 5.32; *Commentary on Isaiah* 6.1; *Letters* 50.1, 52.8. Gregory, however, makes no mention of Jerome in his writings.
[27] In some ways Gregory's experiences at Constantinople were similar to those of John Chrysostom, who became bishop of Constantinople after Gregory's successor: he too became unpopular because of his very chaste and simple way of life and was finally driven into exile, largely as a result of the machinations of another bishop of Alexandria, Theophilus.

late in 379 or early in 380, of Maximus, an Egyptian posing as a Cynic convert to Christianity. The orthodox congregation thought that Maximus was joining them with the support of bishop Peter of Alexandria (Athanasius' successor), but it later became apparent that Maximus was a man of breathtaking impudence and that, if he had Peter's support, it was because Peter hoped Maximus would further Alexandrian interests in Constantinople: in fact this episode can be seen as part of the wider problem of the long-term rivalry between the churches of Constantinople and Alexandria. Gregory was unaware of Maximus' dubious past and of his ambitions for the future, and with characteristic, if pardonable, naivety, welcomed the man. He even composed a eulogy on him as the perfect Christian philosopher, someone who, like Gregory himself, was striving to steer a course between the eremitic and the communal way of life and who had taken a brave stand against the Arians at Alexandria.[28] It is noticeable that Gregory not only often refers with approval in his writings to certain views held by the Cynic philosophers but even portrays himself in terms reminiscent of the descriptions of Cynics like Diogenes,[29] so he and Maximus must have had such sympathies in common, too. Maximus was however working to betray Gregory by winning some of Gregory's supporters over to his side. After the arrival of more of Maximus' supporters from Alexandria, Maximus considered the time was right to put into action his plan to bring Constantinople under the control of Alexandria: one night the Alexandrian priests secretly consecrated Maximus as bishop of Constantinople in the Anastasia church. However, they were interrupted during the consecration ceremony and Maximus fled to Thessalonica where he hoped – in vain, as it turned out – to persuade the emperor Theodosius of the justice of his cause and to insinuate himself as successor to the Arian bishop Demophilus, whom Theodosius was to expel from Constantinople. In fact, Maximus was forced to return to Alexandria in disgrace, though we find him in the

---

[28] See *Oration* 25. Gregory refers to the object of his praises as Hero, but the circumstantial details make it clear that this is Maximus.

[29] See in particular *De Vita Sua* 701.

following year still attempting to get himself recognised as the rightful bishop of Constantinople. Indeed it seems that even as perspicacious a man as Ambrose of Milan was persuaded for a time.[30] But Gregory was now in no doubt as to Maximus' wickedness and unsuitability for such a position, as he makes clear in poem II.1.41 against Maximus, as well as in the *De Vita Sua*.[31]

## The Council of Constantinople 381[32]

It was probably after Theodosius' entry into Constantinople at the end of 380 that arrangements were made for a council to be held there in the early summer of 381. The objectives and achievements of this council (later to be known as the Second General or Ecumenical Council, despite the fact that there was little representation of western bishops) were summarised in a letter sent by the council to Theodosius: its members 'pronounced some short definitions,[33] ratifying the faith of the Nicene Fathers, and anathematising the heresies which have sprung up contrary to it'.[34] Questions of Trinitarian and Christological doctrine were still hotly debated among different parties[35] and the problems arising from the wide variety of beliefs needed to be solved for the sake of the church's unity. At

---

[30] See Ambrose, *Ep.* 13: in 381 Ambrose and the other Italian bishops wrote to Theodosius objecting to the election of Nectarius as bishop of Constantinople on the grounds that Maximus had already been elected bishop! No mention is made of Gregory in this letter. It would seem that a synod held at Rome in the following year finally rejected Maximus' claims to the bishop's throne at Constantinople.

[31] Lines 736–1000.

[32] *De Vita Sua* 1506–1918.

[33] E.g. the Council reasserted the Nicene definition of the three persons of the Trinity as *homoousios*. See H. Chadwick, *The Early Church* (Harmondsworth, 1967), p. 150.

[34] J. Stevenson (ed.), *Creeds, Councils and Controversies*, no. 91. Gregory's *De Vita Sua* and his farewell oration (*Oration* 42) are important sources for knowledge of the Council's course, for few official documents relating to this Council have survived.

[35] Gregory of Nyssa, in his work *De Deitate Filii et Spiritus Sancti* (PG 46.557) gives a vivid description of the mania for theological discussion even among the laity at Constantinople: 'If you ask someone [in the marketplace] the price of a loaf of bread, he will answer, "The Father is greater and the Son is subordinate."'

this council, too, it was decreed that Maximus the Cynic was not a bishop and that those who had been ordained by him were not members of the clergy. Of wider interest is the fact that the Nicene creed was here drastically altered and given the form familiar to us.[36] The president of the council was Meletius of Antioch, who had been the chief champion of orthodoxy after the death of Athanasius of Alexandria in 373 and of Basil of Caesarea in 379. One of the first things to be implemented by him on his arrival in Constantinople was the election of Gregory as bishop of Constantinople, probably in May 381.[37] Gregory had at last agreed to this, as he hoped to be able to work for peace and reconciliation within the church. Soon, however, he became disillusioned, depressed at how deep the schism between east and west seemed to be. Unfortunately, too, Meletius died soon after, with the result that the vexed question of the bishopric of Antioch leapt on to the agenda. For nearly twenty years there had existed side by side at Antioch two rival bishops, Meletius and Paulinus, both claiming to uphold the Nicene faith and differing only in their use of the term *hypostasis* in relation to the persons of the Trinity: each had his own supporters among the bishops of east and west. Gregory, together with Basil and Gregory of Nyssa, had long supported Meletius, but they were unable to persuade the bishops of either Rome or of Alexandria to withdraw support for Paulinus: without the support of these key bishops, the position could only be one of stalemate. To complicate matters further, Theodosius had at first recognised Paulinus but changed his mind when he came to Constantinople; this change is reflected in the fact that he chose Meletius as president of the Council. Interestingly, on Meletius' death Gregory decided that the best course was for everyone to accept Paulinus for the duration of his lifetime, after which one new successor should be chosen. This, it was hoped, would mean an end to

---

[36] See J. N. D. Kelly, *Early Christian Creeds*, third edition (London, 1972), pp. 297–8; H. Chadwick, *The Early Church*, pp. 150–1 on the changes made to the Nicene Creed.

[37] *De Vita Sua* 1525ff.; Socrates, *Historia Ecclesiastica* v.8; R. Ruether, *Gregory of Nazianzus: Rhetor and Philosopher*, p. 45.

the schism, but it was not a view shared by the majority of bishops, who decided in favour of Flavian, one of Meletius' clergy. It was as a result of this rebuff and of the fact that, with the arrival of bishop Timothy of Alexandria (the brother and successor of bishop Peter) and the other Egyptian bishops in June 381, objections were made to the election of Gregory to the bishopric of Constantinople on the grounds that the Nicene canons had forbidden translations from one bishopric to another,[38] that Gregory felt his position was no longer tenable. It is possible that he had been bishop of Constantinople for no more than six weeks. As he tells us in the *De Vita Sua*, he made a speech to the council informing them of his position and was deeply disappointed and hurt when the 150 bishops accepted his resignation with little demur.[39] The emperor, too, agreed that Gregory should withdraw from Constantinople. So Gregory retired to Nazianzus, where for about two years he resumed the episcopal duties, since no successor to his father had yet been appointed. It was not until 383 that Gregory, weakened by illness and misfortune, was able to retire to his estate and devote the remaining years of his life to literary endeavours. It is probable that he died in 390, as we learn from the evidence of Jerome,[40] who praises Gregory as a man of the greatest eloquence, as a teacher of the Scriptures and as the writer of, according to Jerome's estimate, thirty thousand lines of verse and prose.

## Gregory's writings

Most of Gregory's poetical works, as well as many of his letters, seem to have been composed in the years between his departure from Constantinople in 381 and his death in 390, and

---

[38] See Socrates, *Historia Ecclesiastica* v.7.
[39] The historian Sozomen, however, appreciated Gregory's achievement at Constantinople: 'I have to admire this most wise of men for many other reasons but particularly for his behaviour in this matter, for he was not arrogant because of his rhetorical skills nor did he desire to be bishop in order to win empty glory; when the bishops demanded it back, he gave it up without complaining about all the things he had suffered or the dangers he had gone through in his struggle against the heretics.' (Sozomen, *Historia Ecclesiastica* VII.7)
[40] Jerome, *De Viris Illustribus* 117.

during this period his final oration[41] was delivered (at Easter 383). However, we also have other writings from earlier periods of his life. For example, the first extant letter, addressed to Basil, was written in 361, while Gregory was still planning on leading a life of Christian contemplation alongside his friend, and the first oration was delivered at Nazianzus at Easter 362, when Gregory was forced to come to terms with his ordination. In all, we now have 44 orations which are considered to be genuinely his, while of the 244 letters which have survived under his name, 241 are probably authentic. More than 16,000 lines of Gregory's poetry are extant.

Of his orations, the most famous are the five theological ones composed for his congregation at Constantinople.[42] Of the rest, only one is an exposition of a biblical text: this is no.37, in which Gregory discusses the text of Matthew 19:1–12. A few others take as their theme one of the church festivals, such as Epiphany or Pentecost.[43] *Orations* 4 and 5 are of broader historical interest, consisting of virulent attacks on the emperor Julian, particularly for forbidding Christians to teach pagan Greek literature.[44] The vast majority, however, are either speeches in praise of someone or concern some crisis in Gregory's own life. The best-known of the former is Gregory's funeral oration for Basil,[45] but he composed similar speeches for his brother, sister and father,[46] as well as speeches in praise of Athanasius and Cyprian.[47] The latter type are of course of particular interest when set beside his many other autobiographical writings: such are his *Oration 2*, the so-called *Apologeticus*,[48] which he gave before the congregation at Nazianzus after he had been ordained against his will; *Oration 9*, addressed to his father after Gregory had been made

[41] *Oration* 44.
[42] *Orations* 27–31.
[43] E.g. *Oration* 38 on the Epiphany, or 41 on Pentecost.
[44] For Julian's rescript on teachers in the year 362, see J. Stevenson (ed.), *Creeds, Councils and Controversies*, no. 47.
[45] *Oration* 43.
[46] *Orations* 7 on Caesarius, 8 on Gorgonia and 18 on his father.
[47] *Orations* 21 and 24.
[48] This work seems to have influenced John Chrysostom in his *On the Priesthood*, and in Rufinus' Latin translation, Gregory the Great in his *Pastoral Rule*.

bishop of Sasima against his will; *Oration* 10, given on his return after fleeing from episcopal responsibility; *Oration* 12, also addressed to his father after Gregory had been persuaded to assist him at Nazianzus. Of those given at Constantinople, we may note *Oration* 36, in which he responds to accusations that he had aspired to become bishop of Constantinople, and *Oration* 42, his farewell speech after resigning as bishop of Constantinople in the summer of 381,[49] in which he gives an account of his achievements and makes a plea for release from his episcopal responsibilities.

His poems have been divided into two broad sections, the theological and the historical. The theological section is divided into dogmatic and moral poems, while the so-called historical section consists of poems about himself (these form the majority!) and poems concerning other people, including verse epistles, 129 epitaphs and 94 epigrams.[50] Among the moral poems the most notable are perhaps the long poems on virginity[51] (I.2.1) and on virtue (I.2.10); the latter has been referred to as 'the most complete expression of the Cappadocian humanism.'[52] During the time they spent together in retreat at Annesi Gregory also collaborated with Basil on an edition of the *Philocalia*, a selection from the writings of Origen. The drama *Christus Patiens*, often associated with Gregory's name, is now regarded as having been falsely attributed to him.

## The poems in this volume

The section II.1 in Migne's *Patrologia Graeca* 37 contains 99 poems about Gregory himself. The majority,[53] of varying length

---

[49] These orations are printed in volumes 35 and 36 of Migne's Patrologia Graeca.
[50] The poems are printed in volumes 37 and 38 of the Patrologia Graeca.
[51] Jerome refers specifically to this poem in his *De Viris Illustribus* (117), reporting that it takes the form of a discussion between Marriage and Virginity.
[52] L. Bouyer, *A History of Christian Spirituality* (London, 1968), vol. I, p. 343.
[53] This section also contains numerous short poems, many only a few lines long, some dealing with his misfortunes or addressed to those he felt to be his enemies; others are addressed to Christ or the devil but are nevertheless still concerned with Gregory's personal experiences and feelings.

and often drawing on ideas earlier formulated in his orations, mention the misfortunes Gregory felt he had suffered throughout his life but particularly at Constantinople. The most famous of these poems is the *De Vita Sua*, Gregory's longest poem and the one which is of the greatest biographical, historical and theological interest. In it Gregory summarises his early life, referring in particular to his studies at Athens with Basil (an account which can be compared with what he says in the Funeral Oration on Basil (*Oration* 43)), to his difficulty in choosing a way of life that suited him, and to his problematic relations with his father. However, the bulk of the poem is devoted to an account of the two years or so Gregory spent at Constantinople, and is both a denunciation of the way he was treated by others and an apologia for his views and behaviour during this troubled period.

The understanding of Gregory's life gained from this poem can to some extent be supplemented by what he tells us in other poems such as II.1.1 *De rebus suis*, a poem of 634 lines, II.1.12 *De se ipso et de episcopis* of 836 lines or II.1.45 *De animae suae calamitatibus* of 350 lines. In this volume we have decided to set the *Querela de suis calamitatibus* (II.1.19), a slightly shorter poem than those referred to above, beside his *De Vita Sua*. Unlike the latter, which is composed in iambic trimeters, the metre of tragedy, the *Querela* is written in hexameters and is of interest also for the epic dialect it uses, incorporating Homeric vocabulary and word groups throughout, despite its very different subject matter.

Gregory's skill in the elegiac couplet is displayed in the poem *In silentium jejunii* (II.1.34), which also uses the epic dialect. This was written during Lent 382, when Gregory was back at Nazianzus and had put himself under a vow of silence for the forty days of Lent as a form of self-mortification.[54] His aim here conformed to the spiritual aims governing his whole life, as expressed, for example, in the oration[55] written to justify his flight after

---

[54] Gregory mentions his vow of silence during this period in *Letters* 107–19; his silence is the subject also of the shorter poems II.1.35–7 while *Poem* II.1.38 is a 52-line hymn to Christ at Easter when the period of silence was over.
[55] *Oration* 2.

ordination: 'To me, nothing seems preferable to the state of the man who, closing his senses to exterior impressions, escaping from the flesh and the world, re-entering into himself, retaining no further contact with any human beings except when necessity absolutely requires it, conversing with himself and with God, lives beyond visible things and carries within himself the divine images, always pure, untouched by any admixture with the fugitive forms of this earth.'[56] The poem is both a justification for his decision, explaining that he believes the discipline of silence can lead to spiritual purification, and a sharp attack on the harm caused by speech.[57]

The only short poem included here is the *Epitaph* Gregory wrote for himself (II.1.92) which provides a brief summary of his life as he saw it, alluding to the facts that are dealt with in greater detail in his other poems. These four poems are prefaced in this selection by the iambic verses Gregory composed on the subject of his own poetry, *In suos versus* (II.1.39), in which he gives his reasons for writing verse and defends himself against his critics. Within the restrictions of this small volume the intention has been to offer some idea of the different themes, styles and metres with which Gregory worked when writing about his own feelings and experiences.

Gregory's poetic language is exceedingly literary, influenced by his profound knowledge of Greek literature, and especially by Homer and the Greek tragedians, particularly Euripides. His style is also naturally influenced by his rhetorical training and is notable for the number of neologisms he uses.[58] Alongside what derives from his traditional education, we find frequent biblical allusions, particularly to characters in the Old Testament, whom

---

[56] *Oration* 2.7, quoted by Bouyer, *A History of Christian Spirituality*, vol. I, p. 347.

[57] Like Erasmus, who composed his *Lingua*, a bitter attack on the sins of the tongue, after much personal experience of slander, Gregory had suffered from what he deemed to be unjust criticisms of his opinions and behaviour. On Erasmus' treatise and earlier medieval works on the sins of speech, see the introductory note to the *Lingua* by Elaine Fantham, *Collected Works of Erasmus* (Toronto, 1989), vol. 29, pp. 250–6.

[58] For a list of some of the *hapax legomena* in the *De Vita Sua*, see Jungck's edition, p. 25.

Gregory cites as examples. The poems are also marked by a tendency for words and phrases to be repeated a line or two further on, a feature which reinforces the impression of careful artistic construction. The tone of most of these poems is one of grief and bitterness; the style is often allusive and opaque. Gregory tends to communicate through a series of vague generalisations, gnomic statements[59] and metaphors, which sometimes make it hard to glean much biographical information from his autobiographical poems. One of the reasons for the popularity of the *De Vita Sua* may be that in this poem he does speak more directly and concretely about some of the dramatic and moving episodes of his fascinating life. The images he uses here to make his experiences more vivid to the reader tend to be introduced in the manner of similes, less enigmatic than the unexplained metaphors in other poems. For example, Gregory describes the vulnerability of the orthodox church as he found it at Constantinople in terms of a toddler in nappies, tottering around,[60] and himself, in his eagerness to leave Constantinople in 381, as a horse tethered in its stable but restless in its desire to break out into the fields.[61] His ability to conjure up a lively picture is evident also in longer descriptions, as in the famous account of the storm which hit his ship as he sailed from Alexandria to Greece. But Gregory's poem is not just a series of vivid images: his verse comes to life because he manages to maintain the impression that he is addressing the reader as if in conversation, asking for his views and evoking his sympathy. Another remarkable feature of this poem in particular is the manner in which Gregory not only highlights human relations and feelings but depicts them with such perceptiveness, whether with compassion or with harsh irony. His frequent reflections on human nature, and in particular on the human tendency to evil, allow us to feel that we can look into Gregory's heart and see life from his point of view. For all his naivety and gullibility, and despite the pathetic tone

---

[59] e.g. *In suos versus* 42, *De Vita Sua* 143, 967, 1656–7.
[60] *De Vita Sua* 690–4.
[61] *De Vita Sua* 1818–22. There is an allusion here to Homer, *Iliad* 6.506–11; cf. Vergil *Aeneid* 11. 492–7.

of one who has suffered unjustly at the hands of friends and enemies alike, Gregory is admirably perceptive about his own and others' motives, honest about his own weaknesses and forceful in his condemnation of hypocrisy and injustice.

# The poems

# ΕΙΣ ΤΑ ΕΜΜΕΤΡΑ

Πολλοὺς ὁρῶν γράφοντας ἐν τῷ νῦν βίῳ
λόγους ἀμέτρους, καὶ ῥέοντας εὐκόλως,
καὶ πλεῖστον ἐκτρίβοντας ἐν πόνοις χρόνον,
ὧν κέρδος οὐδὲν ἢ κενὴ γλωσσαλγία·
5 ἀλλ' οὖν γράφοντας καὶ λίαν τυραννικῶς,
ὡς μεστὰ πάντα τυγχάνειν ληρημάτων,
ψαμμοῦ θαλασσῶν ἢ σκνιπῶν Αἰγυπτίων·
πάντων μὲν ἂν ἥδιστα καὶ γνώμην μίαν,
ταύτην ἔδωκα, πάντα ῥίψαντας λόγον,
10 αὐτῶν ἔχεσθαι τῶν θεοπνεύστων μόνον,
ὡς τοὺς ζάλην φεύγοντας ὅρμων εὐδίων.
εἰ γὰρ τοσαύτας αἱ Γραφαὶ δεδώκασι
λαβὰς, τὸ, Πνεῦμα, τουτί σοι σοφώτερον,
ὡς καὶ τόδ' εἶναι παντὸς ὁρμητήριον
15 λόγου ματαίου τοῖς κακῶς ὡρμωμένοις.
ποτ' ἂν γράφων σὺ, τοις κάτω νοήμασιν
ἀναμφιλέκτους, ὦ 'τὰν, ἐκτείναις λόγους;
ἐπεὶ δὲ τοῦτο παντελῶς ἀμήχανον,
κόσμου ῥαγέντος εἰς τόσας διαστάσεις,
20 πάντων τ' ἔρεισμα τῆς ἑαυτῶν ἐκτροπῆς
τούτους ἐχόντων τοὺς λόγους συμπροστάτας·
ἄλλην μετῆλθον τῶν λόγων ταύτην ὁδὸν,
εἰ μὲν καλήν γε, εἰ δὲ μή γ', ἐμοὶ φίλην·
μέτροις τι δοῦναι τῶν ἐμῶν πονημάτων.
25 οὐχ, ὡς ἂν οἰηθεῖεν οἱ πολλοὶ βροτῶν,
τῶν πάντα ῥᾴστων, δόξαν ἐκκαρπούμενος

# To his own verses[1]

    Seeing many people in this present age writing
    words without measure which flow forth easily,
    and expending a great deal of time on their efforts
    for which no reward awaits – or only empty chatter;
5  anyway, seeing them writing all too arrogantly
    and realising that all of it is full of worthless matter
    like the sand of the seas or swarms of Egyptian flies,
    I gave them this single piece of advice, the best of all:
    throwing away every word, they should
10 cling only to the divinely inspired ones,
    as those who flee the storm seek the harbour's calm.
    For if the Scriptures accord so many great opportunities,
    this, O Spirit, is the one that seems most sensible to you,
    namely that this should be a defence against all
15 empty talk on the part of those with evil motives.
    When you write, do you, my friend, bring indisputable
    arguments to your thoughts that belong to this lower world?
    Since this is completely impossible,
    now the world has broken up into so many separate parts
20 and everyone has supporting arguments like these
    as a basis for their own escape,
    I have taken another path in my writing and this is it,
    (a good way, I think, but if not, dear to me at least):
    to put something of my own struggles into verse.
25 Not, as many people might think –
    those always ready to jump to conclusions – so as to reap
        glory

---

[1] *Poem* II.1.39. The metre is the iambic trimeter.

κενὴν, ὃ δὴ λέγεται. τοὐναντίον μὲν οὖν
τρέχοντας οἶδα τοῖς ἐμοις, οὕτω γράφειν,
ἀνθρωπαρεισκεῖν μᾶλλον· οἱ γὰρ πλείονες
30 τοῖς σφῶν μέτροις μετροῦσι καὶ τὰ τῶν πέλας
οὔτε προτιμῶν τοῦτο τῶν θείων πόνων·
μή μοι τοσοῦτον ἐκπέσοι θεοῦ λόγος;
    Τί οὖν πέπονθα, τοῦτ' ἴσως θαυμάσετε.
πρῶτον μὲν ἠθέλησα, τοῖς ἄλλοις καμὼν,
35 οὕτω πεδῆσαι τὴν ἐμὴν ἀμετρίαν·
ὡς ἂν γράφων γε, ἀλλὰ μὴ πολλὰ γράφω,
καμὼν τὸ μέτρον. δεύτερον δὲ τοῖς νέοις,
καὶ τῶν ὅσοι μάλιστα χαίρουσι λόγοις,
ὥσπερ τι τερπνὸν τοῦτο δοῦναι φάρμακον,

40 πειθοῦς ἀγωγὸν εἰς τὰ χρησιμώτερα,
τέχνῃ γλυκάζων τὸ πικρὸν τῶν ἐντολῶν.
φιλεῖ δ' ἀνίεσθαί τε καὶ νευρᾶς τόνος·
εἴ πως θέλεις καὶ τοῦτο· εἰ μή τι πλέον,
ἀντ' ἀσμάτων σοι ταῦτα καὶ λυρισμάτων.

45 παίζειν δέδωκα, εἴ τι καὶ παίζειν θέλεις,
μή τις βλάβη σοι πρὸς τὸ καλὸν συλωμένῳ.
τρίτον πεπονθὼς οἶδα· πρᾶγμα μὲν τυχὸν
μικροπρεπές τι, πλὴν πέπονθ'· οὐδ' ἐν λόγοις
πλέον δίδωμι τοὺς ξένους ἡμῶν ἔχειν·

50 τούτοις λέγω δὴ τοῖς κεχρωσμένοις λόγοις
εἰ καὶ τὸ κάλλος ἡμῖν ἐν θεωρίᾳ.
ὑμῖν μὲν οὖν δὴ τοῖς σοφοῖς ἐπαίξαμεν.
ἔστω τις ἡμῖν καὶ χάρις λεόντιος.
τέταρτον εὗρον τῇ νόσῳ πονούμενος

55 παρηγόρημα τοῦτο, κύκνος ὡς γέρων,
λαλεῖν ἐμαυτῷ τὰ πτερῶν συρίγματα,
οὐ θρῆνον, ἀλλ' ὕμνον τιν' ἐξιτήριον.
    πρὸς ταῦτα νῦν γινώσκεθ' ἡμῖν, οἱ σοφοὶ,
τῶν ἔνδον. Εἰ δ' ἥττησθε, τῶν αὐτῶν λόγων

that is insubstantial, as they say. (On the other hand,
I know that those who run my writings down write
so as to win greater popularity. For the majority measure
30 by their own standards the actions of their neighbours, too.)
Nor because I value my verse above the divine works –
may God's word never abandon me to such a degree!
Perhaps you wonder what my motivation was.
First of all I wished, by expending effort on other matters,
35 so to restrain my own lack of measure;
so that in writing I would not write a great amount,
struggling with the metre as I was. Secondly, I wished to present my work
to young people (and especially those who enjoy literature)
as a kind of pleasant medicine,
40 an inducement which might lead them to more useful things,
skilfully sweetening the harshness of the commandments:
for a taut bowstring also needs to be relaxed.
Perhaps you are willing to give this a try; if nothing more,
these verses can be a substitute for songs and lyre-playing.
45 I offer this for your enjoyment, if you should wish to enjoy it a little,
so nothing hinders you in your progress towards the good.
Thirdly, I know I feel – this may seem petty of me,
but I do feel this – I cannot admit
the pagans to have greater literary talent than us.
50 I am speaking of those ornate words of theirs,
for in our eyes beauty lies in contemplation.
And so for you, the wise, we have produced this amusement.
Allow us, too, a certain leonine grace.
Fourthly, while suffering from illness I have found
55 some comfort, like an aging swan,
in singing to myself with the beating of wings,
not a lament but a kind of farewell song.
In addition, you may now understand, you wise men,
my innermost thoughts. But if you give up, the matter

ΕΙΣ ΤΑ ΕΜΜΕΤΡΑ

60 πλεῖστον τὸ χρῆμα· καὶ τὰ παιζόντων λόγοι,
χωρεῖτε· μακρὸν δ' οὐδὲν οὐδ' ὑπὲρ κόρον,
ἀλλ' οὐδ' ἄχρηστον, ὡς ἐγῷμαι παντελῶς.
αὐτοὶ διδάξουσ' οἱ λόγοι θέλοντά σε.
τὰ μὲν γάρ ἐστι τῶν ἐμῶν, τὰ δ' ἔκτοθεν.

65 ἢ τῶν καλῶν ἔπαινος, ἢ κακῶν ψόγος,
ἢ δόγματ', ἢ γνώμη τις, ἢ τομαὶ λόγων,
μνήμην ἔχουσαι τῇ δέσει τοῦ γράμματος.
εἰ μικρὰ ταῦτα, σὺ τέλει τὰ μείζονα.
μέτρον κακίζεις· εἰκότως, ἄμετρος ὢν,

70 ἰαμβοποιὸς, συγγράφων ἀμβλώματα.
τίς γὰρ βλέποντα, μὴ βλέπων, ἐγνώρισεν;
ἢ τίς τρέχοντι, μὴ τρέχων, συνέδραμε
πλὴν οὐ λέληθας, ὃ ψέγεις, ὠνούμενος.
ὃ γὰρ κακίζεις, τοῦτό σοι σπουδάζεται,

75 καὶ σφόδρ' ἀμέτρως, τὸ γράφειν ποιήματα.
ὅταν δ' ἐλέγχῃ, πίστις ἀντεισέρχεται,
καὶ πεζὸς ἡμῖν ναυαγῶν ὁ φίλτατος.
τοιαῦτα τεχνάζεσθε, ὑμεῖς οἱ σοφοί.
ταῦτ' οὐ πρόδηλον ψεῦδος, οὐχὶ διπλόη;

80 πίθηκος ἡμῖν ἀρτίως, λέων δὲ νῦν.
οὕτως ἁλίσκετ' εὐπετῶς δόξης ἔρως.
πλὴν ἴσθι πολλὰ καὶ Γραφαῖς μετρούμενα,
ὡς οἱ σοφοὶ λέγουσιν Ἑβραίων γένους.
εἰ μὴ μέτρον σοι καὶ τὰ νεύρων κρούματα,

60   is more than the words, for words are the stuff of those who play.
     Come on, since there is nothing long or excessive here,
     but neither is it without benefit, at least in my view.
     The words themselves will teach you, if you are willing.
     Some things are my own, some are from other sources –
65   whether praise of the good or censure of the wicked,
     whether teachings or some opinion or sections of speeches
     that are memorable because they are bound fast in writing.
     If this is of little value, produce something better yourself.
     You criticise the metre, understandably so, for you are without measure,
70   a writer of invective, creating malformed offspring.
     For who, being blind, could recognise one who can see?
     Or who, if unable to run, could run to meet someone running?
     You cannot conceal the fact that you practise what you revile,
     for you strive to achieve the very thing you vilify –
75   the writing of poetry, and that completely without measure.
     For whenever he finds fault,[2] it has the opposite effect: confidence grows
     and this wonderful person is for us a prosaic writer who has foundered.
     Compose this kind of thing, you who are so wise.
     Is this not a blatant falsehood, is it not a trick?
80   One moment we have an ape, the next a lion.[3]
     So easily is the desire for glory convicted!
     Know that even in the scriptures there is much in verse,
     as the wise men of the Hebrew race do tell.
     If the sounds produced by the strings do not seem metrical,

---

[2] Throughout this passage, down to line 81, Gregory is referring to the critic of Gregory's poems mentioned in line 69. I am particularly grateful to Professors Mossay and Sicherl for their advice on the text (including the slight emendation to the text of *PG* in line 76) and the meaning of lines 76–7.
[3] On the theme of the pretentious monkey, see U. Beuckmann, *Gregor von Nazianz: Gegen die Habsucht. Einleitung und Kommentar* (Studien zur Geschichte und Kultur des Altertums. NF, 2. Forschungen zu Gregor von Nazianz, 6), (Paderborn etc. 1988), pp. 106–7.

## ΕΙΣ ΤΑ ΕΜΜΕΤΡΑ

85 ὡς οἱ πάλαι προσῇδον ἐμμελεῖς λόγους,
τὸ τερπνὸν, οἶμαι, τοῦ καλοῦ ποιούμενοι
ὄχημα, καὶ τυποῦντες ἐκ μελῶν τρόπους.
Σαοὺλ σε τοῦτο πεισάτω, καὶ πνεύματος
ἐλευθερωθεὶς τοῖς τρόποις τῆς κινύρας.
90 τίς οὖν βλάβη σοι, τοὺς νέους δι' ἡδονῆς
σεμνῆς ἄγεσθαι πρὸς θεοῦ κοινωνίαν,
οὐ γὰρ φέρουσιν ἀθρόαν μετάστασιν.
νῦν μέν τις ἔστω μίξις εὐγενεστέρα.
πῆξιν δ' ὅταν τὸ καλὸν ἐν χρόνῳ λάβῃ,
95 ὑποσπάσαντες, ὡς ἐρείσματ' ἀψίδων,
τὸ κομψὸν, αὐτὸ τἀγαθὸν φυλάξομεν.
τούτου τί ἂν γένοιτο χρησιμώτερον;
σὺ δ' οὐ τὰ ὄψα τῷ γλυκεῖ παραρτύεις,
ὦ σεμνὲ, καὶ σύνοφρυ καὶ συνηγμένε;
100 τί οὖν κακίζεις τὴν ἐμὴν εὐμετρίαν,
τοῖς σοῖς μέτροις σταθμώμενος τὰ τῶν πέλας;
χωρὶς τὰ Μυσῶν καὶ Φρυγῶν ὁρίσματα
χωρὶς κολοιῶν κ' ἀετῶν ὑψώματα.

85 as the men of old used to sing the words in harmony,
producing, I believe, a delightful vehicle for the good,
and using the melodies to influence behaviour,
then let Saul convince you of this, for he was freed
from the spirit by the music of the harp.
90 So what harm do you think there is for the young to be led
by means of dignified pleasure to communion with God?
They do not have to undergo a sudden conversion:
for the moment let there be a more attractive combination,
but when in time the good acquires stability,
95 we will withdraw what is pleasant, like the supports
of an arch, retaining the good alone.
What could be more useful than this?
Do you not add sweetness to your food,
you who are so solemn, frowning and with wrinkled brow?
100 Why then do you find fault with my ability to write verse,
measuring the verses of others by your own standards?
Far apart lie the lands of the Mysians and Phrygians,
far apart are the heights of jackdaws and eagles.

# ΠΕΡΙ ΤΟΝ ΕΑΥΤΟΥ ΒΙΟΝ

Τὸ τοῦ λόγου βούλημα, τῶν ἐμῶν κακῶν
ἐξιστορῆσαι τὴν ὁδόν, εἴτ' οὖν δεξιῶν·
οἱ μὲν γὰρ οὕτως, οἱ δ' ἐκείνως φαῖεν ἄν,
ὅπως ἄν, οἶμαι, καὶ ῥοπῆς ὦσιν τινες.
5 οὐ γὰρ τὸ βούλεσθ' ἀσφαλὲς κριτήριον.
παίζει δὲ μέτρον τῆς ἀνίας φάρμακον,
παίδευμα καὶ γλύκασμα τοῖς νέοις ἅμα,
τερπνὸν παρηγόρημα. πρὸς δ' ὑμᾶς λόγος,
τοὺς ἦν ὅθ' ἡμῶν, ἀλλὰ νῦν ἀλλοτρίους,

10 ὅσοι τε ὁμοδοξοῦντες, εἴτε τις νόθος·
πάντες γὰρ ἡμῖν εὐμενεῖς μεμυκόσιν.
ἄνδρες, τὸ κλεινὸν ὄμμα τῆς οἰκουμένης,
οἳ κόσμον οἰκεῖθ', ὡς ὁρῶ, τὸν δεύτερον,
γῆς καὶ θαλάσσης κάλλος ἠμφιεσμένοι,

15 Ῥώμη νεουργής, εὐγενῶν ἄλλων ἕδος,
Κωνσταντίνου πόλις τε καὶ στήλη κράτους,
ἀκούσατ', ἄνδρες, ἀνδρὸς ἀψευδεστάτου
καὶ πολλὰ μοχθήσαντος ἐν πολλαῖς στροφαῖς,
ἐξ ὧν ὑπάρχει καὶ τὸ γιγνώσκειν πλέον.

# Concerning his own life[1]

### Prologue (1–50)

The purpose of this work is to explore the course
of my misfortunes or, if you like, my successes:
for some would describe it one way, others in another,
each, so I believe, according to his own inclination:
5 but inclination is not a reliable basis for judgement.
The verse form, providing a remedy for pain, adds a
    playfulness,
being both a means of instruction and a source of pleasure
    for the young,
a delightful consolation. To you this work is addressed,
you who once were mine but now are another's,[2]
10 you who share the same beliefs (even if any of you is a
    heretic).
For all are well-disposed to me when my lips are closed.
You men, the shining eye of the earth,
who inhabit the second world, as I see it,
clothed in the beauty of earth and sea,
15 the newly built Rome,[3] the seat of a new nobility,
the city of Constantine and a monument to his power,
listen, you men, to a man who is completely devoid of
    falsehood,
and who has suffered greatly amid many twists of fortune,
out of which there has arisen a greater understanding.

---

[1] *Poem* II.1.11. The metre is the iambic trimeter.
[2] Nectarius took over as Bishop of Constantinople after Gregory's resignation.
[3] See Canon 3 of the Council of Constantinople (J. Stevenson (ed.), *Creeds, Councils and Controversies*, no. 91).

## ΠΕΡΙ ΤΟΝ ΕΑΥΤΟΥ ΒΙΟΝ

20 Κέκμηκε πάντα, καὶ τὰ καλὰ τῷ χρόνῳ
κέκμηκεν. οὐδὲν ἢ στενὸν τὸ λείψανον,
ὡς γῆς συρείσης ὑετῶν λάβρων φορᾷ
κάχληκές εἰσιν οἱ λελειμμένοι μόνον.
οὔπω μέγ' οὐδέν, εἰ τὰ τῶν πολλῶν λέγω,
25 οἳ μηδὲ τὸ πρὶν ἦσαν ἐν τάξει καλῶν,
βοσκηματώδεις καὶ κάτω νενευκότες.
ἡμεῖς δ' ὁ δεινὸς καὶ τραχὺς χαραδρεών·
ἡμῶν τὸ σύστημ' ἔκλυτον, θρηνῶν λέγω,
ὅσοι καθήμεθ' οὐ καλῶς ὑψίθρονοι,

30 λαοῦ πρόεδροι, τοῦ καλοῦ διδάσκαλοι,
ψυχὰς τρέφειν λαχόντες ἐνθέῳ τροφῇ,
αὐτοὶ δὲ λιμώττοντες· ἰατροὶ παθῶν,
νεκροὶ βρύοντες ἀφθόνοις νοσήμασιν·
τρίβων ὁδηγοὶ τῶν ἐπικρήμνων ἴσως,
35 ἃς οὔποθ' ὡδήγησαν οὔθ' ὡδεύκασιν·
οἷς μηδ' ἕπεσθαι δόγμα συντομώτατον
σωτηρίας δίδαγμά τ' εὐστοχώτατον·
ὅσων τὸ βῆμα τοῦ τρόπου κατήγορον,
κιγκλὶς διείργουσ' οὐ βίους, ἀλλ' ὀφρύας.

40 Ἐξ ὧν δ' ὑπήχθην ταῦτα δοῦναι τῷ λόγῳ
– οὐ γὰρ φίλον μοι πολλὰ ῥαψῳδεῖν μάτην –,
ἀκουσάτω πᾶς, οἵ τε νῦν οἵ θ' ὕστερον.
μικρὸν δ' ἄνωθεν τὰς ἐμὰς περιστάσεις
εἰπεῖν ἀνάγκη, κἂν δέῃ μακρηγορεῖν,

45 τοῦ μὴ καθ' ἡμῶν ἰσχύσαι ψευδεῖς λόγους.
οἱ γὰρ κακοὶ φιλοῦσιν, ὧν δρῶσιν κακῶς,
εἰς τοὺς παθόντας περιτρέπειν τὰς αἰτίας,
ὡς ἂν κακῶσι καὶ πλέον τοῖς ψεύσμασιν,
αὐτοὺς δ' ὑπεκλύσωσι τῶν ἐγκλημάτων.
50 ἔστω δὲ τοῦτο τοῦ λόγου προοίμιον.

20  Everything ends in disaster: even good things are by time
    outworn. Little or nothing remains,
    as when the earth is swept away by heavy showers
    and the pebbles are all that is left.
    This is by no means important, if I refer to the situation of
        the many
25  who never, not even earlier, were included in the ranks of
        the good,
    being like cattle with their heads bowed down.
    We,[4] however, are the terrible and violent torrent;
    our community has been broken up, I tell it weeping,
    we who are not worthy to sit on our high thrones,
30  leaders of the people, teachers of virtue,
    appointed to nourish souls with divine food,
    while we ourselves go hungry; healers of suffering,
    we ourselves are corpses teeming with numerous diseases.
    Guides along steep paths we may be,
35  but along these we have never walked or led.
    Not to follow such guides is the most succinct advice
    and the most apposite lesson for salvation.
    The chancel accuses them for their behaviour,
    the altar-screen marks no difference in their lives, only in
        their pride.
40  My reasons for undertaking to give an account of these
        things
    (for I do not like to spin a long story to no purpose),
    let all hear, both my contemporaries and future generations.
    To tell of my situation a little further back in time,
    is necessary, even if it means speaking at length,
45  to prevent false reports of me prevailing.
    For malicious people tend to divert the blame
    for their own wicked deeds onto their victims
    so as to harm them even more by their lies
    while washing themselves clean of accusations.
50  Let this stand as the prologue to my account.

---

[4] In lines 27–39 Gregory seems to be referring to the clergy of the Christian church in general, deeply aware of their weaknesses and failings.

Ἦν μοι πατὴρ καλός τε κἀγαθὸς σφόδρα,
γηραιός, ἁπλοῦς τὸν τρόπον, στάθμη βίου,
πάτραρχος ὄντως, Ἀβραάμ τις δεύτερος,
ὤν, οὐ δοκῶν, ἄριστος, οὐ τὸν νῦν τρόπον·
55 πλάνης τὸ πρόσθεν, ὕστερον Χριστοῦ φίλος,
ἔπειτα ποιμήν, ποιμένων ὅ τι κράτος.
μήτηρ θ', ἵν' εἴπω συντόμως, ὁμόζυγος
ἀνδρὸς τοσούτου καὶ τάλαντον ἀρρεπές,
ἐξ εὐσεβῶν τὸ πρόσθεν εὐσεβεστέρα,

60 θῆλυς τὸ σῶμα, τὸν τρόπον δ' ἀνδρὸς πέρα·
ἄμφω λάλημα κοινὸν ἐξ ἴσου βίῳ.
τῷ τοῦτο δῆλον; πῶς τεκμηριῶ λόγον;
αὐτὴν ἐπάξομ', ὧνπερ εἶπον, μάρτυρα,
ἐμὴν τεκοῦσαν, τῆς ἀληθείας στόμα,

65 κρῦψαί τι μᾶλλον τῶν φανερῶν εἰθισμένην
ἢ τῶν ἀδήλων κομπάσαι δόξης χάριν.
φόβος γὰρ ἦγεν, ὃς μέγας διδάσκαλος.
   Αὕτη ποθοῦσα παιδὸς ἄρρενος γόνον
ἰδεῖν ἐν οἴκῳ, πρᾶγμα ὂν πολλοῖς φίλον,
70 θεῷ προσωμίλησε καὶ δεῖται πόθου
τυχεῖν. ἐπεὶ δ' ἦν δυσκάθεκτος τὴν φρένα,
δῶρον δίδωσιν, ὅνπερ ἠξίου λαβεῖν,
καὶ τὴν δόσιν φθάνουσα τῇ προθυμίᾳ.
καὶ τοίνυν εὐχῆς οὐχ ἁμαρτάνει φίλης,
75 ἀλλ' ἧκεν αὐτῇ δεξιὸν προοίμιον
ὄψις σκιὰν φέρουσα τῶν αἰτουμένων.

## Gregory's life before the move to Constantinople (51–551)

### Birth and childhood (51–100)

I had a father[5] who was very much a gentleman,
an elderly man, simple in his ways, a standard for our life,
truly a patriarch, a second Abraham,
not just seeming but being the best, not like people now.
55 Formerly he had wandered away[6] but later became Christ's friend,
then His shepherd, the model of a strong shepherd.
And my mother, to describe her briefly, was an equal partner
for a man of such qualities, complementing him perfectly.
She came from a devout family, even more devout herself,
60 a woman in body but in her way of life more than a man:
both of them equally famous, their lives equally matched.
What evidence is there for this? How shall I prove this claim?
I shall call her as witness to my words,
my own mother, she who was the very mouthpiece of truth.
65 She was prepared to conceal something that was obvious
rather than boast about private matters to gain glory:
for fear was her guide, which is a powerful teacher.
She longed to see a male child
in her house – something which many wish for –
70 and so she spoke to God and prayed to obtain
her wish. Since she was so determined,
she promised to give the gift she hoped to receive:
thus in her eagerness did she anticipate its granting.
And indeed she did not fail to obtain her dearest wish:
75 there came to her a propitious foretaste,
a vision bringing a foreshadowing of her request.

---

[5] Gregory the elder was probably born about 280, in which case he would have been around fifty when Gregory was born.
[6] Gregory the elder had belonged for many years to a Judeo-pagan sect known as the Hypsistarii before becoming a Christian; see also *Oration* 18.5.

ἐμὸν γὰρ εἶδος ἐμφανῶς παρίσταται
καὶ κλῆσις· ἡδ' ἦν ἔργον ἡ νυκτὸς χάρις.
ἐγὼ γὰρ αὐτοῖς γίνομ', εἰ μὲν ἄξιος
80 εὐχῆς, τὸ δῶρον τοῦ δεδωκότος θεοῦ·
εἰ δ' οὖν ἀπευκτός, τῆς ἐμῆς ἁμαρτίας.
Οὕτω μὲν οὖν παρῆλθον εἰς τοῦτον βίον,
πηλῷ κερασθείς — φεῦ τάλας — καὶ συνθέσει,
ὑφ' ὧν κρατούμεθ' ἢ κρατοῦμεν ὧν μόγις·
85 πλὴν παντὸς ἀρραβῶνα καλλίστου λαβὼν
τὴν γένεσιν αὐτήν· οὐ γὰρ ἀχαριστεῖν θέμις.
ὡς δ' ἧκον, εὐθὺς γίνομαι ἀλλότριος
ἀλλοτρίωσιν τὴν καλήν. τῷ γὰρ θεῷ
παρίσταμ' ὡς ἀμνός τις ἢ μόσχος φίλος,
90 θῦμ' εὐγενές τε καὶ λόγῳ τιμώμενον —
ὀκνῶ γὰρ εἰπεῖν, ὡς Σαμουὴλ τις νέος,
πλὴν εἰ βλέποιμι πρὸς πόθον δεδωκότων.
Τραφεὶς δ' ἐν ἅπασι τοῖς καλοῖς ἐκ σπαργάνων
(τύπους γὰρ εἶχον τοὺς ἀρίστους οἴκοθεν)
95 ἤδη τιν' αἰδῶ τοῦ γέρως ἐλάμβανον,
καί μοι κατὰ μικρόν, ὥσπερ ἐκ γνόφου νέφος,
συνήγεθ' ἡ τοῦ κρείσσονος προθυμία.
πρόσω δ' ἔβαινον συντρέχοντος καὶ λόγου,
βίβλων τ' ἔχαιρον ταῖς θεοῦ συνηγόροις,
100 ἀνδρῶν θ' ὡμίλουν τοῖς ἀρίστοις τὸν τρόπον.

Τοιαῦτα μὲν δὴ ταῦτα· τἀπίλοιπα δέ
οὐκ οἶδ', ὁποίαν τοῦ λόγου τέμω τρίβον.
κρύψω τὰ θαύμαθ', οἷς με προὔτρεψεν θεός,
ἀρχὴν ἀρίστην τὴν προθυμίαν λαβών
105 (οὕτω γὰρ ἕλκειν οἶδεν εἰς σωτηρίαν),
ἢ θῶ προθύμως ἐκλαλήσας εἰς μέσον

For my appearance, together with my name, was clearly
    revealed.
That favour, appearing by night, was genuine,
for I was born to them, if indeed I am worthy
80 of the prayer, the gift of God who granted it.
But if I am not what they prayed for, it is my own fault.
And so I entered into this life,
combined with clay – alas, wretch that I am – and
    composite elements,
which either control us or which we with difficulty control.
85 Yet I take this birth itself as the pledge of all that is best,
for it is not right to be ungrateful.
As soon as I arrived I immediately became another's
by means of a beneficial estrangement; for to God
I was offered like a lamb or a sweet calf,
90 a noble sacrifice and one endowed with reason –
I would hesitate to say, like a second Samuel,
if I did not have in mind the longing of those who offered
    me.
Brought up amidst every kind of virtue from infancy
(for I had the very best models in my own home),
95 I soon took on a certain dignity of age,
and gradually there came upon me, as a cloud out of
    darkness,
a desire for something greater.
I progressed according to the development of reason:
I enjoyed those books that spoke of God
100 and associated with men of the best character.

*Passage to Athens (101–210)*

So much for these matters. As to the rest,
I do not know which path to take in my account.
Shall I conceal the wonders God used to urge me on,
taking my eagerness as his starting-point
105 (for he knows that this is the way to draw us to salvation)?
Or shall I speak out readily and make them public?

τὸ μὲν γὰρ ἀχάριστον, τὸ δ' οὐκ ἔξω τύφου.
σιγᾶν ἄμεινον – ἀρκέσει τό μ' εἰδέναι –,
μὴ καὶ μάχεσθαι τῷ λόγῳ τὰ νῦν δοκῇ

110 πλεῖστον δέοντα τῆς τότε προθυμίας.
ὃ δ' οὖν ἀνάγκη, γνωρίσω τοῖς πλείοσιν.
ἄχνους παρειά, τῶν λόγων δ' ἔρως ἐμέ
θερμός τις εἶχε. καὶ γὰρ ἐζήτουν λόγους
δοῦναι βοηθοὺς τοὺς νόθους τοῖς γνησίοις,

115 ὡς μήτ' ἐπαίροινθ' οἱ μαθόντες οὐδὲ ἕν
πλὴν τῆς ματαίας καὶ κενῆς εὐγλωττίας,
τῆς ἐν ψόφοις τε καὶ λάρυγξι κειμένης,
μήτ' ἐνδεοίμην πλεκτάναις σοφισμάτων.
ἐκεῖνο δ' οὔποτ' εἰς ἐμὴν ἦλθε φρένα,

120 πρόσω τι θεῖναι τῶν ἐμῶν παιδευμάτων.
ὅπερ δὲ πάσχει θερμότης ἀεὶ νέων,
ὁρμαῖς ἀτάκτοις εὐκόλως ῥιπίζεται,
ὡς πῶλος ᾄττων εἰς δρόμους θυμοῦ πλέως,
πέπονθα τοῦτο. τῆς γὰρ ὥρας παντελῶς

125 ἔξω, θαλάσσης οὐκέθ' ἡμερουμένης –
Ταύρου τιν' οὐρὰν οὐκ ἀκίνδυνόν φασιν
οἱ ταῦτα δεινοί, πλοῦν θράσους, ἀλλ' οὐ φρενός –
τότ' οὖν Ἀλεξάνδρειαν ἐκλιπὼν ἐγώ
(κἀνθένδε γάρ τι τῶν λόγων ἐδρεψάμην)

One course seems ungrateful, the other is not free from
   pride.
To keep silent is better – it is enough that I should know –
so that my present situation, which seems completely to lack
110 my early enthusiasm, does not conflict with my account.
Just what is necessary, then, shall I reveal to a wider
   audience.
While my cheek was still beardless, a passionate love of
   letters
possessed me. Indeed I sought to make bastard letters[7]
serve as assistants to the genuine ones,
115 to prevent those becoming arrogant who had learned
   nothing at all
apart from vain and empty glibness of tongue,
(which is merely the product of sounds in the throat),
and myself becoming entangled in the meshes of their
   sophisms.
It had never occurred to me
120 to prefer anything to the subjects I was studying,
but I did undergo a common experience of hot-blooded
   youth –
when one is all too easily swayed by undisciplined forces,
like a mettlesome colt galloping over the racecourse.
For completely outside the season,[8]
125 when the sea was no longer calm
(those who are experts in these matters speak of a
   dangerous
tail of Taurus,[9] when to sail is rash, not sensible),
at that moment I left Alexandria
(I had gone there to cull a few fruits of learning)

---

[7] Gregory is here referring to pagan Greek literature and its relation to Christian writing.
[8] For an account of this storm-tossed crossing, see also *Poem* II.1.1.308ff. and *Oration* 18.31.
[9] Gregory appears to be referring to the autumn rising of the constellation Pleiades which formed the tail of Taurus: its rising marked the beginning of the stormy winter season. For further discussion, see Jungck's edition of *De Vita Sua*, p. 157.

130 ἄρας ἔτεμνον πόντον εὐθὺς Ἑλλάδος.
   Κύπρου τὰ πλευρά· καὶ στάσις τῶν πνευμάτων
   ἔβραζε τὴν ναῦν καὶ τὰ πάντ' ἦν νὺξ μία·
   γῆ, πόντος, αἰθήρ, οὐρανὸς ζοφούμενος·
   βρονταὶ δ' ἐπήχουν ἀστραπῶν τινάγμασιν,
135 κάλοι δ' ἐρόχθουν ἱστίων πληρουμένων.
   ἔκλινεν ἱστός, οἰάκων δ' οὐδὲν σθένος·
   βίᾳ γὰρ ἡρπάζοντο χειρὸς αὐχένες.
   πλῆρες δ' ὑπερτοιχοῦντος ὕδατος σκάφος.
   βοὴ δὲ συμμιγής τε καὶ θρήνων πλέως
140 ναυτῶν, κελευστῶν, δεσποτῶν, ἐπιβάτων[1],
   Χριστὸν καλούντων ἐκ μιᾶς συμφωνίας,
   καὶ τῶν, ὅσοι τὸ πρόσθεν ἠγνόουν θεόν·
   ὁ γὰρ φόβος δίδαγμα καιριώτερον.
   ὃ δ' ἦν ἁπάντων σχετλιώτατον κακῶν,
145 ἄνυδρος ἡ ναῦς· εὐθὺ γὰρ στροβουμένης
   νεὼς ῥαγεῖσα σπείρετ' ἐν βυθῷ σκάφη,
   ἣ τὸν γλυκὺν θησαυρὸν εἶχεν ὕδατος.
   λιμοῦ δ' ἀγὼν ἦν καὶ ζάλης καὶ πνευμάτων
   νεκροὺς γενέσθαι. τοῦδε μὲν λύσιν θεός

150 εἶδεν ταχεῖαν. ἔμποροι γὰρ Φοινίκης
   ἄφνω φανέντες, καίπερ ὄντες ἐν φόβῳ,
   λιταῖς μαθόντες τὸ στενὸν τοῦ κινδύνου,
   κοντῶν ἐρεισμοῖς καὶ χερῶν ἀράγματα
   νεῶν φυγόντες (καὶ γὰρ ἦσαν εὐσθενεῖς)

155 σῴζουσιν ἡμᾶς ποντίους ἤδη νεκρούς,
   ὡς ἐκ θαλάσσης ἐκλιπόντας ἰχθύας
   ἢ λαμπάδα θνήσκουσαν οὐκ οὔσης τροφῆς.
        Ὁ δ' ἠγριοῦτο καὶ πλέον βρυχώμενος
   πόντος καθ' ἡμῶν ἡμέραις ἐν πλείοσιν

---

[1] 140 ἐπιβάτων: sic PG – †ἐπηβόλων† Jungck

130 and setting sail I held course straight for Greece.
Along the coast of Cyprus the winds' uprising
threw our ship into confusion; all became one darkness:
earth, sea, air and blackened sky.
Claps of thunder resounded, accompanied by lightning flashes
135 and the ropes which tied the billowing sails creaked loudly.
The mast leaned over, the rudders were powerless,
for the tillers were violently wrenched from one's hands.
The hull was full of water washing over the ship.
Shouts mingled with weeping were heard
140 from sailors, helmsman, officers and passengers[10] alike
all calling on Christ with one accord,
even those who had been agnostics hitherto:
for fear provides an opportune lesson.
Of all our misfortunes the most terrible
145 was that the ship was without water, for when it began to pitch,
the barrel containing the sweet treasure of water
broke open and was scattered over the deep.
Hunger, choppy seas and winds competed
to see which could turn us into corpses first. God found a means of
150 swift release from all this: for Phoenician merchants
suddenly appeared, and although they were themselves afraid,
when they understood from our entreaties the gravity of our situation,
they used their poles and hands to prevent a crash
between the ships (for they were very strong),
155 thus saving us, we who were already corpses of the sea,
like fish washed up from the waves
or like a light flickering out from lack of oil.
The sea, however, continued to rage against us,
roaring even louder for several days.

---

[10] I have chosen the reading given in *PG* in preference to that given by Jungck which seems less fitting in the context.

160 οὔθ' οἳ πλέοιμεν εἰδότων πολλαῖς στροφαῖς
οὔτε τιν' ὁρώντων ἐκ θεοῦ σωτηρίαν.
πάντων δὲ τὸν κοινὸν θάνατον δεδοικότων
ὁ κρυπτὸς ἦν ἔμοιγε φρικωδέστερος.
καθαρσίων γάρ, οἷς θεούμεθ', ὑδάτων

165 ἠλλοτριούμην ὕδασι ξενοκτόνοις.
τοῦτ' ἦν ὀδυρμός, τοῦτ' ἔμοιγε συμφορά,
τούτῳ βοὰς ἔπεμπον, ἐκτείνων χέρας,
ὑπερκτυπούσας κυμάτων πολὺν ῥόθον,
ῥήξας χιτῶνα, κείμενος πρηνὴς τάλας.
170 ὃ δ' ἐστὶν οὐ πιστὸν μὲν, ἀψευδὲς δ' ἄγαν,
πάντες παρέντες τὴν ἑαυτῶν συμφοράν
ἐμοὶ συνῆγον ἐκβοὰς εὐκτηρίους,
πλωτῆρες εὐσεβοῦντες ἐν κοινοῖς κακοῖς·
οὕτω συνήλγουν τοῖς ἐμοῖς παθήμασιν.
175      Σὺ καὶ τότ' ἦσθα, Χριστέ μου, σωτὴρ μέγας,
καὶ νῦν ἐλευθερῶν με κυμάτων βίου.
ἐπεὶ γὰρ οὐδὲν ἐλπίδος χρηστῆς ὑπῆν,
οὐ νῆσος, οὐκ ἤπειρος, οὐκ ὀρῶν ἄκρα,
οὐ πυρσός, οὐ πλωτῆρσιν ἀστέρες σκοποί,

180 οὐ μικρόν, οὐ μεῖζόν τι τῶν ὁρωμένων,
τί μηχανῶμαι; τίς πόρος τῶν δυσχερῶν;
πάντων ἀπογνοὺς τῶν κάτω πρὸς σὲ βλέπω,
ζωή, πνοή μου, φῶς, κράτος, σωτηρία,
φοβῶν, πατάσσων, μειδιῶν, ἰώμενε,

185 πλέκων τὸ χρηστὸν τοῖς ἐναντίοις ἀεί.
πάντων δ' ὑπομνήσας σε τῶν πρὶν θαυμάτων,
187 οἷς τὴν μεγίστην χεῖρά σου γνωρίζομεν,
190 Αἰγυπτίων μάστιξιν ἐκτετριμμένων,
188 πόντου ῥαγέντος Ἰσραὴλ ὁδευκότος,

160 We did not know where we were sailing (we kept going
      round in circles)
   nor could we see any rescue coming from God.
   Although we all feared a common death,
   more terrifying to me was the death concealed:
   for by those murderous waters I was being kept away
165 from the purifying waters[11] by which we are made divine.
   This was the source of my grief, this was my misfortune,
   for this reason I shouted out, stretching forth my hands,
   (shouts which echoed above the great roar of the waves),
   and tore my clothes, lying prostrate in my misery.
170 It is an incredible fact but absolutely true
   that everyone disregarded their own troubles
   and joined with me in cries of prayer –
   sea-farers showing their piety in shared misfortunes.
   Thus did they share the pain of my sufferings.
175 Even then you were, my Christ, a great saviour,
   just as now you save me from the storms of life.
   For when there was no longer any hope of a happy
      outcome –
   no island, no mainland, no cliffs on the coastline,
   no beacon, no stars to guide the sailors,
180 nothing either large or small that one could see –
   what was I to do? What way was there out of these
      difficulties?
   Despairing of everything here below I looked to you,
   my life, my breath, my light, my strength, my salvation,
   you who terrify and strike, smile and heal,
185 ever entwining the good with its opposite.
   I reminded you of all your former miracles
   in which we recognise your powerful hand:
190 of the Egyptians utterly destroyed by the plagues,[12]
188 of the sea which parted to allow Israel to cross it,[13]

---

[11] i.e. in baptism.
[12] Text altered so that these events should be referred to in the order in which they occur in the Old Testament; on the plagues sent to harass the Egyptians, see Exodus 7–11.
[13] Exodus 14: 21–2.

189 χειρῶν ἐπάρσει δυσμενῶν ἡττημένων,
191 αὐτης στρατάρχαις τῆς κτίσεως δουλουμένης,
σάλπιγξι τειχῶν καὶ δρόμῳ πορθουμένων,
προσθείς τε τἀμὰ τοῖς πάλαι βοωμένοις,
"σός", εἶπον, "εἰμὶ, καὶ τὸ πρὶν καὶ νῦν ἔτι.
195 σὺ δίς με λήψῃ, κτῆμα τῶν σοι τιμίων,
γῆς καὶ θαλάσσης δῶρον, ἐξηγνισμένον
εὐχῇ τε μητρὸς καὶ φόβοις ἐξαισίοις.
σοὶ ζήσομ', εἰ φύγοιμι δισσὸν κίνδυνον.
σὺ ζημιώσῃ λάτριν, εἰ προσοῖό με.

200 καὶ νῦν μαθητὴς ἐν σάλῳ· τίνασσέ μοι
τὸν ὕπνον ἢ πέζευε, καὶ στήτω φόβος."
Ταῦτ' εἶπον· ἡ δ' ἔληξε πνευμάτων στάσις,
πίπτει δὲ πόντος, ἡ δὲ ναῦς εὐθύπλοος.
καὶ τοῦτο δ' ἐστὶν ἐμπόρευμα τῆς ἐμῆς
205 εὐχῆς· τὸ γὰρ πλήρωμα τῆς νεὼς ἅπαν
ἀπῆλθον εὐσεβοῦντες εἰς Χριστὸν μέγαν,
διπλῆν λαβόντες ἐκ θεοῦ σωτηρίαν.
Ῥόδον δ' ὑπερβαλόντες μικρὸν ὕστερον
εἰς Αἰγινήτην ὅρμον (Αἰγιναία γὰρ
210 ἡ ναῦς) πλέοντες οὐρίᾳ κατήραμεν.


Ἔπειτ' Ἀθῆναι καὶ λόγοι. τἀκεῖσε δέ
ἄλλοι λεγόντων, ὡς μὲν ἐν φόβῳ θεοῦ
ἀνεστράφημεν πρῶτα τὰ πρῶτ' εἰδότες·
ὡς δ' ἐν νέων ἀκμῇ τε καὶ φορᾷ θράσους,
215 ἄλλων σὺν ἄλλαις φατρίαις οἰστρουμένων,
οὕτω διεξήειμεν ἥσυχον βίον

189 of the enemies defeated by the raising of hands,[14]
191 of creation itself obeying the leaders of the army,[15]
of walls destroyed by a procession with trumpets.[16]
I added my own entreaties to those of old,
saying, 'I am yours now, too, as before.
195 Accept me a second time, the possession of those dear to
you,
a gift from both land and sea, consecrated
by my mother's prayer and by overpowering fear.
For you will I live if I escape the double danger,[17]
but if you abandon me you will lose a servant.
200 Now again one of your disciples is in a storm: for my sake
shake off your sleep and walk; let fear be stilled.'[18]
These were my words. The storm abated,
the sea subsided, the ship sailed on a straight course –
all this as a result of my prayer.
205 All the ship's passengers and crew
went on their way praising the great Christ,
for they had received from God a double salvation.
After passing Rhodes a little later
and sailing before a favourable wind, we docked
210 (it being an Aeginetan ship) in the harbour at Aegina.

## *Student life at Athens*[19] *(211–236)*

Then came Athens and studies – but of what happened
there
let others tell: how we lived
in fear of God, aware that first things are first;
how among the youth's elite, driven by recklessness,
215 all racing around frantically in different gangs,
we led a life of such calm –

---

[14] Exodus 17: 11.
[15] Numbers 20:9–12 and Joshua 10: 12–13.
[16] Joshua 6.
[17] i.e. physical and spiritual death.
[18] See Mark 4: 37-41 for an account of Jesus' calming of the storm.
[19] Cf. *Oration* 43.14-24 for another account of Gregory's student days.

— πηγή τις, οἶμαι, πόντιος καθ' ὑδάτων
γλυκεῖα πικρῶν, ὥσπερ οὖν πιστεύεται —
οὔθ' ἑλκόμενοι πρὸς τῶν φερόντων εἰς βλάβην,
220 ἕλκοντες αὐτοί τ' εἰς τὰ κρείσσω τοὺς φίλους.
    Καὶ γὰρ με καὶ τοῦτ' εὖ πεποίηκεν θεός·
συνῆψεν ἀνδρὶ τῷ σοφωτάτῳ φέρων,
μόνῳ βίον τε καὶ λόγον πάντων ἄνω.
τίς οὗτος; ἢ γνώσεσθε ῥᾳδίως λίαν.
225 Βασίλειος ἦν, τὸ μέγ' ὄφελος τοῦ νῦν βίου.
τοῦτον λόγου τε καὶ στέγης καὶ σκεμμάτων
κοινωνὸν εἶχον. εἴ τι δεῖ καὶ κομπάσαι·
ξυνωρὶς ἦμεν οὐκ ἄσημος Ἑλλάδι.
τὰ πάντα μὲν δὴ κοινά, καὶ ψυχὴ μία
230 δυοῖν δέουσα σωμάτων διάστασιν.
ὃ δ' εἰς ἓν ἡμᾶς διαφερόντως ἤγαγεν,
τοῦτ' ἦν· θεός τε καὶ πόθος τῶν κρεισσόνων.
ἐξ οὗ γὰρ εἰς τοσοῦτο θάρσους ἤλθομεν,
ὥστ' ἐκλαλῆσαι καὶ τὰ καρδίας βάθη,

235 πλέον συνεσφίγγημεν ἀλλήλοις πόθῳ.
τὸ γὰρ ὁμόγνωμον πιστὸν εἰς συμφυΐαν.


    Τί λοιπόν; ἡ πατρίς τε καὶ βίου τύποι.
καὶ γὰρ πολὺς τέτριπτο τοῖς λόγοις χρόνος·
ἤδη τριακοστόν μοι σχεδὸν τοῦτ' ἦν ἔτος.
240 ἐνταῦθ' ἐπέγνων, οἷον εἰς ἡμᾶς πόθον
οἵαν τε δόξαν εἶχον οἱ συμπαίστορες.
παρῆν ὁ καιρός — καὶ παρῆν πολὺς πόνος.

like a spring, so to speak, of sweet water
believed to exist beneath the bitter waters of the sea.
Nor were we seduced by those who led the way to trouble;
220 instead we ourselves drew our friends on to higher things.
And indeed, God granted me this favour too:
he took me and attached me to the wisest man,
the only person, in his life and thought, superior to all.
Who was this man? No doubt you will easily recognise him.
225 It was Basil,[20] the great benefactor of our age.
With him I shared my studies, my lodgings and
my thoughts. And if I might boast a little,
we formed a pair famous throughout Greece.
All things we held in common and one soul
230 united our two separate bodies.[21]
What particularly brought us together
was this: God and a desire for higher things.
For from the moment we achieved such a degree of confidence
that we divulged to each other even the deep secrets of our hearts,
235 we were bound together all the more closely by our longing,
for shared ideals are a strong incentive to close friendship.

### Return home (237–276)

What came then? My country and the choice of a way of life.
For indeed much time had been spent in study
and already I had nearly reached my thirtieth year.
240 Then I realised what great affection
and what respect our companions had for us:
the moment of departure had arrived, and with it much grief.

---

[20] Basil of Caesarea, 329/30–379.
[21] Cf. Acts 4: 32 and the proverbial statements from antiquity referring to friends holding all in common and forming one soul in two bodies. Cf. Carolinne White, *Christian Friendship in the Fourth Century* (Cambridge, 1992).

έδει περιπλοκῶν τε καὶ στυγνῶν λόγων,
τῶν ἐξοδίων μνήμης τ' ἐμπυρευμάτων.
245 τῷ μὲν βίᾳ τε καὶ μόγις, εἶξαν δ' ὅμως,
εἰπόντι πολλὰς αἰτίας τῆς ἐξόδου.
ἐμοὶ δὲ καὶ νῦν προτρέχει τὸ δάκρυον
τῆς τηνικαῦτα συγχύσεως μεμνημένῳ.
πάντες περιστάντες με σὺν πολλῷ τάχει,

250 ξένοι, συνήθεις, ἥλικες, διδάσκαλοι,
ὅρκοις, ὀδυρμοῖς, καὶ τι μιγνύντες βίας
(τὸ γὰρ φιλεῖν ἔπειθε τολμᾶν καὶ τόδε)
ἀπρὶξ κατεῖχον μηδ' ἄν, εἰ γένοιτό τι,
πέμψειν λέγοντες ἐκεῖθεν - οὐδὲ γὰρ πρέπειν
255 ἡμῶν Ἀθήνας ἐκπεσεῖν τὰς τιμίας –
ὡς δὴ λόγων δώσοντες ἐκ ψήφου κράτος·
ἕως ἔκαμψαν - καὶ γὰρ ἦν δρυὸς μόνης
θρήνοις τοσούτοις ἀντιβῆναι καὶ λόγοις –
οὐ μὴν τελείως· καὶ γὰρ ἀνθεῖλκεν πατρίς

260 πίστει κρατοῦσα τῶν ὑφ' ἡλίῳ σχεδόν,
ἐν ᾗ φιλοσοφεῖν τῶν καλῶν ἐφαίνετο,
γονεῖς τε γήρᾳ καὶ χρόνῳ κεκμηκότες.
   Ἔτ' οὖν Ἀθήναις μικρὸν ἐμμείνας χρόνον
ἔκλεψα μικροῦ λάθρᾳ τὴν ἐκδημίαν·

265 ἦλθον, λόγους ἔδειξα, τήν τινων νόσον
ἔπλησ' ἀπαιτούντων με τοῦθ' ὥς τι χρέος.
οὐ γὰρ κρότων ἔμοιγε καὶ ψόφων λόγος
οὐδὲ βλακευμάτων τε καὶ λυγισμάτων,
οἷς οἱ σοφοὶ χαίρουσιν ἐν πλήθει νέων.

It was a time for embraces and sad words,
words of farewell which serve to kindle memories.
245 Basil they allowed to leave, with difficulty and under
pressure,
after he had given them many reasons for departure,
but as for me, even now my tears flow forth
when I remember my confusion at that time.
Suddenly they all surrounded me –
250 strangers, close friends, fellow students and teachers –
using oaths and lamentations to hold me, not without some
violence
(for their affection drove them to dare even this).
They said that whatever happened
they would not let me leave that place; it was not right
255 that we should be lost to highly honoured Athens;
they intended, they said, to vote me the prize in rhetoric.
At last they forced me to submit (for only an oak tree
could have withstood such powerful laments and
arguments),
but not completely, for I was pulled the opposite way by my
country –
260 which is firmer in its faith than almost any beneath the
sun:
there to lead a life of philosophy seemed an excellent
thing –
and also by my parents, worn out by old age and the
passing of time.
And so, after I had stayed in Athens a little while longer,
I departed secretly, unknown to almost anyone.
265 When I arrived home I gave a sample of my eloquence to
satisfy
the excessive desire of those demanding this of me as if it
were a debt.
But to me rhetoric was not a matter of noisy applause
or of showy expressions or verbal contortions
in which the sophists delight amidst crowds of young men.

270 πρῶτον δὲ τοῦτο φιλοσοφῆσαι προυθέμην,
ῥῖψαι θεῷ καὶ τἆλλα καὶ πόνους λόγων,
ὡς οἱ παρέντες μηλοβότους τὰς οὐσίας
ἢ χρυσὸν ἀθροίσαντες εἰς ἅλμης βυθούς.
ἀλλ' ὃ προεῖπον, τοις φίλοις ὠρχησάμην.
275 ταῦτ' ἦν ἀγώνων ὥσπερ ἐγγυμνάσματα
ἢ καὶ προτέλεια μειζόνων μυστηρίων.

Ἔδει δὲ λοιπὸν ἀνδρικῶν βουλευμάτων.
ἔνδον καθίζω τῶν φίλων κριτήριον,
ἐμῶν λογισμῶν γνησίων παραινετῶν.
280 στρόμβος κατεῖχε τὴν ἐμὴν δεινὸς φρένα
τὸ κρεῖσσον ἐκζητοῦντος ἐν τοῖς κρείσσοσι.
τὸ μὲν τὰ σαρκὸς εἰς βυθοὺς ῥῖψαι πάλαι
δεδογμένον τ' ἦν καὶ τότ' ἤρεσκεν πλέον.
αὐτῶν δέ μοι σκοποῦντι τῶν θείων ὁδῶν
285 οὐ ῥᾷστον εὑρεῖν τὴν ἀμείνω καὶ λίαν.
ἄλλων γὰρ εἵνεκ' ἄλλο καλὸν ἢ κακὸν
ἐφαίνεθ' ὥσπερ πολλαχοῦ τῶν πρακτέων.
τοιοῦτο τοὐμόν, ὥς τινι προσεικάσαι,
μακράν τιν' οἷον ἐννοῶν ἐκδημίαν

290 πλοῦν μὲν πεφεύγειν καὶ πόνους θαλασσίους,
ὁδὸν δ' ἀνίχνευον, ἥτις εὐπορωτέρα.
Ἠλίαν εἶχον ἐν λόγῳ τὸν Θεσπίτην
καὶ τὸν μέγαν Κάρμηλον ἢ ξένην τροφήν,
τοῦ Προδρόμου τὸ κτῆμα, τὴν ἐρημίαν,

270 I had set this as the first step in the philosophic life:
    to cast everything before God, including my attempts at oratory,
    like those who gave up their land to be grazed by sheep,
    or who threw their gold into the depths of the sea.[22]
    However, as I said before, I danced for my friends.
275 These were, so to speak, preparatory exercises
    or even preliminary initiations to greater mysteries.

*The search for the right way of life*[23] *(277–336)*

    The time had come for manly decisions:
    at home I set up a tribunal of my friends
    to act as sincere advisors in my deliberations.
280 My thoughts were in a terrible whirl
    as I sought in higher things to find what was higher.
    To cast the things of the flesh into the depths
    I had long ago decided, and now the idea pleased me even more.
    But when I actually considered the divine ways
285 it was hard to decide which path was definitely the better.
    Each thing seemed good or bad depending on the arguments,
    as is often the case when action needs to be taken.
    To draw a comparison: it was as if
    in planning a long journey to a foreign land,
290 I had rejected a voyage by ship and the dangers of the sea
    but was still trying to work out the most direct route.
    I admired Elijah the Tishbite[24]
    and the great Carmel[25] or the strange food,
    the property of the Precursor, the desert,[26]

---

[22] Gregory has in mind here the stories about various Presocratic philosophers; see e.g. Diogenes Laertius 6.87 and Jerome, *Adversus Jovinianum* II.9.
[23] Cf. *Poem* I.2.8, a comparison of different ways of life.
[24] See 1 Kings 17: 1.
[25] See 1 Kings 18: 19.
[26] Matthew 3: 1–4.

295 παίδων Ἰωναδάβ τε ἄσκευον βίον·
θείων τε βίβλων αὖθις ἐκράτει πόθος
καὶ πνεύματος φῶς ἐν λόγου θεωρίᾳ,
πρᾶγμ' οὐκ ἐρήμης ἔργον οὐδ' ἡσυχίας —
ἕως ἐπ' ἄμφω πολλάκις μετακλιθείς

300 τέλος διαιτῶ τοῖς πόθοις τοῦτον τρόπον
καὶ τὴν πλάνην ἔστησα τοῦ νοῦ μετρίως.
ὁρῶν γὰρ, οὓς μὲν πρακτικὸς τέρπει βίος,
ἄλλοις μὲν ὄντας χρησίμους τῶν ἐν μέσῳ,
αὑτοῖς δ' ἀχρήστους καὶ κακοῖς στροβουμένους,

305 ἐξ ὧν τὸ λεῖον ἦθος ἐκκυμαίνεται,
τοὺς δ' ἐκτὸς ὄντας εὐσταθεῖς μὲν πως πλέον
καὶ πρὸς θεὸν βλέποντας ἡσύχῳ νοΐ,
αὑτοῖς μόνοις δὲ χρησίμους φίλτρῳ στενῷ
καὶ ζῶντας ἔξαλλόν τε καὶ τραχὺν βίον,

310 μέσην τιν' ἦλθον ἐρημικῶν καὶ μιγάδων,
τῶν μὲν τὸ σύννουν, τῶν δὲ τὸ χρηστὸν φέρων.
    Προσῆν δὲ μεῖζον καὶ χάρις τῶν τιμίων,
λέγω δὲ τοὺς φύσαντας, οἷς ὑπόχρεως.
τούτων τὸ γῆρας (καὶ γὰρ εὐσεβέστατον

315 γονεῦσι πρώτην ἐκ θεοῦ τιμὴν νέμειν,
ἐξ ὧν ὑπάρχει καὶ τὸ γινώσκειν θεόν)
ἔθαλπον, ἐστήριζον ἐκ παντὸς σθένους,

295 and the simple way of life of the sons of Jonadab.[27]
Then again a desire for the holy scriptures got the upper hand
as did the light of the spirit in the contemplation of the word –
practices not suited to the desert or a life of calm.
After swinging to and fro between these positions many times,
300 I at last reconciled my desires in the following way,
and giving each position its due, checked the vacillations of my mind:
I realised that those who enjoy a practical life
are useful to others who are in the thick of things
but do not benefit themselves; they are distracted by the wicked, too,
305 who disrupt their calm disposition. On the other hand,
those who have withdrawn are in some way more stable
and with a tranquil mind can keep their gaze directed towards God,
but they only benefit themselves, for their love is a narrow one
and strange and harsh is the life they lead.
310 So I chose a middle path between solitude and involvement,[28]
adopting the meditative ways of the one, the usefulness of the other.
There was, too, a greater consideration,[29] my gratitude to those I loved,
I mean my parents, to whom I was endebted.
I tended their old age (for the most important duty in a devout life
315 is to render the greatest honour after God to your parents,
for it is from them that we gain our knowledge of God),
and supported them with all my strength,

---

[27] Jeremiah 35: 6–7.
[28] As so often in his life, Gregory seeks a position of compromise, here couched in terms of the philosophical 'middle way'.
[29] See Gregory, *Letter* 1 to Basil and *Oration* 2.103.

## 34 ΠΕΡΙ ΤΟΝ ΕΑΥΤΟΥ ΒΙΟΝ

ἐχειραγώγουν, ὡς ἐμαυτῷ δεξιόν
θεῖναι τὸ γῆρας, γῆρας ἰλεούμενος.
320 θερίζομεν γάρ, οἷά περ καὶ σπείρομεν.
Τοῦτ᾽ ἦν μέρος μοι φιλοσόφου παιδεύσεως·
τὸ μὴ δοκεῖν τὸν πρῶτον ἐκπονεῖν βίον,
εἶναι δὲ μᾶλλον ἢ δοκεῖν θεῷ φίλον.
στέργειν μὲν οὖν δεῖν ᾠόμην καὶ πρακτικούς,

325 ὅσοι λελόγχασ᾽ ἐκ θεοῦ τιμήν τινα
λαοὺς ἄγοντες ἐνθέοις τελέσμασιν.
πλείων δέ μ᾽ εἶχε τῶν μοναστικῶν πόθος,
καίπερ δοκοῦντα συντετάχθαι πλείοσιν·
τρόπων γὰρ εἶναι τὴν μονήν, οὐ σωμάτων.

330 τὸ βῆμα δ᾽ ἦν μοι σεπτόν, ἀλλ᾽ ἑστηκότι
πόρρωθεν, ὡς φῶς ἡλίου τῶν ὄψεων
ταῖς ἀσθενούσαις. πάντ᾽ ἂν ἤλπισα πλέον
ἢ τοῦτο δέξασθ᾽ ἐν πολλαῖς στροφαῖς βίου.
μηδὲν μέγ᾽ εἴπῃς, συντόμως, ἄνθρωπος ὤν.

335 ἀεὶ κολούει τὰς ἐπάρσεις ὁ φθόνος.
μηδὲν λάβῃς ἔξωθεν, τἀμὰ δὲ σκόπει.

Οὕτω φρονοῦντι δεινὸς ἐμπίπτει κλόνος.
ὁ γὰρ πατήρ με, καίπερ ἀκριβέστατα
γνώμην γινώσκων τὴν ἐμήν, οὐκ οἶδ᾽ ὅθεν,
340 ἴσως δὲ φίλτρῳ πατρικῷ κινούμενος
(δεινὸν δὲ φίλτρον ἐστὶ σὺν ἐξουσίᾳ),
ὡς ἂν κατάσχοι ταῖς πέδαις τοῦ πνεύματος

led them by the hand, so as to make for myself
a happy old age by making their old age comfortable:
320 for we reap exactly what we sow.[30]
This was part of my education as a philosopher:
not merely to seem to be training for the highest form of
    life,
but to be, rather than seem, the friend of God.
And so I thought it necessary also to respect men of
    action[31]
325 who have won from God a place of honour
because they lead the people by means of holy mysteries.
But I was still possessed by a greater love for the solitary
    life,
although outwardly I appeared to be involved in the
    community:
solitude is more a matter of attitude than physical situation.
330 I revered the altar, but as one who stands at a distance,
for it affected me like sunlight falling on
weak eyes. I expected anything rather than
that I should receive this amid all the vicissitudes of life.[32]
In short: make no great claims, for you are just a human
    being.
335 Envy always puts a stop to high ambitions.
You need take no examples from outside, just consider my
    experience.

*Gregory's ordination (337–385)*

While I was in this frame of mind, a terrible shock befell me.
For although my father was well aware
of my views, he forced me to accept a place
340 inferior only to the bishop's throne – I don't know why.
Maybe he was motivated by fatherly love
(for terrible is the love which is combined with power),

---

[30] Cf. Galatians 6: 7.
[31] Gregory here refers to the secular clergy.
[32] Gregory is referring to his ordination as priest.

ὧν τ' εἶχε τιμήσειε τοῖς ἀμείνοσιν,
κάμπτει βιαίως εἰς θρόνων τοὺς δευτέρους.
345 οὕτω μὲν οὖν ἤλγησα τῇ τυραννίδι
— οὔπω γὰρ ἄλλως τοῦτ' ὀνομάζειν ἰσχύω,
καί μοι τὸ θεῖον πνεῦμα συγγιγνωσκέτω
οὕτως ἔχοντι —, ὥστε πάντων ἀθρόως,
φίλων, φυσάντων, πατρίδος, γένους λυθείς,
350 ὡς οἱ μύωπι τῶν βοῶν πεπληγότες,
εἰς Πόντον ἦλθον τῆς ἀνίας φάρμακον
θήσων ἐμαυτῷ τῶν φίλων τὸν ἔνθεον.
ἐκεῖ γὰρ ἤσκει τὴν θεοῦ συνουσίαν,
νέφει καλυφθεὶς ὡς σοφῶν τις τῶν πάλαι·
355 Βασίλειος οὗτος ἦν, ὃς ἐν ἀγγέλοις τὰ νῦν.
τούτῳ τὸ λυποῦν ἐξεμάλθασσον φρενός.
 Ἐπεὶ δ' ὁ μὲν γήρᾳ τε κάμνων καὶ πόθῳ
ἐδεῖτο πολλὰ παιδὸς ὁ χρηστὸς πατήρ
τιμὴν παρασχεῖν ταῖς τελευταίαις πνοαῖς,
360 ἐμοὶ δ' ἔπεσσεν ὁ χρόνος τὴν συμφοράν,
ὡς μήποτ' ἐχρῆν, αὖθις εἰς βυθὸν τρέχω
δείσας στεναγμὸν πατρικῶν κινημάτων,
μή μοι τὸ φίλτρον εἰς κατάραν ἐκπέσῃ·
τοιοῦτόν ἐστιν ἁπλότης ὠργισμένη.
365  Μικρὸν μέσον τι, καὶ πάλιν τρικυμία,
οὐκ ἔστιν εἰπεῖν ὅσσον ἀγριωτέρα.
οὐδὲν δὲ χεῖρον πάντα γνωρίσαι φίλοις.
ἀρχήν τιν' ἔπραττ' οὑμὸς ἀδελφὸς κοσμικήν
— ἀδελφὸς οὑμός, ὦ κάκισθ', ὅσον σθένεις —
370 ἡ δ' ἦν ταμείων πίστις. ἐν δ' ἀρχῇ μέσῃ
θνήσκει, κυνῶν δὲ πλῆθος ἐξανίσταται
τοῖς τοῦ θανόντος χρήμασιν καὶ λειψάνοις.

and wished to bind me with the shackles of the spirit[33]
and honour me with the best of what he had.
345 I suffered such pain as a result of this tyrannical behaviour
(for I cannot call it by any other name;
may the Holy Spirit forgive me for feeling thus),
that all of a sudden I severed my ties with everything,
friends, parents, home and family;
350 just like the cow stung by a gadfly,[34]
I made for Pontus, seeking a remedy
for my pain from that holy friend of mine.
For he was there practising communion with God,
concealed in a cloud like one of the wise men of old.[35]
355 Basil it was, he who is among the angels now –
through him I hoped to soothe the agony in my soul.
But when my good father, weakened by old age
and longing, kept begging his son
to respect his last breaths,
360 and when time had tempered my suffering,
I ran back into the abyss,[36] as I should never have done,
for I feared my father's angry reproaches,
or that his love for me should turn into a curse:
single-mindedness, when angered, is capable of this.
365 After a short interval there came another mighty wave –
how far more devastating I am unable to describe.
But it is better to reveal all to one's friends.
My brother held some worldly position –
O most wicked one,[37] what power you have –
370 involving responsibility for the state finances. In mid-term
he died[38] and a pack of dogs sprang up to prey upon
the dead man's money and estate.

---

[33] Jungck interprets this as referring to the Holy Spirit.
[34] Gregory may here have in mind Io, the girl whom Zeus metamorphosed into a cow to protect her from Hera, but who was stung by a gadfly and ran through Greece into Asia and then into Egypt.
[35] i.e. Moses (Exodus 19: 16–19).
[36] See *Oration 1*. Gregory's ordination was shortly followed by that of Basil.
[37] Gregory is referring here to Satan.
[38] Gregory's *Oration 7* was composed as a funeral oration for his younger brother Caesarius.

πάντ' ἐσπάρασσον οἰκέται, ξένοι, φίλοι.
τίς γὰρ πεσούσης οὐ ξυλεύεται δρυός;
375 Ἐγὼ δ', ὅσον μὲν ἧκεν εἰς ἐμὸν λόγον,
οὔποτ' ἂν ἔδεισα πραγμάτων ἐπιδρομάς·
πτηνὸν γὰρ εἰμι ῥᾳδίως μετάρσιον.
ὅμως δ' ἀνάγκη πάντα τῷ καλῷ πατρί
συνδιαφέρειν, καὶ χρηστὰ καὶ τἀναντία,
380 κοινωνὸν ὄντα πραγμάτων, οὐ χρημάτων.
ὡς δ' οἱ βάσιν τὸ πρῶτον οὐ πεπηγότες
ἅπαξ ὀλισθήσαντες εἰς κρημνοῦ βάθος
πίπτουσιν, οὐκέτ' ὄντες αὑτῶν ἐγκρατεῖς,
οὕτως ἔμοιγε τῶν κακῶν γεγευμένῳ
385 ἄλλοις ἔπ' ἄλλο δεινὸν ἐξηγείρετο.


Ἧκέν ποθ' ἡμῖν - τἀμμέσῳ σιγήσομαι,
τοῦ μὴ δοκεῖν βλάσφημον ἐκφέρειν λόγον
κατ' ἀνδρός, ὃν νῦν εὐλογῶν ἐπαυσάμην —
ἀλλ' ἧκεν ἡμῖν τῶν φίλων ὁ φίλτατος,

390 Βασίλειος — οἴμοι τῶν λόγων· ἐρῶ δ' ὅμως —,
ἄλλος πατήρ μοι φορτικώτερος πολύ·
τὸν μὲν γὰρ ἐχρῆν καὶ τυραννοῦντα στέγειν,
τὸν δ' οὐκ ἀνάγκη τῆς ἑταιρίας χάριν
βλάβην φερούσης, οὐκ ἀπαλλαγὴν κακῶν.


395 οὐκ οἶδ' ἐμαυτοῦ τὰς ἁμαρτίας πλέον,
αἳ πολλὰ δή με πολλάκις δεδήχασιν,
μέμψωμ', ὑπερζέοντος ὡς ἀεὶ νέου
τοῦ συμπεσόντος, ἢ σὲ τῆς ἐπάρσεως,
ἀνδρῶν ἄριστε, ἣν δέδωκεν ὁ θρόνος;

Servants, strangers, friends tore everything apart,
for when an oak tree falls, who does not gather wood?
375 I would never, on my own account,
have feared the onslaught of practical problems,
for I am a bird flying effortlessly, high in the air.
But yet it was necessary to help my good father
to endure it all, both the good things and the bad,
380 sharing his troubles but not his wealth.
Just as those who from the start have no firm foundation,
when once they slip, they fall right to the bottom
of the precipice, no longer in control of themselves,
in the same way I found that once I tasted misfortune,
385 one disaster followed upon another.

### Gregory's consecration as bishop of Sasima (386–485)

Then there came to visit us (I will pass over in silence what happened
in the meantime, lest I should seem to be insulting
a man whom I have just recently been praising),[39]
there came to visit us the dearest of my friends,
390 Basil, – my words cause me grief but I will still speak them –
who behaved like a second father to me, but one far more oppressive:
for I had to love my father even when he acted like a tyrant,
but I did not need to love Basil for friendship's sake
when it brought injury instead of release from suffering.
395 I do not know whether I should blame my sins more,[40]
for they have certainly often bitten me hard
(the incident rankles as sharply as ever in my mind),
or blame you, best of men, for the high-handedness
that came with your elevation to the throne.

---

[39] i.e. in Gregory's *Oration* 43, the funeral oration probably given in Basil's memory on 1 January 382, the third anniversary of his death.

[40] See Gregory's *Letter* 59.3.

400 ὡς τῶν γε λοιπῶν εἵνεχ', ἱλήκοις λόγῳ,
τάχ' οὐδ' ἂν αὐτὸς ἠξίους ὑπερζυγεῖν·
οὔκουν τὸ πρόσθεν, ὦ φέριστ', οὐδ' ἠξίους·
εἰ δ' ἠξίους, τυχόν σε τῶν εὖ εἰδότων
ἄμφω κατέσχεν ἄν τις εὐγνώμων κριτής.

405 τί οὖν πέπονθας; πῶς τοσοῦτον ἀθρόως
ἔρριψας ἡμᾶς; ὡς ὄλοιτ' ἐκ τοῦ βίου
νόμος φιλίας οὕτω σεβούσης τοὺς φίλους.
λέοντες ἦμεν ἐχθές, ἀλλὰ σήμερον
πίθων ἔγωγε· σοὶ δὲ μικρὸν καὶ λέων.

410 εἴ τοί γε πάντας – φθέγξομ' ὑψηλὸν λόγον –
οὕτως ἑώρας τοὺς φίλους, οὐ χρῆν γ' ἐμέ.
ὃν καὶ φίλων ἔμπροσθεν ἦγες ἦν ὅτε,
πρὶν ᾗς ὑπερνεφῶν τὰ πάντ' ἔχων κάτω.
    Τί, θυμέ, βράζεις; εἶργε τὸν πῶλον βίᾳ.


415 πρὸς νύσσαν αὖθις οἱ λόγοι. ἐκεῖνος ἦν
ψεύστης ἔμοιγε, τἆλλα δ' ἀψευδέστατος,
ὅς μου λέγοντος ταῦτ' ἀκούσας πολλάκις,
ὡς νῦν μὲν οἰστὰ πάντα, κἂν χείρω πέσῃ,
εἰ δ' ἐκλίποιεν οἱ τεκόντες τὸν βίον,

420 κἀμοὶ τὰ πράγματ' ἐκλιπεῖν ἅπας λόγος,
ὡς ἄν τι κερδάναιμι τῆς ἀνεστίου
ζωῆς πολίτης ῥᾷστα ὢν παντὸς τόπου –
ταῦτ' οὖν ἀκούων καὶ συναινῶν τῷ λόγῳ
ὅμως βιάζετ' εἰς ἐπισκοπῆς θρόνον,
425 αὐτὸς πατήρ τε δίς με τοῦτο πτερνίσας.

400 As regards other matters, were you to look graciously on
    what I say,
  perhaps you would not consider yourself superior;[41]
  at least you did not do so in earlier days, my dearest friend.
  If you had, maybe one of those who knew us both well,
  a fair-minded judge, would have restrained you.
405 So what happened to you? How could you cast me off
  so suddenly? May the kind of friendship which treats its
    friends
  in such a way be banished from this life.
  We were lions yesterday but today
  I am an ape.[42] But to you even a lion is of little worth.
410 Even if you had regarded all your friends in this way,
  (for I will make a proud claim) you should not have
    regarded me so,
  I whom you once preferred to all your other friends
  before you were raised above the clouds and considered all
    beneath you.
  But why, my soul, do you seethe? Restrain the untamed colt
    by force.
415 My words must turn towards the winning-post. That man
  was false to me but in other respects he was most honest.
  He had often heard me say this,
  that I could bear it all for the time being, even if things got
    worse,
  but if my parents were to depart this life,
420 then I would have every reason to depart from public affairs
  so that I might draw some benefit from a life without ties
  and effortlessly become a citizen of every place.
  Basil heard me say this and expressed agreement,
  and yet he forced me onto the bishop's throne,
425 he and my father who thus tricked me twice over.[43]

---

[41] See Gregory, *Letter* 48 addressed to Basil in 372 where he writes, 'I blame the episcopal throne which suddenly raised you higher than us', and *Oration* 43. 58–9.
[42] See Plato, *Republic* 590b.
[43] Cf. the opening of *Oration* 10.

Μήπω ταραχθῆς, πρὶν ἂν ἐκμάθῃς τὸ πᾶν.
εἰ πλεῖστον ἐσκέψαντο δυσμενεῖς χρόνον,
ὅπως ἀτιμάσαιεν, οὐκ ἄλλον τινά
εὑρεῖν ἂν αὐτοὺς οἴομ' ἢ τὸν νῦν τρόπον.
430 ποθεῖς ἀκοῦσαι; πάντες οὐκ ἐροῦσί σοι,
ὅσοις τὸ πρᾶγμ' ἔδοξε τῶν οὐκ ἐνδίκων;
ἐγὼ μὲν οἷον ἐμπαρέσχον τῷ φίλῳ
ἐμαυτόν, οἶδε Πόντος, οἶδε καὶ πόλις
ἡ Καισαρέων καὶ πάντες οἱ κοινοὶ φίλοι.
435 μικροπρεπὲς γὰρ ταῦτ' ὀνειδίζειν ἐμέ.
τὸν μὲν γὰρ εὖ παθόντα μεμνῆσθαι πρέπει,
ὧν εὖ πέπονθε, τὸν δράσαντα δ' οὐδαμῶς.
ὁ δ' οἷος ἡμῖν, πειθέτω τὰ πράγματα.

Σταθμός τίς ἐστιν ἐν μέσῃ λεωφόρῳ
440 τῆς Καππαδοκῶν, ὃς σχίζετ' εἰς τρισσὴν ὁδόν,
ἄνυδρος, ἄχλους, οὐδ' ὅλως ἐλεύθερος,
δεινῶς ἀπευκτὸν καὶ στενὸν κωμύδριον.
κόνις τὰ πάντα καὶ ψόφοι καὶ ἅρματα,
θρῆνοι, στεναγμοί, πράκτορες, στρέβλαι, πέδαι,

445 λαὸς δ' ὅσοι ξένοι τε καὶ πλανώμενοι.
αὕτη Σασίμων τῶν ἐμῶν ἐκκλησία·
τούτοις μ' ὁ πεντήκοντα χωρεπισκόποις
στενούμενος δέδωκε — τῆς εὐψυχίας —
καὶ ταῦθ', ἵν' ἁρπάζοντος ἄλλου πρὸς βίαν

450 περικρατήσῃ τὴν καθέδραν καινίσας.
ἡμεῖς γὰρ αὐτῷ τῶν ἀρηΐων φίλων
τὰ πρῶτα — καὶ γὰρ ἦμεν ἄλκιμοί ποτε,

(Do not get upset until you have heard the whole story.)
If my enemies had spent a long time plotting
as to how they might insult me, I do not think
they could have found any better means than this.
430 Do you want to hear about it? Will not everybody tell you,
everyone who thought it an unfair proceeding?
Pontus knows and the city of Caesarea knows
as well as all the friends we have in common,
how I submitted to my friend's authority.
435 It would be petty of me to reproach him for that;
it is right that he who receives benefits, not he who gave them
should be mindful of the benefits received.
Let the facts demonstrate how he behaved towards me.
There is a staging-post half-way along the highway
440 through Cappadocia, where the road divides into three,[44]
a place without water, without vegetation, completely uncivilised,
an utterly dreadful and cramped little settlement.
It is all dust and noise and chariots,
cries and groans, officials, instruments of torture and shackles,
445 a population consisting only of visitors and vagrants.
This was Sasima, my congregation!
This was what he appointed me to, he who was surrounded
by fifty suffragan bishops[45] – what magnanimity on his part!
He did this so that by creating a new see he would get the upper hand
450 over another man[46] who was trying to seize it by force.
For among his friends who were capable of fighting he regarded me
as holding first place – indeed I was a brave fighter once

---

[44] Sasima lay at the junction of the roads from Tyana, Archelais and Mokissus. See W. M. Ramsay, *The Historical Geography of Asia Minor* (London, 1890), p. 293.
[45] i.e. as bishop of Caesarea.
[46] Bishop Anthimus of Tyana.

καὶ δεινὸν οὐδὲν τραύματ' ηὐλογημένα.
πρὸς τοῖς γὰρ ἄλλοις, οἷς ἀπηριθμησάμην,
455 οὐδ' ἦν ἀναιμωτί γε τοῦ θρόνου κρατεῖν·
μεταίχμιον γὰρ ἀντεπισκόπων δύο
τοῦτ' ἦν, συνερρώγει τε δεινός τις μόθος,
οὗ δημιουργὸς ἡ τομὴ τῆς πατρίδος
δύω πόλεις τάξασα μικρῶν μητέρας.

460 ψυχαὶ πρόφασις, τὸ δ' ἔστιν ἡ φιλαρχία·
ὀκνῶ γὰρ εἰπεῖν, οἱ πόροι τε καὶ φόροι,
ἐξ ὧν δονεῖται πᾶς ὁ κόσμος ἀθλίως.
  Τί οὖν με ποιεῖν, πρὸς θεοῦ, δίκαιον ἦν;
στέργειν; δέχεσθαι τῶν κακῶν τὰς ἐμβολάς;

465 βάλλεσθ' ἀωρί; συμπνίγεσθαι βορβόρῳ;
μηδ' ἔνθα θείην εὐπορεῖν γῆρας τόδε
ἀεὶ βιαίως ἐκ σκέπης ὠθούμενον;
μηδ' ἄρτον ἔξων τῷ ξένῳ διακλάσαι,
πένης πένητα λαὸν εὐθύνειν λαχών,
470 ὧν μὲν κατορθώσαιμι, μηδὲ ἓν βλέπων,
ὧν δ' αἱ πόλεις ἔχουσιν, εὐπορῶν κακῶν,
τρυγῶν ἀκάνθας, οὐκ ἀπανθίζων ῥόδα,
τὰ δεινὰ γυμνὰ τῶν καλῶν καρπούμενος;
ἄλλην ἀπαίτει μ', ἢν θέλεις, εὐψυχίαν,

475 τὴν δὲ πρότεινε τοῖς ἐμοῦ σοφωτέροις.
  Τοιαῦτ' Ἀθῆναι καὶ πόνοι κοινοὶ λόγων,
ὁμόστεγός τε καὶ συνέστιος βίος,
νοῦς εἷς ἐν ἀμφοῖν, οὐ δύο, θαῦμ' Ἑλλάδος·
καὶ δεξιαί, κόσμον μὲν ὡς πόρρω βαλεῖν,

480 αὐτοὺς δὲ κοινὸν τῷ θεῷ ζῆσαι βίον
λόγους τε δοῦναι τῷ μόνῳ σοφῷ λόγῳ.
διεσκέδασται πάντα, ἔρριπται χαμαί,

and blessed wounds are no misfortune.
As well as everything else I have enumerated,
455　it was impossible to take possession of this throne without bloodshed.
It was a no-man's land between two rival bishops
and a dreadful fight broke out,
the cause of which was the division of our native province
and the setting up of two city sees as mothers of smaller provinces.
460　Souls were the pretext, but the real cause was desire for power.
I hesitate to say it, but the wretched fact is that it is
revenues and taxes that motivate the whole world.
What then, in God's name, was the right course for me?
Was I to acquiesce? Should I just accept the onslaughts of misfortune?
465　Allow myself to be beaten prematurely? Suffocate in dust?
Was I not even to find a place to rest my aging limbs,
but always to be driven from my home by force?
Was I to be without bread to break with a guest,
be penniless in charge of a penniless flock,
470　unable to see a single thing I could successfully accomplish,
possessing in abundance only those evils with which cities are filled,
gathering thorns without a rose to cull,
reaping terrible things stripped of anything good?
Please demand a different kind of magnanimity from me,
475　and offer this to those who are wiser than I.
So much for Athens and our shared commitment to our studies,
our life together sharing hearth and home:
one mind, not two, in both of us, we were the marvel of Greece.
So much for our pledges to cast the world aside
480　and live a shared life dedicated to God,
devoting our rhetorical skills to the Word who alone is wise:
all this has been scattered, dashed to the ground,

αὖραι φέρουσι τὰς παλαιὰς ἐλπίδας.
ποῦ τις πλανηθῇ; θῆρες, οὐ δέξεσθέ με,
485 παρ' οἷς τὸ πιστὸν πλεῖον, ὡς γ' ἐμοὶ δοκεῖ;

Ἔσχεν μὲν οὕτω ταῦτα, συντόμως φράσαι.
ἐπεὶ δ' ἐκάμφθην, οὐ φρόνημ', ἀλλ' αὐχένα —
τί φῶ πόθεν δὲ τὴν ἐμὴν ὠδῖνά σοι
πᾶσαν παραστήσαιμι κέντρα μοι πάλιν,
490 πάλιν φυγάς τις καὶ δρομαῖος εἰς ὄρος
κλέπτων φίλην δίαιταν, ἐντρύφημ' ἐμόν.
τί μοι τὸ κέρδος; οὐ γὰρ εὔτονος φυγάς
ἦν, ὡς ἔοικε. πάντα δ' εἰδὼς καρτερεῖν
ἓν τοῦτ' ἀγεννής· πατρὸς οὐ φέρω χόλον.
495 πρῶτον μὲν οὖν ἀγῶνα ποιεῖται πατήρ
ἐνιδρῦσαί με Σασίμοις· ὡς δ' ἠσθένει,
ὁ δεύτερος πλοῦς ἀλλὰ μὴ κάτω μένειν,
αὐτῷ δὲ συμπονοῦντα (καὶ γὰρ ἦν βαρύς
ταῖς σαρξὶν ἤδη) συνελαφρίζειν πόνους,

500 χεῖρας προτείνων, τῆσδε τῆς γενειάδος
ἁπτόμενος, οἵοις πρός με χρώμενος λόγοις.
"Πατήρ σε λίσσεθ', υἱέων ὦ φίλτατε,
πατὴρ ὁ πρέσβυς τὸν νέον, τὸν οἰκέτην
ὁ δεσπότης φύσει τε καὶ διπλῷ νόμῳ.
505 οὐ χρυσὸν αἰτῶ σ', οὐ λίθους οὐδ' ἄργυρον,
οὐ γῆς ἀρούρας, τέκνον, οὐδ' ὅσα τρυφῆς.
ζητῶ σ' Ἀαρὼν καὶ Σαμουὴλ πλησίον
θεῖναι θεῷ τε τίμιον παραστάτην.

and the winds carry off our former hopes.
Where was I to go in my wanderings? Wild beasts, will you
   not welcome me?
485 For as far as I can see there is greater loyalty among you.

*Flight and return (486–525)*

This was how matters stood, to put it briefly.
When I had been forced to bend, not my will, but my
   neck –
what can I say? How can I present to you the full extent
of my suffering? Once again I felt the goads,[47]
490 once again I turned fugitive and ran off into the mountains,
secretly to find the life I loved and which was my delight.
But what did I gain from that? I was no competent fugitive
it seems, for though I am able to endure all things,
this one thing I am bad at: I cannot bear my father's anger.
495 First of all my father struggled to establish me
at Sasima, but when he failed to do that,
the next best thing was for me not to remain in such a
   lowly rank,
but to work as his auxiliary (for he was already slow
of body) and help to lighten his burden.
500 Stretching out his hands, he touched this beard of mine
and spoke to me in the following words:
'Dearest of sons, your father entreats you,
the old father entreats the young man, the master
the servant, servant by nature and by the twofold law.[48]
505 It is not money I ask you for, not precious jewels or silver,
neither acres of land, my child, nor items of luxury.
I am asking you to set yourself beside Aaron and Samuel[49]
as a worthy minister of God.

---

[47] Cf. line 348ff. for Gregory's earlier flight from priestly responsibility. This time, it seems, he did not go as far as Basil's monastic settlement in Pontus.
[48] Jungck explains this as referring to the respect due to the elder Gregory as father and bishop.
[49] Aaron helped his brother Moses (Exodus 4: 14ff.) and Samuel (1 Samuel 2: 11) assisted the priest Eli.

ὁ δοὺς ἔχει σε· τέκνον, μὴ μ' ἀτιμάσῃς,
510 ὡς ἵλεώ γε τοῦ μόνου τύχοις πατρός.
καλὸν τὸ αἴτημ', εἰ δὲ μή γε, πατρικόν.
οὔπω τοσοῦτον ἐκμεμέτρηκας βίον,
ὅσος διῆλθε θυσιῶν ἐμοὶ χρόνος.
δὸς τὴν χάριν, δός — ἢ τάφῳ μ' ἄλλος δότω.

515 ταύτην ὁρίζω τῆς ἀπειθείας δίκην.
δὸς τὰς βραχείας ἡμέρας τῷ λειψάνῳ.
τὰ δ' εἰσέπειτα σοὶ φίλως βουλευτέα."
     Ἐπεὶ δ' ἤκουσα ταῦτα καὶ ψυχὴ βάρους
μικρὸν διέσχεν ὥσπερ ἥλιος νέφους —

520 τί γίνεται; ποῖ τἀμὰ καταστρέφει πάθη;
ἐνουθέτησ' ἐμαυτόν, ὡς οὐδὲν βλάβος
ἕως καθέδρας πατρὸς ἐκπλῆσαι πόθον.
"οὐ γὰρ καθέξει τοῦτ'", ἔφην, "ἄκοντά με,
ὃν οὔτε κήρυγμ' οὔθ' ὑπόσχεσις κρατεῖ."
525 οὕτως ἀνήγαγέν με νικήσας φόβος.


     Ἐπεὶ δ' ὑπεξῆλθον μὲν οἱ γονεῖς βίου
κλῆρον λαχόντες, εἰς ὃν ἔσπευδον πάλαι,
ἐγὼ δ' ἐλείφθην οὐ καλῶς ἐλεύθερος,
τῆς μὲν δοθείσης οὐδ' ὅλως ἐκκλησίας

530 προσηψάμην, οὐδ' ὅσσον λατρείαν μίαν
θεῷ προσενεγκεῖν ἢ συνεύξασθαι λεῷ

He who gave you holds you. My child, do not treat me dishonourably,
510 if you hope to find the one and only Father merciful to you.
My request is proper; even if it were not, it is still a father's request.
You have not yet measured out as much life
as is equal to the time I have passed in ministry.
Grant this favour, grant it or allow another to lay me in my grave:
515 that is the punishment I lay down for your disobedience.
Grant to me the few days which remain.
As to what happens afterwards, you can decide as you think fit.'
When I heard these things and when my soul had come clear
a little from its heaviness, like the sun breaking out from a cloud,
520 what happened? Where will my sufferings end?
I thought to myself there could be no harm
in fulfilling my father's desire with regard to the bishop's throne.
'For this will not hold me against my will,' I said,
'since there is no contract or promise restraining me.'
525 And thus did fear triumphant lead me back.

*Adminstration at Nazianzus and withdrawal to Seleucia (526–551)*

But when my parents departed this life[50]
to receive the reward which long had been their aim,
I was left behind, now free but in unfortunate circumstances,
for I was in no way committed to the church
530 entrusted to me – to the extent that I did not offer
a single sacrifice to God or join the congregation in prayer;

---

[50] Gregory's parents died within months of each other in 374.

ἢ χεῖρα θεῖναι κληρικῶν ἑνί γέ τῳ·
τῆς πατρικῆς δέ – καὶ γὰρ οὐκ ἀνίεσαν
ὀρκοῦντες, ἐμπίπτοντες εὐλαβῶν τινες,

535 πολλῶν ἀτελέστων μηνύοντες ἐξόδους –
χρόνον βραχὺν μὲν ὡς ξένος ἀλλοτρίας
ἔσχον τιν' ἐπιμέλειαν, οὐκ ἀρνήσομαι,
τοῦτ' αὐτὸ φάσκων τοῖς ἐπισκόποις ἀεί
αἰτῶν τε δῶρον ἐκ βάθους τῆς καρδίας,

540 στῆσαί τιν' ἄνδρα τῷ πτολίσματι σκοπόν,
λέγων ἀληθῆ, ἓν μέν, ὡς οὔπω τινά
εἰληφὸς εἴη γνωρίμῳ κηρύγματι,
τὸ δεύτερον δέ, ὡς πάλαι δεδογμένον
εἴη φυγεῖν με καὶ φίλους καὶ πράγματα.

545     Ὡς δ' οὐκ ἔπειθον τοὺς μὲν ἐκ πολλοῦ πόθου
κρατεῖν θέλοντας, τοὺς δ' ἴσως ὑπέρφρονας,
πρῶτον μὲν ἦλθον εἰς Σελεύκειαν φυγάς,
τὸν παρθενῶνα τῆς ἀοιδίμου κόρης
Θέκλας· "τάχ' ἂν πεισθεῖεν ἀλλ' οὕτω", λέγων,

550 "χρόνῳ καμόντες ἡνιάς δοῦναί τινι."
καί μοι διῆλθεν οὐ βραχὺς τῇδε χρόνος.

neither did I ordain even one priest.[51]
But I will not deny that for a short time I looked after my
    father's church
like a stranger looking after someone else's property,[52]
535 for some pious people plagued me and would not yield
in their attempts to make me swear an oath,
telling me of the deaths of many unbaptised.
But all the time I kept saying to the bishops,
begging them from the bottom of my heart to grant this
    favour,
540 that they should appoint someone else as bishop of this
    town.[53]
I told them honestly that for one thing I had not yet
been elected by means of an official contract,
and secondly, that I had long ago decided
that I would flee from friends and administrative duties.
545 When I failed to persuade them (some wanted to get their
    own way
due to their great love for me, others perhaps from a sense
    of superiority),
first I went as a fugitive to Seleucia,
to the retreat of the famous virgin
Thecla.[54] I told myself. 'Perhaps in time they will get fed up,
550 and be persuaded to hand over the reins to someone else',
and there I spent a considerable time.

---

[51] Gregory's insistence that he performed none of his episcopal duties at Sasima is motivated by his eagerness to prove that he was never really bishop there and that therefore his election as bishop of Constantinople was not uncanonical.
[52] See Gregory, *Letter 182.5*.
[53] i.e. Nazianzus.
[54] According to the *Acts of Paul and Thecla*, Thecla was converted to Christianity by St Paul at Iconium. Gregory seems to have withdrawn to the monastery near her tomb at Meriamlik, near Seleucia in Cilicia. Cf. *Peregrinatio Aetheriae* 23.1–5 for a description of the area in the fourth century.

Ἐπεὶ δ' ἐπιστὰς τοῖς ἐμοῖς αὖθις κακοῖς,
ὧν μὲν ἐνόμιζον, εὗρον οὐδὲ ἓν καλῶν,
ὧν δ' ἐκπεφεύγειν πραγμάτων, πολὺ στῖφος,

555 ὑπερφανέντων ὥσπερ ἐκ προθεσμίας,
ἐνταῦθα δή μοι τοῦ λόγου τὸ σύντονον.
ἐρῶ δ', ἃ λέξω, καίπερ εὖ ἐγνωκόσιν,
ἵν' ἡμᾶς οὐκ ἔχοντες ἀλλὰ τὸν λόγον
ἔχητε τοῦτον, τῆς ἀνίας φάρμακον,

560 ἐχθροῖς ὄνειδος, μαρτυρίαν δὲ τοῖς φίλοις
ὧν ἠδικήμεθ' οὐδὲν ἠδικηκότες.
Δύω μὲν οὐ δέδωκεν ἡλίους φύσις,
δισσὰς δὲ Ῥώμας, τῆς ὅλης οἰκουμένης
λαμπτῆρας, ἀρχαῖόν τε καὶ νέον κράτος,

565 τοσοῦτο διαφέροντε ἀλλήλων, ὅσον
τὴν μὲν προλάμπειν ἡλίου, τὴν δ' ἑσπέρας,
κάλλει δὲ κάλλος ἀντανίσχειν συζύγως.
τούτων δὲ πίστιν ἡ μὲν ἦν ἐκ πλείονος
καὶ νῦν ἔτ' ἐστὶν εὔδρομος, τὴν ἑσπέραν
570 πᾶσαν δέουσα τῷ σωτηρίῳ λόγῳ,
καθὼς δίκαιον τὴν πρόεδρον τῶν ὅλων
ὅλην σέβουσα τὴν θεοῦ συμφωνίαν·
ἡ δ' ἦν τὸ πρόσθεν ὀρθόπους, νῦν δ' οὐκέτι
— ταύτην λέγω δὴ τὴν ἐμήν, εἶτ' οὐκ ἐμήν —,
575 ἀλλ' ἐν βυθοῖς ἔκειτο τῆς ἀπωλείας,
ἐξ οὗ τὸ κοῦφον ἄστυ καὶ πλῆρες κακῶν
πάντων Ἀλεξάνδρεια, θερμότης ἄνους,

## Constantinople (552–1918)

*Introduction to Gregory's work at Constantinople (552–606)*

But when I found myself up against my misfortunes once again
and realised that I had found none of the benefits I had expected,
but only a vast number of the very problems I had fled from,
555 which appeared as if by appointment –
here I come to the serious part of my account:
I shall say what I have to say, even though I speak to those who know it well,
so that although you do not have me, you may have
this account which can act as a remedy for pain,
560 a reproach to my enemies, and a testimony to my friends
of the ways I was wrongly treated despite having done no wrong.
Nature has given us not two suns,
but two Romes, beacons of the whole world,
one ancient power and one new,
565 differing from one another to this extent, that
the one outshines the sun, the other the evening star,[55]
but in their beauty they are equally balanced.
With regard to faith, one of them has long been
and still is on the right path, uniting the whole West
570 by means of the message of salvation,
and (as is right for the principal among all the churches),
worshipping the whole harmony of God.
The other city once stood upright, but now no longer –
I mean this city of mine, or rather which is not mine;
575 instead it lay in the depths of destruction,
ever since Alexandria, that vain city, filled
with every wickedness, irrational in its recklessness,

---

[55] i.e. Constantinople in the East, Rome in the West.

ἔπεμψ' Ἄρειον, τὸ βδέλυγμ' ἐρημίας,
ὃς πρῶτος εἶπεν "ἡ τριὰς οὐ σεπτέα",

580 ὅρους δ' ἔθηκεν ἀξίας φύσει μιᾷ
τεμὼν ἀνίσως τὴν ἀμέριστον οὐσίαν,
ἕως κατετμήθημεν εἰς πολλὰς ὁδούς.
Ὅμως δὲ καίπερ ἀθλιωτάτη πόλις
οὕτως ἔχουσα κατὰ τὸν ἐκ χρόνου νόμον

585 — ἔθος γὰρ ἐγχρονίζον εἰς νόμον τελεῖ —
θανοῦσά τ' οἰκτρὸν ἐξ ἀπιστίας μόρον
εἶχεν τι μικρὸν ζωτικῆς σπέρμα πνοῆς,
ψυχὰς τελείας τῷ λόγῳ τῆς πίστεως,
λαὸν βραχὺν μέν, τῷ θεῷ δὲ πλείονα,

590 ὃς οὐκ ἀριθμεῖ πλῆθος, ἀλλὰ καρδίας,
πιστὸν φύτευμα, κλῆμα τιμιώτατον.
τούτοις — ἐδόξαμεν γὰρ ἐν θεῳ τινες
εἶναι βίῳ τε καὶ λόγῳ τῶν γνωρίμων
καίπερ ἀεὶ ζήσαντες ἄγροικον βίον —
595 ἔπεμψεν ἡμᾶς ἡ χάρις τοῦ πνεύματος
πολλῶν καλούντων ποιμένων καὶ θρεμμάτων
λαοῦ βοηθοὺς καὶ λόγου συλλήπτορας,
ὡς ἂν καταψύξαιμεν εὐσεβεῖ ῥοῇ
ψυχὰς ἀνύδρους καὶ χλοαζούσας ἔτι

600 τροφῇ τ' ἐλαίου συγκραθῇ λύχνῳ τὸ φῶς,
γλῶσσαι δὲ λάβροι καὶ πολύστροφοι πλοκαί,

sent forth Arius, that abomination of the desert.[56]
He was the first to say,' The Trinity should not be worshipped,'
580 imposing different degrees of honour on the one nature,
chopping into unequal parts the being which cannot be divided,
until we were split and walked along separate paths.[57]
Nevertheless, although this city was in a most wretched state
according to the law which is the product of time
585 (for custom continuing over a long period ends up as law),
dying a pitiable death as a result of the poor condition of its faith,
it did have left some tiny seed of life-giving breath:
there were a few souls perfect in the word of faith,
just a small congregation,[58] it is true, but larger in God's eyes
590 (for he counts not the number but the hearts),
a faithful growth, a most precious branch.[59]
To these the grace of the Holy Spirit sent me
(for I had a reputation for devoutness
because of my way of life and my eloquence
595 although I had always led a provincial life),
at the invitation of many shepherds and their flocks,
to assist the congregation and help defend the Word.
They hoped that with a stream of correct doctrines
I might revive souls parched but still producing green growth,
600 and that if the lamp were fed with oil, the light might shine.
They also hoped that the turbulent tongues and twisted contortions

---

[56] It seems to have been in 318 or 319 that Arius put forward his belief in a subordinationist theory of the Person of Christ.
[57] I.e. the Christian church was split between different beliefs on the nature of the Trinity, a split which the Council of Nicaea had been unable to mend.
[58] This was the minority of Christians who still held to the tenets of the faith set out at the Council of Nicaea in 325.
[59] Cf. John 15: 5.

ἐξ ὧν τὸ ἁπλοῦν οἴχεται τῆς πίστεως,
ἱστοί τ' ἀράχνης, σαθρὰ δεσμωτήρια,
τὰ κοῦφα συνδέοντες, ἰσχυροῖς γέλως,
605 ῥαγεῖεν ἢ λυθεῖεν ἐν στερροῖς λόγοις,
οἵ τ' ἐμπεσόντες ἐκφύγοιεν τοὺς βρόχους.


Οὕτω μὲν ἦλθον, οὐχ ἑκών, ἀλλ' ἀνδράσιν
κλαπεὶς βιαίοις, ὡς λόγου συνήγορος.
καὶ γάρ τις ἐθρυλεῖτο καὶ συνήλυσις
610 ἐπισκόπων νέηλυν αἵρεσιν, λόγον
ἐπεισαγόντων ταῖς φίλαις ἐκκλησίαις,
ὃς τὴν πρὸς ἡμᾶς τοῦ θεοῦ λόγου κρᾶσιν,
ἣν οὐ τραπεὶς ἐδέξατ' ἄνθρωπον λαβών
ἔμψυχον, ἔννουν, ἐμπαθῆ τὰ σώματος,

615 Ἀδὰμ ὅλον τὸν πρόσθε πλὴν ἁμαρτίας,
ταύτην τεμὼν ἄνουν τιν' εἰσάγει θεόν
ὥσπερ δεδοικώς, μὴ θεῷ μάχηθ' ὁ νοῦς
– οὕτω γὰρ ἂν δείσαιμι καὶ σαρκὸς φύσιν,
μᾶλλον γὰρ αὕτη, καὶ θεοῦ πορρωτάτω –

620 ἢ τῶν μὲν ἄλλων δεομένων σωτηρίας
τὸν νοῦν δ' ὀλέσθαι παντελῶς δεδογμένου,
ὃς δὴ μάλιστα τῷ θεῷ μου σωστέος,
ὃς καὶ μάλιστ' ὤλισθεν ἐν πρώτου πλάσει·
ὃ γὰρ δέδεκτο, καὶ παρεῖδε τὸν νόμον,

which had caused the simplicity of the faith to be lost –
spiders' webs, grim prisons
which the strong ridicule but which trap the naive –
605 might be destroyed or undone by means of powerful words,
and that those who had been trapped might escape the
noose.

### The Apollinarians (607–651)

And so I arrived, not of my own will but summoned
by forceful men, to defend the Word,
for there was talk of a group of bishops
610 introducing their teaching, a new-fangled heresy,[60]
into our beloved churches.
This heresy cut the union between us and the Word of God,
a union He did not change when He adopted it, taking
upon Himself
man together with the human soul, mind, physical feelings,
615 the whole of the original Adam but without the sin.
Instead it posited a God without a mind,
as if it feared that the mind would conflict with God –
I would fear this more as regards the nature of the flesh,
for this would be more at odds and much further from
God –
620 or they thought that while everything else needed
salvation,
they had decided that the mind was utterly irredeemable;
in fact, I believe that the mind particularly needs to be
saved by God,
since it in particular was corrupted at the first man's
creation.
For that which received the law also transgressed it,

---

[60] This heresy was Apollinarism. The followers of Apollinarius, wishing to emphasise the full deity of Christ, posited that instead of a human spirit in Christ there was the divine Logos, so that while He possessed perfect Godhead, He did not possess complete manhood. From an orthodox point of view this meant, as we see from Gregory's criticisms, that Christ was unable to save the whole of human nature. The heresy was condemned at the Council of Constantinople.

625 ὃ δ' ἦν παριδόν, τοῦτο καὶ προσλήψιμον.
μὴ τοίνυν ἥμισύν με σῳζέτω λόγος
ὅλον παθόντα, μηδ' ἀτιμούσθω θεός
ὡς οὐχ ὅλον λαβών με, πηλὸν δὲ μόνον,
ψυχὴν δ' ἄνουν τε κἀλόγου ζῴου τινός,

630 ὃ καὶ σέσωσται δηλαδὴ τῷ σῷ λόγῳ.
Καὶ ληξάτω τοιαῦτα εὐσεβῶν ἅπας.
ἴσον τι γὰρ πταίουσιν ἐξ ἐναντίας
τοῖς εἰσάγουσιν ἀσκόπως υἱοὺς δύο,
τὸν ἐκ θεοῦ τε καὶ τὸν ἐκ τῆς παρθένου,

635 οἱ τὴν κάτω τέμνοντες εὐαρμοστίαν,
οἱ μὲν ξέοντες, οἱ δὲ διπλοῦντες κακῶς.
εἰ γὰρ δύω, δέδοικα μὴ ἓν τῶν δύο,
ἢ προσκυνῶμεν ἀνθ' ἑνὸς δύω θεούς,
ἢ τοῦτο μὴ πάθωμεν εὐλαβούμενοι

640 πέμπωμεν ἔξω τοῦ θεοῦ τὸ σύνθετον.
ὧν μὲν γὰρ ἡ σάρξ, οὐδὲν ἂν πάθοι θεός.
θεοῦ δ' ὅλου μετέσχεν ἀνθρώπου φύσις,
οὐχ ὡς προφήτης ἤ τις ἄλλος ἐνθέων
– ὃς οὐ θεοῦ μετέσχε, τῶν θεοῦ δέ γε –,

645 ἀλλ' οὐσιωθεῖσ' ὥσπερ αὐγαῖς ἥλιος.
οὗτοι μὲν οὖν ἔρροιεν ἐκ μέσου λόγου,
εἰ μὴ σέβοιεν ὡς ἓν ἄνθρωπον θεόν,
τὸν προσλαβόντα σύν γε τῷ προσλήμματι,
τὸν ἄχρονόν τε καὶ τὸ συμμιγὲς χρόνῳ,

625 but what transgressed must also be welcomed back.
I do not wish the Word to save only half of me
when the whole of me is affected; God should not be insulted,
as if he had failed to adopt my whole being but only assumed the clay,
together with a soul devoid of mind, the soul of an irrational creature
630 which, no one denies, has been saved by your Word.
Everyone who holds correct beliefs should abandon such ideas.
For these heretics make a similar mistake – but in the opposite way –
to those who unthinkingly posit two Sons,
one issuing from God and the other from the Virgin.[61]
635 Both groups destroy the harmony of the earthly dispensation,
the one group by diminishing it, the other by wickedly duplicating it.
For if there were two Sons, I fear one of two things:
either we would worship two gods instead of one
or, while taking care to avoid this,
640 we would banish the composite nature of God:
God would suffer none of the things experienced by the flesh.
Human nature participates in the whole God,
not like a prophet or some other divinely inspired person,
who participates not in God but only in divine qualities;
645 rather, God is in it as the sun is in its rays.
These men should be gone from the discussion
if they do not worship the God-Man as one being,
the one who assumed and that which was assumed,
the timeless and that which was involved in time,

---

[61] Gregory here refers to the teachings of Paul of Samosata, a third-century bishop of Antioch, who held a view of Christ similar to that of the later Nestorians. According to this view, the incarnate Christ was composed of both a human and a separate divine person.

650 τὸν ἐκ μόνου πατρός τε καὶ μητρὸς μόνης,
δύω φύσεις εἰς Χριστὸν ἐλθούσας ἕνα.


Τὰ δ' ἡμέτερα πῶς καὶ τίν' ἔσχε τὸν τρόπον;
πολλοῖς συνηνέχθημεν ἐλθόντες κακοῖς.
πρῶτον μὲν ἐξέζεσε καθ' ἡμῶν ἡ πόλις
655 ὡς εἰσαγόντων ἀνθ' ἑνὸς πλείους θεούς.
θαυμαστὸν οὐδέν· ἦσαν οὕτως ἠγμένοι,
ὥστ' ἀγνοεῖν παντάπασιν εὐσεβῆ λόγον,
πῶς ἡ μονὰς τριάζεθ', ἡ τριὰς πάλιν
ἑνίζετ' ἀμφοῖν ἐνθέως νοουμένοιν.


660 καὶ πρός γε τοῖς πάσχουσι δῆμος ἕλκεται,
ὡς τῷ τότε σφῶν προστάτῃ καὶ ποιμένι
οἶκτον λαβόντι τοῦ πάθους ὑπέρμαχον,
δῆμος τοσοῦτος καὶ φρονήματος πλέως,
ᾧ μὴ τὸ νικᾶν πάντα ἔσχατος ψόγος.

665 λίθους παρήσω τὴν ἐμὴν πανδαισίαν,
ὧν ἕν τι μέμφομ'· οὐ γὰρ ἦσαν εὔστοχοι
τούτων τυχόντες, ὧν τυχεῖν κενὸς φόνος.

650 a being from one father and one mother alone,
two natures in Christ becoming one.

*Struggles against his first opponents (652–727)*

As to my affairs, what state were they in?
On my arrival I came up against many problems.
Firstly, the city was seething with anger against me
655 on the grounds that I was introducing many gods instead of one.[62]
This was not surprising. They had been led in such a way
that they were altogether unable to recognise orthodox teaching –
how a unity could become a trinity and how the trinity
could become one again, while both are understood as divine.
660 Moreover, the people are drawn towards those who suffer,
and so they were to their leader and shepherd at that time,[63]
who received their pity as a champion of his suffering.[64]
To those people, numerous and full of pride,
defeat in any matter was the ultimate reproach.
665 I shall pass over the stones,[65] that banquet of mine,
but one thing about it I will criticise: they were not well aimed,
striking their targets in vain attempts to kill.

---

[62] This would be the accusation of the Arians who denied the divinity of Christ; to them Gregory, in emphasising the twofold divine nature of God the Father and God the Son, would appear to be positing two Gods.

[63] Demophilus, the Arian bishop of Constantinople.

[64] The Arians continued to support Demophilus even after he left Constantinople: the historians Socrates and Sozomen recount how the emperor asked Demophilus to subscribe to the Nicene faith so as to unify the church once more. But Demophilus refused and led his Arian flock out of the city, thereby leaving the churches of Constantinople to the orthodox congregation after forty years of Arian occupation. (Socrates *HE* V.7 and Sozomen VII.12.)

[65] It seems that Gregory's opponents attacked him and his congregation with stones at Easter 379. Cf. *Poem* II.1.12.103 'Of himself and the bishops'; II.1.15.11 'Of himself on his return from Constantinople'; II.1.33.12 'To Christ'; *Letter* 77.3.

ἔπειθ' ὑπάρχοις ὡς φονεὺς εἰσηγόμην
βλέπουσιν ὑψηλόν τι καὶ μετάρσιον,

670 οἷς εἷς νόμος τὸν δῆμον ἵλεων ἔχειν,
ὁ δεινὸν οὐδὲν πώποτ' οὐδ' εἰργασμένος
οὐδ' ἐννοήσας ὡς μαθητὴς τοῦ λόγου.
καὶ μοι παρέστη τοῦ λόγου συνήγορος
Χριστὸς βοηθῶν τῳ συνηγόρῳ λόγων,
675 ὃς καὶ λεόντων οἶδεν ἐκσῴζειν ξένους
καὶ πῦρ δροσίζειν εἰς ἀναψυχὴν νέων,
κῆτος δὲ ποιεῖν εὐσεβῶν εὐκτήριον·
οὗτος μ' ἐδόξασ' ἐν ξένῳ κριτηρίῳ.
  Ἔπειτα δεινὸς τῶν ἐμῶν οἰδεῖ φθόνος
680 εἰς Παῦλον ἑλκόντων με κἀπολλώ τινα,
τοὺς μήτε σαρκωθέντας ἡμῖν πώποτε
μήτ' ἐκχέαντας αἷμα τιμίου πάθους·
ἀφ' ὧν καλούμεθ', οὐχὶ τοῦ σεσωκότος;[2]
οἷς συνδονεῖται πάντα καὶ συσσείεται –

685 ὡς εὐδρομούσης τἆλλα τῆς ἐκκλησίας.
πῶς δ' ἄν ποτ' ἢ ναῦς ἢ πόλις, πῶς δ' ἂν στρατός
ἢ καὶ χοροῦ πλήρωμα, πῶς δ' οἶκος φίλος
σταίη πλέον τὸ βλάπτον ἢ κρατοῦν ἔχων;
τοῦτ' οὖν ἔπασχε τηνίχ' ὁ Χριστοῦ λεώς·

690 πρὶν γὰρ παγῆναι καὶ τυχεῖν παρρησίας,

---

[2] 683 σεσωκότος; PG – σεσωκότος· Jungck

Then like a murderer myself I was brought before the magistrates
who looked at me with proud and supercilious stares:
670 they have one rule – namely, to keep the people happy.
I had never yet done anything wrong
nor even thought it, as a disciple of the Word.
And there stood beside me, to defend my account,
Christ who helps those who stand up for his words,
675 He who had the power to save strangers from the lions[66]
and to turn fire into dew to cool the young men[67]
and to make the whale into an oratory for the pious.[68]
He it was who glorified me in the hostile courtroom.
Then there arose among my supporters terrible dissension
680 as they dragged me to some Paul and to some Apollos,[69]
men who had never become incarnate for us
nor shed the blood of precious suffering.
Shall we call ourselves after them rather than after our saviour?[70]
On account of them all was shaken and thrown into confusion –
685 as if everything was going well in the church in all other respects!
But how could a ship or a city, how could an army
or even all the members of a chorus, how could our own dear house[71]
stand firm when it contains more destructive powers than controlling ones?
This, then, is what the people of Christ endured at that time.
690 Before it could achieve stability and had learned to express itself,

---

[66] Daniel 6.
[67] Daniel 3: 19ff.
[68] Jonah 2: 1–2.
[69] Cf. 1 Corinthians 1: 12ff. Gregory here refers to the way he was torn between the different sides in the long-standing Antiochene schism.
[70] I follow the text of PG rather than that of Jungck in taking this line as a question.
[71] I.e. the small congregation of Nicene Christians.

πρὶν ἐκλυθῆναι σπαργάνων τῶν παιδικῶν,
οὔπω τελείως τὴν βάσιν ἐρηρεισμένος,
ἐκόπτετ', ἐρριπτεῖτο, ἐσπαράσσετο
ἐν ὄψεσιν τεκόντων εὐγενὴς τόκος

695 ἀτεκνίαν πεινῶσι τὴν ἐμὴν λύκοις.
οὐ γὰρ φορητὸν ἄνδρα τὸν πενέστατον,
ῥικνόν, κάτω νεύοντα καὶ δυσείμονα,
γαστρὸς χαλινοῖς, δάκρυσιν τετηκότα
φόβῳ τε τοῦ μέλλοντος, ὡς δ' ἄλλων κακοῖς,

700 οὐδ' εὐφυῶς ἔχοντα τῆς προσόψεως,
ξένον, πλανήτην, γῆς σκότῳ κεκρυμμένον
τῶν εὐσθενούντων καὶ καλῶν πλέον φέρειν.
 Σχεδὸν γὰρ αὐτῶν ταῦτα ἐξηκούετο·
"θωπεύομεν, σὺ δ' οὐχί· τιμῶμεν θρόνους,
705 σὺ δ' εὐλάβειαν· ἀρτύσεις ἡμῖν φίλαι,
σοὶ δ' εὐτέλεια, καὶ τρυφῆς ἔσθων ἅλας
τῆς ὀφρυώδους ἁλμυρὸν καταπτύεις.
δουλεύομεν καιροῖς τε καὶ λαῶν πόθοις
ἀεὶ διδόντες τῷ πνέοντι τὸ σκάφος,
710 χαμαιλεόντων τε τρόπον καὶ πολυπόδων
πολλὰς τιθέντες τοῖς λόγοις ἀεὶ χρόας.
σὺ δ' ἡμῖν ἄκμων ἀνήλατος, τῆς ὀφρύος.
ὥσπερ μιᾶς γε πίστεως οὔσης ἀεί
στενοῖς τὸ δόγμα τῆς ἀληθείας σφόδρα,

715 σκαιὰν βαδίζων πάντοτε τοῦ λόγου τρίβον.
πόθεν δὲ σοι, βέλτιστε, καὶ γλώσσῃ λάλῳ
τὸν λαὸν ἕλκειν, τοὺς δὲ βάλλειν εὐστόχως
κακῶς φρονοῦντας ἐν πολυσχιδεῖ πλάνῃ,
διπλοῦν τιν' ὄντα τοῖς φίλοις καὶ τοῖς ξένοις,

before it could be delivered from the swaddling-clothes of
    infancy,
while it was as yet unable to stand absolutely firm on its
    legs,
this child of noble ancestry was knocked down, hurled, torn
    to pieces
before the very eyes of its parents,
695 by wolves hungering after me in my childlessness.
They found it intolerable that a man of such abject poverty,
withered, bent and shabbily dressed,
wasted by the restraints imposed on the stomach and by
    tears
as well as by fear of what was to come and by the
    wickedness of others,
700 not possessed of a handsome appearance,
a stranger, a vagrant, buried in the darkness of the earth,
should have more success than fine, strong men.
This is the kind of thing they could be heard to say:
'We are flatterers, you are not. We value thrones,
705 you value piety. We like delicacies,
you like plain fare and when you eat the salt of luxury
you spit out the salty taste of arrogance.
We are slaves to circumstance and to the people's whims,
always letting our boat run with whatever wind is blowing.
710 Like the chameleon and the polyp,
we continually change the colours of our words.
But you, in your stubbornness, are to us an immovable
    anvil.
In the belief that the faith has always been one,
you put excessive restrictions on the teaching of the truth,
715 ever treading a twisted path in your sermons.
How is it that you, sir, with your fluent tongue
attract the people, but take shots of deadly accuracy
at those who, in their many different errors, hold misguided
    views?
You are two different people, one to your friends and one to
    outsiders,

## ΠΕΡΙ ΤΟΝ ΕΑΥΤΟΥ ΒΙΟΝ

720 τοῖς μὲν λίθον μάγνητα, τοῖς δὲ σφενδόνην;''
Ταῦτ' εἰ μὲν οὐκ ἔσθ', ὥσπερ οὐκ ἔστιν, κακά,
τί δυσχεραίνεις ὥς τι πάσχων ἔκτοπον;
εἰ δ' ἔστι καὶ σοὶ τοῦτο φαίνεται μόνῳ,
κρῖνον δικαίως ὡς θεοῦ παραστάτης

725 ξαίνειν με τὸν πταίοντα, τὸν λαὸν δ' ἔα,
ὃς οὐδὲν ἠδίκηκεν ἢ στέργων ἐμέ
ἡττημένος τε τῶν ἐμῶν διδαγμάτων.


Τὰ πρῶτα μὲν δὴ καὶ φέρειν οἷός τε ἦν.
εἰ γὰρ με καὶ τὸ καινὸν ἐπτόει βραχύ,
730 ὡς ἀθρόως τις ὠσὶν ἐμπεσὼν ψόφος
ἢ τοῖς ἀπείροις ἀστραπῆς αὐγῆς τάχος,
ἀλλ' ἦν ἔτ' ἁπλὴξ καὶ φέρειν πάντα σθένων·
ἥ τ' ἐλπὶς οὖσα πραγμάτων ἐλευθέρων,
τοῦ μὴ πάλιν μοι ταὐτὸ συμπεσεῖν πάθος,
735 ἔπειθε ῥᾷον διαφέρειν τὴν συμφοράν.
ἃ δ' ἦλθεν ἡμῖν αὖθις ἐκ τούτων κακά —
ὢ πῶς ἂν ἐκφράσαιμι τοὺς ἐμοὺς πόνους
ὢ τῶν κακῶν πορισταί, δαῖμον βάσκανε,
πῶς ἴσχυσας τοσοῦτον ἐκπλῆσαι κακόν;
740 οὐχ αἷμά μ' οὐδὲ βάτραχος, οὐ σκνιπῶν νέφος
οὐδὲ κυνόμυια οὔτε τις κτηνῶν φθορά,
οὐ φλυκτίς, οὐ χάλαζ', οὐκ ἀκρίς, οὐ σκότος,
οὐ πρωτοτόκων ὄλεθρος, ἔσχατον κακῶν,
ἔκαμψεν ἡμᾶς (ταῦτα γὰρ τῶν ἀγρίων

745 Αἰγυπτίων μάστιγες ἐκβοώμεναι).
καὶ πρός γ' Ἐρυθρᾶς κῦμα συγκλύσαν λεών.
τί δ' ὦσεν ἡμᾶς; κουφότης Αἰγυπτίων.

720 a magnet to your friends, a dangerous missile to others.'
'If these things are not, as indeed they are not, wrong,
then why are you annoyed as if you experienced something
     unusual?
But if they are wrong and they appear so to you alone,
then, as a fellow fighter for God, make a fair judgment
725 to have me, the guilty party, flogged, but let the people be,
for their only crime lies in loving me
and in being influenced by my teachings.'[72]

## Maximus the Cynic (728–1112)

At first I was able to bear this,
for although this bizarre situation frightened me for a while,
730 like a sudden noise assailing the ears
or lightning flashing with unexpected speed,
I was yet uninjured and strong enough to bear everything.
And the hope that I would have freedom of action
and that the same misfortune would not befall me again,
735 persuaded me more easily to endure my situation.
But the terrible things which befell me subsequently –
alas, how can I describe what I went through?
Oh, you bringer of misfortunes, you envious demon,
how could you produce so much evil?
740 It was not blood or frogs, nor swarms of gnats,
not flies or any pestilence afflicting cattle,
not boils or hail, not locusts or darkness,
not the death of the firstborn sons (the last of the
     plagues)[73]
which crippled me (for these, together with
745 the Red Sea's waves which washed over the people,
were the famous punishments inflicted on the cruel
     Egyptians).
What was it that threw me headlong? The Egyptians'
     fickleness.

[72] Lines 721–7 form Gregory's answer to his critics.
[73] For the plagues, see Exodus 7–11.

ὡς δ' ὦσεν, εἰπεῖν ἄξιον· στήλη γὰρ ἂν
αὕτη γένοιτο τῶν κακῶν αἰωνία.

750 Ἦν τίς ποθ' ἡμῖν ἐν πόλει θηλυδρίας,
Αἰγύπτιον φάντασμα, λυσσῶδες κακόν,
κύων, κυνίσκος, ἀμφόδων ὑπηρέτης,
ἆρις, ἄφωνον πῆμα, κητῶδες τέρας,
ξανθὸς μελάνθριξ, οὖλος ἁπλοῦς τὴν τρίχα –

755 τὰ μὲν παλαιά, τὰ δ' ἀρτίως εὑρημένα·
τέχνη γάρ ἐστι δημιουργὸς δευτέρα.
πλεῖστον γυναικῶν ἔργον, εἴτ' οὖν ἀρρένων,
χρυσοῦν, ἑλίσσειν τὴν φιλόσοφον σισόην.
τὰ τῶν γυναικῶν ἐν προσώποις φάρμακα
760 σοφοὶ φερόντων· εἰς τί γὰρ μόναι σοφαί
τὴν ἀπρεπῆ τε καὶ κακὴν εὐμορφίαν,
ἢ πρόγραμμ' ἐστὶ καὶ σιωπῶν τοῦ τρόπου,
ὡς οὐκ ἐχόντων Μαξίμους καὶ ἀρρένων;
ἡ κουρὰ τοῦτ' ἔδειξε λανθάνον τέως.
765 τοιαῦτα θαύμαθ' ἡμῖν ἐκ τῶν νῦν σοφῶν,
διπλοῦν τιν' εἶναι τὴν φύσιν τὸ σχῆμά τε
ἀμφοῖν μερίζειν τοῖν γενοῖν τρισαθλίως,
κόμην γυναιξίν, ἀνδράσιν βακτηρίαν.
ἐξ ὧν ἐκόμπαζ' ὥς τι τῇ πόλει δοκῶν,

770 ὤμους σκιάζων βοστρύχοις ἀεὶ φίλοις,
πέμπων λογισμοὺς σφενδονωμέναις κόμαις,
πᾶσαν φέρων παίδευσιν ἐν τῷ σώματι.
    Πολλὰς διελθὼν οὗτος, ὡς ἀκούομεν,
ὁδοὺς πονηράς – ἅστινας δ' ἄλλοις μέλοι,

As to how it threw me, it is worth relating. May my
 account stand
as an everlasting monument to my suffering.
750 There was amongst us in the city at that time an effeminate
 creature,
a phantom from Egypt, a pestilential fanatic,
a dog,[74] a puppy, a street-walker,
a disaster with no sense of smell, no bark, a great hulking
 monster,
a raven-haired blond, his hair both straight and curled,
755 (the one his original state, the other recently acquired,
for art is a second creator).
To dye the philosopher's curls gold and curl them
is usually women's work, but now it became men's.
Let these wise men wear women's cosmetics
760 on their faces, for why should wise women alone
possess this unseemly and foul beauty
(which offers a silent indication of their character),
as if men did not have their Maximuses too?
This was revealed by his curls, hitherto concealed.
765 Such are the wonders we owe to our present-day sages –
that a person is ambiguous as to nature and shape,
having thrice-wretchedly a share of both sexes,
in hairstyle like women but like men in carrying a staff.[75]
He liked to show these things off, as if he were of some
 importance in the city,
770 with his darling curls falling over his shoulders,
shooting forth his clever ideas with swinging locks
and wearing all his learning on his body.
Numerous were the wicked ways, so we hear, along which
this man had passed – but let others concern themselves
 with that,

---

[74] This term of abuse is also a reference to Maximus' Cynic beliefs, for the term Cynic was derived from this adjective meaning 'dog-like'. In the following passage Gregory plays constantly with this double meaning.
[75] This was one of the marks of a Cynic.

## ΠΕΡΙ ΤΟΝ ΕΑΥΤΟΥ ΒΙΟΝ

775 οὐ γὰρ τὰ πάντ' ἔμοιγε ἐκζητεῖν σχολή·
βίβλοι δ' ὅμως φέρουσιν ἀρχόντων ὅσαι –
ταύτῃ τελευτῶν ἐγκαθέζεται πόλει.
οὐδὲν γὰρ εἶχε βρῶμα τῶν εἰωθότων·
ὀξὺ βλέπων δὲ καὶ σοφῶς ὀσφρώμενος –
780 σοφὸν γὰρ ἔστω καὶ τὸ πικρῶς συντεθέν,
τὸ δ' ἐστὶν ἡμᾶς τῆς καθέδρας ἐκβαλεῖν
τοὺς οὔτ' ἔχοντας, οὔθ' ὅλως τιμωμένους,
πλὴν τοῦ φυλάξαι καὶ καταρτίσαι λεών·
σοφώτερον δέ, καὶ γὰρ οὐ διὰ ξένων,

785 αὐτῶν δ' ἀφ' ἡμῶν συμπλέκει τὸ δρᾶμ' ὅλον,
ὡς ἂν σοφιστὴς τῶν κακῶν καὶ συνθέτης,
τῶν ταῦτ' ἀήθων καὶ πλοκῆς πάντῃ ξένων,
ἄλλην δὲ τιμᾶν δεινότητ' εἰθισμένων·
εἰπεῖν σοφόν τι καὶ λέγοντα θαυμάσαι

790 βίβλων τε θείων ἐκλέγειν τὴν καρδίαν.
  Καινόν τιν' εἰπεῖν ἐν κακοῖς λόγον θέλω·
ἐχρῆν τὸν αὐτὸν πᾶσιν εἶναι δὴ τρόπον,
ἢ τὸν κακῶν ἄπειρον ἢ τὸν ποικίλον.
ἧττον γὰρ ἐβλάπτοντ' ἂν ἔκ τινων τινες
795 ἀντιζυγούντων ἢ συνεστώτων τρόπων·
νῦν δ' εἰσὶ θήρα τῶν κακῶν οἱ βελτίους.
τίς ἡ τοσαύτη σύγχυσις τοῦ πλάσματος;
ὡς σφόδρ' ἀνίσως ἐζύγημεν ἐκ θεοῦ.
τίς τὸν κάκιστον ὄψεται τῶν μετρίων
800 δολοῦντα, συμπλέκοντα, μηχανώμενον,
κλέπτονθ' ἑαυτὸν μυρίαις ἀεὶ στροφαῖς;
τὸ μὲν γὰρ εὐκίνητον εἰς μοχθηρίαν
τηρεῖ τὰ πάντα καὶ βλέπει τὰ καίρια·
τὸ δ' εἰς ἀρετὴν πρόχειρον εἰς ὑποψίαν
805 τῶν χειρόνων ἀργόν τε καὶ νωθὲς φύσει.
οὕτως ἁλίσκετ' εὐχερῶς ἡ χρηστότης.
  Πῶς τοῦτο ποιεῖ καί – σκοπεῖθ' – ὡς ποικίλως.

775 for I have not the time to search it all out,
the police records can reveal what they were –
before he finally settled in this city.
For he was not after any ordinary food:
with his sharp eyes and keen sense of smell
780 (I will admit it was a clever plot which caused me pain),
he was out to throw me off the bishop's throne,
I who have nothing, not even a respected position,
apart from my duty to protect my congregation and set them straight.
Even cleverer was the fact that he constructed this whole drama
785 using me myself rather than strangers;
he was a true sophist and worker of wickedness,
while I was inexperienced in these matters, a total stranger to guile,
accustomed to valuing a different kind of cleverness:
saying something wise and admiring anyone else who could do so,
790 and extracting deeper meanings from the holy scriptures.
I should like to make a novel observation about the wicked:
everyone ought to have a consistent character,
either cunning, or innocent of evil.
For people would harm each other less
795 if their characters were openly hostile or in agreement,
but as it is, the good are a prey to the wicked.
What great confusion exists in creation!
How very unequally we are yoked together by God.
Which of the moderates will recognise a wicked person
800 plotting, intriguing, contriving,
always managing to conceal himself by a thousand tricks?
For he who is disposed to depravity
watches everything and keeps a look out for opportunities,
while he who is disposed to virtue is by nature
805 slow and reluctant to suspect the worst;
in this way is goodness easily entrapped.
Watch how skilfully he achieves his aim –

Αἰγύπτιόν τιν' ἄλλον ὄψει Πρωτέα.
τῶν εὐνοούντων γίνεται καὶ τῶν σφόδρα
810 πιστῶν. τίς οὕτως ὡς ἔμοιγε Μάξιμος
στέγης, τραπέζης, δογμάτων, βουλευμάτων
κοινωνός; οὐδὲν θαῦμα· καὶ γὰρ ἦν μέγα·
κύων ὑλακτῶν δῆθεν τοὺς κακόφρονας
καὶ τῶν ἐμῶν πρόθυμος αἰνετὴς λόγων.

815 ὁμοῦ δὲ ταῦτα, καί τι τῶν ἐν βήματι
λαβὼν νόσημα, λεῖμμα τῆς πρώτης νόσου,
τὸ δ' ἦν ἄπαυστος ζῆλος, ἔμφυτον κακόν –
οὐ ῥᾳδίως γὰρ κάμπτεται πονηρία –,
τούτοις βραβεύων ἀνίσως, αὑτῷ φίλως,
820 δύω συνεργοῖς χρώμενος τῆς πικρίας,
πρώτῳ τε δευτέρῳ τε ἀνθρωποκτόνοις,
μόγις ποτ' ἐξέρρηξεν ἀσπίδος τόκον.
ὁ πρῶτος ἦν Βελίας, ἄγγελός ποτε,
ὁ δεύτερος δὲ τοῦδε λαοῦ πρεσβύτης
825 τὸν νοῦν τι μᾶλλον ἢ τὸ σῶμα βάρβαρος,
ὃς οὐ παροφθείς, οὐδὲν ἐκμελὲς παθών,
τὰ πρῶτ' ἔχων τιμῆς τε καὶ θρόνων ἀεί –
ἄκουε, Χριστέ, καὶ Δίκης ὄμμ' ἀπλανές,
εἰ δὴ καλεῖν ἐνταῦθα Χριστὸν ἄξιον –

830 μῖσος πονηρὸν καὶ κακότροπον ἀθρόως
ὤδινεν. οἴ μοι· πῶς ἀποκλαύσω; σκότος
αἰθρία λαμπρά, καὶ τὸ συντεθὲν κακόν
πόρρωθεν ἦλθεν ἡμίν, Αἰγύπτου νέφος.
    Κατάσκοποι μὲν πρῶτον, οὓς τῆς ἐκκρίτου
835 γῆς Ἰσραήλ ποτ' ἐξέπεμψ' ὁ γεννάδας·
πλὴν οὐκ Ἰησους οὐδὲ Χάλεβ οἱ σοφοί,
ἀλλ' εἴ τις ὕβρις ἐν νέοις καὶ πρεσβύταις,
Ἄμμων, Ἀπάμμων, Ἁρποκρᾶς, Στίππας, Ῥόδων,
Ἄνουβις, Ἑρμάνουβις, Αἰγύπτου θεοί,

you will recognise a second Proteus from Egypt!
He associates with those who are well-disposed to me
810 and totally reliable. Was there anyone who shared
my house, my table, teachings, plans
as Maximus did? No wonder: for indeed he was a strong personality,
a dog that pretended to bark at those who harboured wicked thoughts
and praised my words enthusiastically.
815 But at the same time he was catching some of the disease
which priests are prone to, a remnant of that first sickness,
I mean unceasing jealousy, that inborn evil,
(for wickedness does not easily give in).
He used two accomplices in his cruel plan,
820 proving to them an unjust leader, but indulgent to himself,
both of them murderous characters.
Only then did the offspring of the serpent burst forth.
The first was Belial, once an angel,
the second was a priest of this people,
825 even more a barbarian in mind than in looks.
Though he had not been overlooked or treated in any way unfairly,
and still held first place in priestly rank –
listen, Christ, and you, the unerring eye of Justice,
if indeed it is proper to call on Christ in this instance –
830 he suddenly revealed a wicked and malicious
hatred. Alas! How may I express my sorrow? The bright sky
turned to darkness and this evil plot, like a storm from Egypt,
came from afar and burst upon us.
First of all came spies, like those once sent forth
835 by the father[76] of Israel, the chosen land –
although it was not those wise men Joshua and Caleb,
but rather all the most insolent of the young men and old,
Ammon, Apammon, Harpocras, Stippas, Rhodon,
Anubis, Hermanubis, the gods of Egypt,

---

[76] i.e. Moses. See Numbers 13: 2–3 and 14: 6.

840 πιθηκόμορφοι καὶ κυνώδεις δαίμονες,
δύστηνα ναυταρίδια καὶ παράφθορα,
εὔωνα, μικροῦ κέρματος πολλοὺς θεοὺς
ῥᾷστ' ἂν προθέντα, εἴπερ ἦσαν πλείονες.
Ἔπειτα μικρὸν ὕστερον οἱ πεπομφότες
845 τούτους, στρατηγοὶ τῆς φάλαγγος ἄξιοι
ἤ, τῶν κυνῶν εἰπεῖν τι προσφυέστερον,
οἱ ποιμένες. πλέον γὰρ οὐδὲν φθέγξομαι
— καίπερ σφαδᾴζων ἔνδοθεν πολλοῖς λόγοις
ὥσπερ τις ἀσκὸς δέσμιος γλεύκους ζέων
850 ἢ καὶ φυσητὴρ χαλκέως γέμων πνοῆς —
αἰδοῖ τε τοῦ πέμψαντος, εἰ καὶ κουφόνους,
αὐτῶν τ' ἐκείνων, οἷς τι συγγνώμης τυχόν
μετῆν ὑποσπασθεῖσιν ἐξ ἀγροικίας,
ὅποι φέροιεν οἱ κακοί, κινουμένοις,

855 οὓς ἐνθάδ' ἡμῖν ἐδημιούργησε φθόνος.
σοφοί, τὸ πρόβλημ' εἴπατ' — οὐκ ἔμοιγε γὰρ
τοῦτ' εὐσύνοπτον, πλήν τις εἰ φράζοι σοφῶν —·
πῶς Πέτρος αὐτός, ὁ βραβεὺς τῶν ποιμένων,
πρώην μὲν ἡμᾶς ἐγκαθίστη γράμμασιν
860 οὕτω προδήλως διπλόης ἐλευθέροις,
ὡς αὐτὰ πείσει τὰ πρὸς ἡμᾶς γράμματα,
καὶ συμβόλοις ἐτίμα τῆς ἱδρύσεως,
νῦν δ' ἧκεν ἡμῖν ἔλαφος ἀντὶ παρθένου;
ταῦτ' οὐ πρόδηλα, ταῦτα δεῖθ' ἑρμηνέως.
865 Ὤφθη τε τούτων σκηνικώτερόν ποτε
πολλῶν πονηρῶς ἐν βίῳ πεπαισμένων;
ὀφθήσεται δὲ ἄλλο παιγνικώτερον;
οἶνον τις εἶπε συμπότης πάντων κρατεῖν,

840 ape-shaped and dog-like demons,
a despicable and corrupt crew,
easily bribed, men who for a small sum would readily
offer many gods for sale, if only there were more to offer.
Then, a little later, came those who had sent
845 these men, leaders, or rather shepherds
(to use an expression more appropriate for dogs),
worthy of these troops. For I will say nothing more –
though I am ready to burst with all the words inside me,
like a stoppered wineskin filled with fermenting new wine[77]
850 or like a blacksmith's bellows full of air –
out of respect for him who sent them,[78] even if he was thoughtless,
and for those people themselves with whom one may sympathise
because they erred out of ignorance,
swept away in whichever direction they were carried
855 by those evildoers whom jealousy had created for me here.
You who are wise, explain this problem (for I cannot
understand it easily unless some clever person explains it):
how was it that Peter himself, the leader of the shepherds,
not long ago installed me by means of letters
860 so clearly free from ambiguity,
(as the wording of his letters to me proves),
and honoured me with the insignia of office,
yet now a deer has been substituted for the virgin?[79]
These matters are not at all clear and need an interpreter.
865 Of all the sorry scenes played on life's stage,
has anything more melodramatic than this been seen?
Will anything else more ridiculous be seen?
Some boozer once said that it is wine which has supreme power,

---

[77] Job 32: 19 (Septuagint).
[78] Peter, bishop of Alexandria, to whom reference is also made in line 858.
[79] See Euripides *Iphigenia in Tauris* 28: Iphigenia, the daughter of Agamemnon, was to be sacrificed to Artemis so that the becalmed Greek fleet might be able to set sail for Troy; at the last moment Artemis saved Iphigenia by substituting a deer to be sacrificed in place of the girl.

## ΠΕΡΙ ΤΟΝ ΕΑΥΤΟΥ ΒΙΟΝ

ἄλλος γυναῖκα, τὴν δ' ἀλήθειαν σοφός·
870 ἐγὼ δ' ἂν εἶπον χρυσόν, ὡς ἔχει κράτος.
τούτῳ τὰ πάντα ῥαδίως πεσσεύεται.
οὔπω τὸ δεινόν, εἰ τὰ τοῦ κόσμου μόνα
πλέον παρ' ἡμῖν ἰσχύει τοῦ πνεύματος.
πόθεν δ' ὁ χρυσὸς τῷ κυνί, ζητητέον.

875 πρεσβύτερον ἐκ Θάσου τιν' ἥκοντ' ἐνθάδε
χρυσὸν φέροντα τῆς ἐκεῖσ' ἐκκλησίας,
ἐφ' ᾧ πρίασθαι Προικονησίας πλάκας,
τοῦτον περισήνας καὶ λαβὼν συμπράκτορα
πολλαῖς τε δήσας ἐλπίσιν τὸν ἄθλιον –

880 οἱ γὰρ κακοὶ τάχιστα μίγνυνται κακοῖς –
τὸν χρυσὸν εἶχεν εἰς ἅπανθ' ὑπηρέτην,
πιστὸν συνεργόν, γνήσιον συνέμπορον.
τεκμήριον δέ· καὶ γὰρ οἱ πρώην ἐμέ
σέβοντες, ὡς ἄχρηστον, ἄχρυσον φίλον

885 περιφρονοῦσι φίλτατοι καὶ ῥαδίως
κλίνουσι πρὸς τὸ χεῖρον ὡς ῥοπὴ ζυγοῦ.
    Νὺξ ἦν· ἐγὼ δ' ἔκαμνον· οἱ δ' ὥσπερ λύκοι
κλέπται φανέντες ἀθρόως μάνδρας ἔσω,
πολλοὺς ἔχοντες μισθίους ἐκ τοῦ στόλου,
890 ἐξ ὧν Ἀλεξάνδρεια ῥᾷστ' ἀνάπτεται –
καὶ γὰρ συνεμπίπτουσι τῷ στόλῳ σαφῶς –,
κεῖραι προθυμοῦντ' εἰς καθέδραν τὸν κύνα,
πρὶν ἤ τι λαῷ, πρὶν κτίλοις ἐκκλησίας,
πρὶν ἡμῖν αὐτοῖς, ὡς κυσὶν γοῦν, γνωρίσαι.

895 οὕτω φασὶν καὶ ταῦτα προστεταγμένοι.
οὕτως Ἀλεξάνδρεια τιμᾷ τοὺς πόνους.

another said that women do, while the wise man says truth does.⁸⁰
870 But I say that it is gold which has the power:
for this all things are readily gambled away.
Nor is it strange, seeing that in this world
purely material things have greater power than the spiritual.
But, one might ask, where did this dog obtain the money?
875 A priest from Thasos arrived in Constantinople
bringing gold belonging to the church over there,
intending to buy tablets of Prokonnesian marble.⁸¹
Maximus fawned on him and made him his accomplice,
binding the poor man to the project with numerous promises –
880 for the wicked are very quick to gang up with the wicked.
And so the gold became Maximus' servant to use as he wished,
a trustworthy accomplice, a valuable partner.
The proof is this: my closest friends
who had recently shown me respect, now scorned me
885 as a friend of no good and no gold,
and readily inclined towards the worse like a pair of scales.
It was night and I lay sick. Like thieving wolves
they appeared suddenly within the fold,
with a crowd of hired mercenaries from the fleet,
890 who stirred up the Alexandrians without difficulty –
for they burst in openly together with the crew.
They were keen to shear the dog for the bishop's throne,
not waiting to inform the congregation or the rams of the church
or ourselves, not even in our position as sheepdogs.
895 They claimed that they had been ordered to do this.
This is how Alexandria rewards my efforts!

---

⁸⁰ Cf. III *Esdras* (= I Ezra) 3: 10–12, a book that the Council of Trent relegated to the apocrypha.
⁸¹ Prokonnesus had marble quarries of such quality that the island was renamed Marmara.

οὕτω δικάσαι τις ὑμῖν ἄλλος εὐμενής.
       Ἦν ὄρθρος· ὁ κλῆρος δέ — καὶ γὰρ ἐγγύθεν
ᾤκουν — ἀνήφθη καὶ τάχιστα τὸν λόγον
900 ἄλλῳ δίδωσιν ἄλλος. εἶτ' ἐγείρεται
φλὸξ λαμπρὰ λίαν· ὦ πόσων μὲν ἐν τέλει,
πόσων ξένων δὲ συρρυέντων καὶ νόθων.
οὐκ ἦν γὰρ ὅστις οὐκ ἐμεμήνει τοῖς τότε
τοιαῦθ' ὁρῶντες τἀπίχειρα τῶν πόνων.

905 τί μακρὰ τείνω; ἐκ μὲν ἡμῶν αὐτίκα
χωροῦσιν ὀργῇ, τοῦ σκοποῦ τῷ μὴ τυχεῖν
ἀλγοῦντες. ὡς δ' ἂν μὴ μάτην ὦσιν κακοί,
τὸ λεῖπον ἐκπληροῦσι τῇ σκηνῇ τέλος.
εἰς γὰρ χοραύλου λυπρὸν οἰκητήριον

910 ἀχθέντες οἱ σεμνοί τε καὶ θεῷ φίλοι
λαόν τ' ἔχοντες τῶν ἀποβλήτων τινάς
κυνῶν τυποῦσι τὸν κάκιστον ποιμένα,
κείραντες οὐ δήσαντες οὐδὲ σὺν βίᾳ·
κύων γὰρ ἦν πρόθυμος εἰς τὰ κρείσσονα.

915 τομὴ δ' ὑπῆλθε βοστρύχους εὐφορβίους
λύουσ' ἀμόχθως τὸν πολὺν χειρῶν πόνον,
τοσοῦτον αὐτῷ καὶ μόνον δεδωκυῖα,
ὅσον γυμνῶσαι τὸ τριχῶν μυστήριον,
τριχῶν, ἐν αἷς ἔκειτο τὸ σθένειν ἅπαν,

920 ὥσπερ λέγουσι τῷ κριτῇ Σαμψών ποτε,
ὃν ἡ κόμη προὔδωκεν ἐξυρημένη,
τριχῶν, ἀώρου κἀνεμοφθόρου θέρους,
ἅς τις γυνὴ τέτμηκεν εἰς ἐχθρῶν χάριν.
       Ποιμὴν δὲ δειχθεὶς ἐκ κυνῶν ποιμένων
925 πάλιν κύων πέφηνε· τῆς ἀτιμίας.

May another Judge be as well-disposed to you!
Then dawn came. The clergy (who lived nearby)
grew excited and very quickly passed
900 the news one to the other. Then there flared up
a flame of great brightness: what a huge crowd gathered! –
people in high office, outsiders and those who were not true Christians.
For everyone went wild at what had happened
when they realised the reward for all my efforts.
905 But why prolong my account? They[82] immediately rushed out
in anger from my church, furious at failing to achieve
their goal. But to prevent their wickedness being fruitless,
they performed the rest of their farce to its conclusion:
these worthy men, these friends of God, were led off
910 to the miserable little place where the choir-master lived,
accompanied by a congregation consisting of a few outcasts.
The most abominable of the dogs they made into their shepherd,
shearing him without the need to tie him up or use force,
for this dog was eager to grasp at higher things.
915 The shears went for his abundant locks,
effortlessly destroying all the hard work his hands had wrought.
All that this brought him was this one thing –
it laid bare the secret of his hair,
the hair in which lay all his strength,
920 as was once the case, they say, with Samson the judge
who was betrayed by the cutting of his hair,
the hair which, like a field of ripe corn prematurely blasted by the wind,
a woman cut to gratify his enemies.
When he had been exhibited as a shepherd by the dogs,
925 he again appeared as a dog among the shepherds. What a disgrace!

---

[82] i.e. those who had attempted to consecrate Maximus as bishop.

κύων ἔρημος, μήτε τῆς κόμης ἔτι
φέρων τὸ κάλλος, μήτε τὴν ποίμνην στρέφων,
αὖθις μακέλλων ὀστέοις ἐπιτρέχων.
δράσεις δὲ δὴ τί τὴν καλὴν κόμην; πάλιν
930 θρέψεις φιλεργῶν; ἢ μενεῖς τοῖος γέλως;
ἄμφω γὰρ αἰσχρά, καί τι τοῖν δυοῖν μέσον
οὐκ ἔστιν εὑρεῖν οὐδὲ ἕν – πλὴν ἀγχόνης.
θήσεις δὲ ποῦ μοι τὰς τρίχας, πέμψεις δὲ ποῦ;
σκηναῖς θεάτρων, εἰτέ μοι, ἢ παρθένοις;


935 τίσιν δὲ τούτων αὖθις; ἢ Κορινθίαις
ταῖς σαῖς, μεθ' ὧν τὰ θεῖα ἐξησκοῦ ποτε
μόνος μόναις τε πανσόφως κοινούμενος;
ἀνθ' ὧν σε θήσω μᾶλλον οὐρανοῦ κύνα.
  Εὐθὺς μὲν οὖν τοσοῦτον ἤλγησεν πόλις
940 τοῖς τηνικαῦτα συμβεβηκόσιν κακοῖς,
ὥστ' ἐπρίοντο πάντες· ἐξέχει θ' ἅπας
λόγους ἀηδεῖς τοῦ βίου κατηγόρους,
θυμοῦ φέροντος ἃ φρένες συνεκρότουν.
ἄλλος τι δ' ἄλλο ἠράνιζεν εἰς ἑνός
945 κακοῦ τελείου πάντοθεν συμφωνίαν.
ὥσπερ γὰρ ἐν τοῖς σώμασιν συνανίσταται
πάθη τὰ μικρὰ ταῖς μεγάλαις ἀρρωστίαις,
κἂν ἠρεμοῦντα τῷ σθένειν τέως τύχῃ,
οὕτως ἐκείνου πάντα τὰ πρόσθεν κακά

950 ἐστηλίτευσεν ἡ τελευταία στάσις.
ἀλλ' οὐκ ἐμοῦ γε ταῦτ' ἂν ἐξέλθοι ποτέ.
ἴσασιν οἱ λέγοντες· ἐνδάκνω δ' ἐγώ

An abandoned dog, no longer adorned
with beautiful hair, nor rounding up his flock,
but once more chasing after butchers' bones.
What will you do with your beautiful hair?[83] Will you put all that effort
930　into growing it again? Or remain as you are, a laughing-stock?
Both alternatives are shameful and between the two
it is impossible to find a way of compromise – except the noose![84]
Where will you put the hair, where will you send it?
To the theatre, for use on the stage? Or to the virgins? Do tell me!
935　To which of them, then? To your Corinthian ladies,[85]
with whom you used to practise holy rites,
most cunningly associating alone with them alone?
For this I shall rather set you as the dog-star in the sky.
Immediately the city suffered such pain
940　on account of the terrible events then taking place,
that it made everyone grind their teeth. All poured forth
bitter words in accusation against his way of life,[86]
while their hearts endured the turmoil of their minds.
Each one made his own contribution to the harmony
945　of the one altogether perfect disaster.
For just as in the body minor ailments
make their presence felt at the same time as serious illnesses,
hitherto dormant on account of the general state of health,
so all this man's previous misdeeds
950　were made public in the final coup.
But may my lips never expound these things:
those who speak of them know them. But I bite my lips in shame

---

[83] Damasus, bishop of Rome, also alludes with contempt to Maximus' long hair, in his *Letter* 5.
[84] Possibly a reference to the fate of another traitor, Judas Iscariot.
[85] i.e. courtesans.
[86] i.e. Maximus'.

## ΠΕΡΙ ΤΟΝ ΕΑΥΤΟΥ ΒΙΟΝ

τῶν πρόσθεν αἰδοῖ καίπερ ἠδικημένος.
"Τί οὖν; σὺ τοῦτον οὐ χθὲς εἶχες ἐν φίλοις
955 καὶ τῶν μεγίστων ἠξίους ἐγκωμίων;"
τάχ' ἄν τις ἀπαντήσειε τῶν ταῦτ' εἰδότων
καὶ τὴν τότ' εὐχέρειαν αἰτιωμένων,
ὑφ' ἧς ἐτίμων καὶ κυνῶν τοὺς χείρονας.
ἄγνοιαν ἠγνόησα μίσους ἀξίαν.

960 ἐξηπατήθην ὡς Ἀδὰμ γεύσει κακῇ.
ὡραῖον ἦν τὸ πικρὸν εἰς ὄψιν ξύλον.
τὸ σχῆμά μ' ἠπάτησε τῆς ὁρωμένης
ἄχρι προσώπου πίστεως καὶ ῥημάτων.
πιστοῦ γὰρ ἀνδρὸς οὐδὲν εὐπειθέστερον
965 πρὸς εὐλάβειαν ῥᾳδίως ὁρμωμένου
ἢ οὖσαν ἢ δοκοῦσαν, ὦ χρηστοῦ πάθους·
ὃ βούλεται γάρ, τοῦθ' ἕκαστος οἴεται.
   Τί χρῆν με ποιεῖν; εἴπατ', ὦ σοφώτατοι.
τί δ' ἄν τις ὑμῶν ἄλλο τι πρᾶξαι δοκεῖ
970 οὕτως ἔτι στενῆς τε τῆς ἐκκλησίας
οὔσης τόθ', ὥστε καὶ καλάμης τι συλλέγειν;
ἐξουσίαν γὰρ οὐ τοσαύτην ὁ στενός,
ὅσην δίδωσι καιρὸς ὁ πλάτους γέμων.
μέγιστον ἦν μοι καὶ πατῶν αὐλὴν κύων

975 ἐμὴν σέβων τε Χριστὸν ἀνθ' Ἡρακλέους.
τῷ δ' ἦν τι μεῖζον· τὴν ἐπ' αἰσχίστοις φυγὴν
πίστιν πεποίηθ' ὡς θεοῦ πάσχων χάριν.
μαστιγίας ἦν, ἀλλ' ἐμοὶ νικηφόρος.
εἰ τοῦτο δεινόν, οἶδα πολλὰ πολλάκις

980 τοιαῦθ' ἁμαρτών. ἆρα συγγνώσεσθέ μοι,
ἄνδρες δικασταί, τῆς καλῆς ἁμαρτίας;

at past events, even though I was unjustly treated.
'What then? Did you not but yesterday count this man a friend of yours
955 and consider him worthy of the highest praises?'[87]
Such might be the objection of one who knew what happened
and who accused me of naivety at the time,
which caused me to think highly of the vilest of dogs.
My failure to recognise my lack of perception was detestable.
960 Like Adam I was deceived by a sinful tasting;
beautiful to behold was the bitter tree.
The appearance of faith deceived me
since I could not see behind his face and words.
For no one is easier to persuade than a trusting man
965 who is readily attracted to piety
whether real or apparent – what a worthy weakness!
For each person believes what he wants to believe.
What should I have done? Tell me, you who are so wise.
Would any of you have acted differently,
970 seeing that the congregation was still so weak
at the time, that one even had to gather some of the stubble?
For difficult circumstances do not offer the same opportunities
as do the right conditions, filled with plenty.
It was a great thing for me that this dog should patter
975 through my hall and worship Christ instead of Heracles.
There was also another point: he assured me that his exile,
due to his most shameful behaviour, had been undertaken for God's sake.
He was a scoundrel, but to me he was a hero.
If this is strange, I know that I have often made
980 many similar mistakes. Will you forgive me,
you gentlemen of the jury, for my error? – I meant well.

---

[87] Probably an allusion to the eulogy (*Oration* 25) given by Gregory in honour of Maximus (there referred to as Hero).

ἦν μὲν κάκιστος, ἀλλ' ἐτίμων ὡς καλόν.
Ἢ φθέγξομαί τι καὶ νεανικώτερον;
ἰδού, προτείνω τὴν ἄκαιρον καὶ λάλον
985 γλῶσσαν· ὁ θέλων ἀνηλεῶς ἐκτεμνέτω.
τί δ' οὐχὶ τέτμητ'; ἢ δοκεῖ σοι καὶ σφόδρα,
ἢ μακρὰ σιγᾷ καὶ πλέον σιγήσεται,
ἴσως δίκας τίνουσα τῆς ἀκαιρίας,
ὡς ἂν μάθῃ μὴ πᾶσιν εἶναι δεξιά;

990 κἀκεῖνο δ' οἷον· προστεθήτω γὰρ μόνον·
ὄντως ἀσυλλόγιστον ἡ πονηρία.
ὃν γὰρ τὸ χρηστὸν οὐκ ἐποίησ' ἥμερον,
τί ἂν δράσειεν ἄλλο τῶν πάντων ποτέ;
καὶ οὗ τοσοῦτός ἐστιν ἡ τιμὴ ψόγος,
995 τούτου τί φήσεις τὸν τρόπον; ἢ κακὸν μέγα;
ταῦτ' εἰ μέν ἐστι πιστά, μὴ ζήτει πλέον·
εἰ δ' οὐκ ἀληθῆ, μηδὲ τὰ πρόσθεν δέχου.
τούτων τί ἂν γένοιτο δυσμαχώτερον;
οὕτω μὲν ἔνθεν ἠλάθη κακῶς κακός,
1000 εἰπεῖν δ' ἀληθὲς μᾶλλον ὡς καλῶς κακός.
Ἐπεὶ δὲ φύλοις βαρβάρων κακὸν φέρων
βασιλεὺς ἑῷος εἶχεν ὁρμητήριον
τὴν Θεσσαλονίκην, τηνικαῦτα τί πλέκει
κύων ὁ παγκάκιστος ἄθρει μοι πάλιν·
1005 ἄρας τὸ συρφετῶδες Αἰγύπτου στῖφος —
λέγω δὲ τοὺς κείραντας αὐτὸν ἀπρεπῶς —
ὡς τὴν καθέδραν βασιλικῷ προστάγματι
πήξων ἑαυτῷ τῷ στρατοπέδῳ προστρέχει.
κἀκεῖθεν αὖθις ὡς κύων ἀπορριφεὶς

1010 ὀργῇ τε πολλῇ χὠρκίοις φρικώδεσιν —
οὔπω γὰρ ἦν τὰ ὦτα διατεθεὶς κακῶς
οὐδεὶς καθ' ἡμῶν, ἀλλ' ἔτ' εἶχον ὑγιῶς —
εἰς τὴν Ἀλεξάνδρειαν αὖθις φθείρεται,
ὀρθῶς γε ποιῶν τοῦτο καὶ μόνον σοφῶς.

He was most wicked but I esteemed him as if he were good.
Or shall I say something even more daring?
Look, I am sticking out this troublesome and talkative
985 tongue of mine: whoever wishes to may mercilessly cut it
    out.
Why has it not been cut off? Or do you think indeed it has,
since it has long been silent and will be silent even longer,
paying the penalty, perhaps, for its vexatiousness,
that it might learn not to be friendly to everybody?
990 So much for that! Let me just add one more thing:
wickedness is truly not susceptible to reason.
For if friendly treatment cannot tame someone,
what other means of all those possible could ever do so?
And if respecting such a man wins such reproach,
995 what should one say of his character? A great evil?
If this reasoning convinces you, do not ask further.
But if it is not true, do not accept my previous arguments;
yet what could be more irrefutable than these?
And so this wretch was banished in a wretched manner,
1000 or rather, to tell the truth, rightly banished as a wretch.
At the time when the eastern emperor had made his
military base at Thessalonica during his campaign
against the barbarian tribes,[88] what was that most vile
dog devising? Listen to me once more.
1005 Gathering together the Egyptian dregs, that vulgar mob,
(I mean those who had shorn him in unseemly fashion),
he hastened to the imperial camp, hoping that by royal
    decree
he might secure for himself the bishop's throne.
But when he had once more been cast out like a dog,
1010 in terrible rage and with oaths which made one shudder
(for as yet nobody's ears were unfavourably disposed
towards me but still were sound),
he made his way back to Alexandria:
this time at least, just for once, he acted rightly and wisely.

---

[88] During the summer of 380.

1015 Πέτρῳ γάρ, ᾧ δίσχιστος ἡ γραφίς ποτ' ἦν
πάντα γράφοντι ῥᾳδίως τἀναντία,
μισθοφορικόν τι τῶν ἀνεστίων ἔχων
ἐπιφύεται καὶ τὸν γέροντ' ἀποστενοῖ,
ἢ τοῦτον αἰτῶν, ὅνπερ ἤλπισε, θρόνον

1020 ἢ τοῦ παρόντος μὴ μεθήσεσθαι λέγων,
ἕως ὑπάρχου τὴν κινουμένην φλόγα,
μὴ ταῖς παλαιαῖς προστεθῇ τι συμφοραῖς,
ὡς εἰκὸς ἦν δείσαντος ἔξω πέμπεται.
καὶ νῦν δοκεῖ μὲν ἠρεμεῖν, δέος δέ μοι,
1025 μὴ που τὸ δεινὸν καὶ χαλάζης ἔγκυον
νέφος συνωσθὲν ἐκ βιαίου πνεύματος
τοῖς οὐ δοκοῦσι τὴν χάλαζαν ἐκχέῃ.
οὐ μή ποτ' ἤρεμον γὰρ ἡ μοχθηρία
οὐδὲν φρονήσει, κἂν σχεθῇ παραυτίκα.
1030    Τοιαῦτα φιλοσοφοῦσιν οἱ νυνὶ κύνες —
κύνες ὑλάκται, τοῦτο καὶ μόνον κύνες.
τί Διογένης τοιοῦτον ἢ Ἀντισθένης;
τί δαὶ πρὸς ὑμας ὁ Κράτης; διάπτυε
τοὺς περιπάτους Πλάτωνος· οὐδὲν ἡ Στοά.

1035 ὦ Σώκρατες, τὰ πρῶτα μέχρι νῦν φέρεις.
φθέγξωμ' ἐγώ τι πιστότερον τῆς Πυθίας;
"ἀνδρῶν ἁπάντων Μάξιμος σοφώτατος."
    Ἐγὼ δὲ τληπαθὴς μέν, εἰ καί τις βροτῶν,
ἤμην τ' ἀπ' ἀρχῆς, εἰμί τε πλέον τὰ νῦν,
1040 πόνοις μὲν ἐκ γῆς, κινδύνοις δὲ ποντίοις,
ἐξ ὧν ἐσώθην — καὶ χάρις πολλὴ φόβοις.
οὗτοι δεδώκασίν με τοῖς ἄνω σαφῶς

1015 Accompanied by a hired gang of vagrants
Maximus attached himself to Peter,[89] whose double-edged pen
was ready once to write utterly contradictory things.
Maximus drove the old man into a corner,
demanding of him this episcopal seat, which he hoped to get,
1020 or threatening not to let go of the existing one.[90]
At last he was sent away because the governor feared
(not without reason) that this raging fire
might cause new disasters in addition to the earlier ones.
At the moment he seems to be quiet, but I fear
1025 that somehow this terrible cloud, swollen with hail,
driven together by a violent wind,
might discharge hail on those who least expect it.
For wickedness will never be peaceably
disposed, even if it is held in check for a while.
1030 Such is the philosophy of today's Cynics,
barking dogs – that is all their Cynicism consists in.
What do you have in common with Diogenes or Antisthenes?
What has Crates to do with you lot? Spit upon
the school of Plato. The Stoa is nothing.
1035 Only till now, Socrates, have you held first place.
Shall I pronounce an oracle more reliable than the Pythian?
'Of all men Maximus is the wisest.'[91]
If any mortal has had much to endure, surely it is I –
I have suffered from the beginning but now do so even more,
1040 both with regard to hardships on land and dangers at sea,
from which I was saved – and I am most grateful to my fears:
they have permitted me to aim unhesitatingly at things on high

---

[89] Bishop of Alexandria.
[90] Gregory seems to be referring in line 1019 to the episcopal seat of Alexandria, and in line 1020 to that of Constantinople.
[91] The oracle at Delphi had said that Socrates was the wisest of all men.

πάντων ὑπερκύψαντα τῶν πλανωμένων.
ὅμως δὲ τὴν τότ' οὐ φέρων ἀτιμίαν
1045 καὶ τῆς ἀφορμῆς ἀσμένως δεδραγμένος,
ὡς τὸν κάκιστον ᾐσθόμην κεκαρμένον,
πάντων μὲν ἡμῖν τῶν φίλων ἐγκειμένων,
οἳ καί με φρουρᾶς εἶχον εἴσω λαθρίου
τηροῦντες ὁρμάς, ἐξόδους, ἀναστροφάς,
1050 πάντων δ' ὁρώντων τὴν πάλην τῶν δυσμενῶν,
οἳ τὴν τομὴν ᾤοντο τοῦ λόγου λύσιν –
ταῦτ' οὖν ὁρῶν τε καὶ φέρειν οὐ καρτερῶν
ἀνδρός τι πάσχω (καὶ γὰρ οὐκ ἀρνήσομαι)
ἁπλουστέρου τι μᾶλλον ἢ σοφωτέρου.

1055 πρύμναν γάρ, ὡς λέγουσι, κρούομ' αὐτίκα,
οὐκ εὐμαθῶς μέν· οὐ γὰρ ἄν τις ᾔσθετο.
    Νῦν δ' ἐξιτήριός τις ἐρράγη λόγος,
ὃν ἐξέπεμψα πατρικῶν σπλάγχνων πόνῳ.
ὁ δ' ἦν· "φυλάσσεθ', ἣν δέδωκα, τριάδα,
1060 τέκνοις ποθεινοῖς εὐπορώτατος πατήρ,
καὶ τῶν ἐμῶν μέμνησθε, φίλτατοι, πόνων."
λαὸς δ' ἐπειδὴ τοῦτον ἤκουσεν λόγον,
τῶν δυσκαθέκτων ἐκβοήσαντός τινος
ἀνίστατ' εὐθὺς ὥσπερ ἐκ καπνοῦ βίας

1065 ἑσμὸς μελισσῶν καὶ βοαῖς ἐκμαίνεται·
ἄνδρες, γυναῖκες, παρθένοι, νεανίαι,
παῖδες, γέροντες, εὐγενεῖς, οὐκ εὐγενεῖς,
ἄρχοντες, ἠρεμοῦντες, ἐκ στρατοῦ τινες,
ζέων, ἕκαστος ἴσον ὀργῇ καὶ πόθῳ,
1070 ὀργῇ κατ' ἐχθρῶν καὶ πόθῳ τοῦ ποιμένος·
ἀλλ' οὐκ ἐμὸν γὰρ τῇ βίᾳ κάμψαι γόνυ,
οὐδ' ἀσπάσασθαι τὴν ἄθεσμον ἵδρυσιν,

and to raise my head above all that is changeable.
However, at that time I was unable to endure the shame
1045 and therefore gladly grasped the opportunity,[92]
once I realised that most wicked man had been shorn,
and that all my friends supported me
(in fact they kept me under secret guard,
watching out for attacks and sorties),
1050 while all could see the intrigues of the enemy
who believed our divisions spelled the dissolution of the faith –
when I saw all this and found myself unable to bear it,
I behaved (I will not deny it) more like
a naive person than someone clever:
1055 all at once I turned my ship around, so to speak,
but not expertly; if I had, no one would have noticed.
As it was I let out some words hinting at my departure,
words I uttered in the pain caused by my fatherly affections.
This was what I said: 'Defend the Trinity which I, your father,
1060 most eager to provide for you, have given my beloved children,
and remember, my dearest ones, all that I have gone through.'
When the people heard these words,
and someone who could not be restrained shouted out,
they immediately erupted like a swarm of bees
1065 driven out by smoke, and began to shout wildly.
Men, women, young girls and boys,
children, old men, nobly born and commoners,
officials, ordinary citizens, some soldiers:
they all seethed with anger and desire alike,
1070 anger at my enemies and desire for their shepherd.
But it is not my way to yield to violence
or to accept an unlawful appointment:

---

[92] This was the opportunity for Gregory to leave Constantinople, which he was in fact unable to do at this point.

ὃς οὐδὲ τὴν ἔνθεσμον ἤνεγκ' ἄσμενος.
Ἄλλην τρέπονται τοῦ πόθου ταύτην ὁδόν.
1075 ὅρκοις τε πολλοῖς καὶ λιταῖς κεχρημένοι
τὸ γοῦν παραμεῖναι καὶ βοηθεῖν ἠξίουν
καὶ μὴ προέσθαι τοῖς λύκοις τὸ ποίμνιον.
πῶς ἂν δυναίμην καρτερεῖν τὸ δάκρυον;
Ἀναστασία, ναῶν ὁ τιμιώτατος,
1080 ἣ πίστιν ἐξήγειρας ἐν γῇ κειμένην,
κιβωτὲ Νῶε, τὴν ἐπίκλυσιν μόνη
κόσμου φυγοῦσα καὶ φέρουσα δεύτερον
κόσμον τὸν ὀρθόδοξον ἐν τοῖς σπέρμασιν,
σοὶ μὲν πολὺς καὶ πάντοθεν ἐπιρρεῖ λεώς
1085 ὡς τοῦ μεγίστου κινδύνων ἑστηκότος
ἡμῶν γενέσθαι τὸ κρατεῖν ἢ τοῦ πόθου·
ἐγὼ δ' ἄφωνος ἐν μέσῳ σκότου γέμων,
οὐδ' ὡς καταστείλαιμι τὰς φωνὰς ἔχων,
οὐδ' ὡς ὑποσχοίμην τι τῶν αἰτουμένων.
1090 τὸ μὲν γὰρ οὐχ οἷόν τε, τῷ δ' ὑπῆν φόβος.
Ἔθλιβεν αὐχμός, σώματ' ἦν διάβροχα.
φωναὶ δ' ἔλειπον, αἱ γυναῖκες ἐν φόβῳ,
καὶ τῶν, ὅσαι μάλιστα εἶεν μητέρες,
παίδων ὀδυρμός, ἐνδεδώκει δ' ἡμέρα.
1095 ὤμνυ δ' ἕκαστος μὴ πρὶν ἐνδώσειν πόνων,
κἂν ἐνταφῆναι τῷ νεῷ δέῃ καλῶς,
ἢ τῶν ποθουμένων τιν' ἐκβαλεῖν λόγον.
οἷον τις εἰπεῖν ἐξεβιάσθη πόνῳ —
φεῦ τῆς ἀκοῆς, ἣ μὴ τότ' εὐθὺς ἐφράγη.

1100 "συνεκβαλεῖς" γὰρ εἶπε "σαυτῷ τριάδα."
ἕως φοβηθείς, μή τις ἐκβῇ κίνδυνος,
ὅρκον μὲν οὐδ' ὥς — καὶ γάρ εἰμ' ἀνώμοτος,
ἵν' ἐν θεῷ κἀγώ τι κομπάσω μικρόν,
ἐξ οὗ λέλουμαι πνεύματος χαρίσματι —,

in fact I was unwilling to accept even a lawful one.
Then their longing drives them to a different course:
1075 with numerous oaths and prayers they entreat me
to consent at least to stay and help them
and not to hand the flock over to the wolves.
How could I restrain my tears?
Anastasia, the most highly honoured of all the churches,
1080 you who awakened the faith that lay buried in the earth,
you ark of Noah, you who alone escaped
the universal flood, bearing a second
world, a world of orthodoxy, in your seeds,
to you streams from every quarter a great crowd of people
1085 at the moment when the greatest uncertainty exists
as to whether I or they will succeed in our desire.
I stand speechless in their midst, filled with despair,
for I do not know how to restrain their cries
or how I can promise any one of their demands:
1090 for I was unable to do the first, afraid to do the second.
The heat was oppressive, our bodies soaked in sweat,
their voices were giving out, the women were frightened,
especially those of them who were mothers,
the children were crying, day had faded.
1095 But each one swore he would not give up his efforts –
even if he had to be buried in the church itself [93] –
until I should yield to some of their demands.
Then someone, by desperation forced to speak,
(alas for the sense of hearing! I wish I had lost mine right then!)
1100 said, 'Then you will throw out the Trinity together with yourself.'
As I was afraid that a dangerous situation might ensue
I gave an oath, or rather (for I have never sworn an oath –
if I, too, may boast a little in God [94] –
since I was washed by the grace of the spirit),

[93] Cf. Augustine's account of similar behaviour on the part of Ambrose's supporters in Milan when threatened by the Arian faction in the city: *Confessions* IX 7.15.
[94] Cf. 2 Corinthians 11: 16 and 1 Corinthians 1: 31 = 2 Corinthians 10: 17.

1105 λόγον δ' ἔδωκα τῷ τρόπῳ πιστούμενον
μενεῖν, ἕως φανῶσι τῶν σκοπῶν τινες
— καὶ γὰρ τότ' ἠλπίζοντο —, προσδοκῶν τότε
λύσειν ἐμαυτὸν φροντίδων ἀλλοτρίων.
οὕτω διεκρίθημεν ἀλλήλων μόγις,

1110 νικῶντες ἄμφω τῇ σκιᾷ τῆς ἐλπίδος·
οἱ μὲν γὰρ ὡς ἔχοντες ἡμᾶς ἐφρόνουν,
ἐγὼ δὲ μικρὸν ὡς μενῶν ἔτι χρόνον.


Ἦν ταῦτα. θεῖος δ' αὖθις ἤστραπτεν λόγος,
τάχιστα πυκνωθέντος ὥσπερ ἑρκίου
1115 ἢ καὶ φάλαγγος τοῦ πεπονθότος μέρους
τάχει στρατηγίας τε καὶ πλήθει χερός.
οἱ γὰρ τὸ πρόσθεν δέσμιοι τῶν δογμάτων
καὶ τοῦτ' ἔχοντες εἰς τὸ συγκεῖσθαι μόνον
ὁρῶντες, οἷ' ἔπασχον, ἔστεργον πλέον.



1120 τοὺς μὲν γὰρ ἦγεν ἡ τριὰς λαλουμένη,
μακρὸν ἀποδημήσασα τοῦ λόγου χρόνον —
ὀκνῶ γὰρ εἰπεῖν, ὡς πάλαι τεθαμμένη —,
τὸ πατρικὸν κήρυγμα καὶ προσήλυτον.
ἦν γάρ ποτ', εἶτ' ἔληξεν, εἶτ' ἦλθεν πάλιν

1125 τὴν ἐκ τάφων ἀνάστασιν πιστουμένη.
τοῖς δ' ἦν λόγος τις τῶν ἐμῶν ἴσως λόγων,
οἱ δ' ὡς ἀθλητῇ καρτερῷ προσέτρεχον,
οἱ δ' ὡς ἑαυτῶν ἔργον εἶχον ἀσμένως.

1105 I gave my word (which was believed because of my
          character)
    that I would stay until some of the bishops arrived
    (for they were expected at that time).[95] I hoped that then
    I could free myself from all my concerns for others.
    And so we parted at last,
1110 both sides victorious, but both deceived by hope:
    for they believed I now was in their hands,
    while I thought I would only stay a while.

*Success in supporting orthodoxy (1113–1272)*

    So matters stood. All at once the divine word shone forth,
    and was swiftly reinforced (like a rampart
1115 or like the part of an army which has suffered losses),
    thanks to the fast action of the leadership and the number
          of troops.
    For those who had hitherto been held captive by my
          teachings
    and for whom this was the sole reason for their attachment
          to me
    felt greater affection for me when they saw what I was
          suffering.
1120 Some were drawn by my preaching of the Trinity
    which for a long time had been banished from sermons –
    I hesitate to say 'had long been buried' –
    this doctrine belonging to our fathers and to outsiders alike:
    for it existed once, then disappeared, then returned once
          more,
1125 thus giving credence to the idea of resurrection from the
          grave.
    There were those who perhaps valued my preaching skills,
    while some rushed to me as if I were a strong champion,
    and others welcomed me as their own creation.[96]

[95] A reference to the planned Council of bishops to be held in 381.
[96] Gregory here alludes to those who had invited him to be in charge of the orthodox Christians at Constantinople, i.e. those referred to in line 596.

οἱ μέν, πύθεσθε ταῦτα τῶν εὖ εἰδότων,

1130 οἱ δ', ἐκδιηγήσασθε τοῖς οὐκ εἰδόσιν –
εἴπερ τινὲς τοσοῦτον ὑμῶν μακρόθεν
ἢ τῆς κρατούσης νῦν Ἰταλῶν ἐξουσίας –,
ὡς ἂν λαληθῇ ταῦτα καὶ τοῖς ὕστερον
ὡς ἄλλο τῶν καινῶν τι τοῦ βίου κακῶν,
1135 ὧνπερ ὁ μάταιος ὁλκὸς ἡμερῶν φέρει
πλεῖον τὸ χεῖρον ἐμπλέκων τῷ κρείσσονι.
Οὔπω λέγω τὸν ὀρθὸν ἐν πίστει λεών,
τὸν τῆς ἐμῆς ὠδῖνος εὐγενῆ τόκον,
οὓς ἔστιν εἰπεῖν οὐδενὸς πεφηνότος
1140 τῶν συμφρονούντων τῷ παρόντι προστρέχειν,
ὡς τοὺς ἀνύδρους ταῖς φανείσαις ἱκμάσι,
λιμοῦ βοηθὸν τὸν λόγον ποιουμένους,
ἢ φωτὶ μικρῷ τοὺς ἄγαν σκουτουμένους.
τί δ' ἄν τις εἴποι τῶν ξένων τῆς πίστεως,

1145 ὅπως ἔχαιρον τῷ λόγῳ, μεμνημένος;


Πολλαὶ μέν εἰσιν αἱ παρέξοδοι λίαν
τῆς ἀπλανοῦς τε καὶ τεταγμένης ὁδοῦ
πᾶσαι φέρουσαι πρὸς βυθοὺς ἀπωλείας,
εἰς ἃς διεῖλεν ὁ φθορεὺς τὴν εἰκόνα,
1150 ὡς ἂν παρείσδυσίν τιν' ἐντεῦθεν λάβοι
γνώμας τεμών, οὐ γλῶσσαν ὡς πάλαι θεός.
ἐντεῦθέν εἰσιν αἱ νόσοι τῶν δογμάτων·
οἱ θεῖον οὐδὲν εἰδότες ἢ φορὰν μόνην,

Some of you must learn these things from those who know well,
1130 while you others, explain them to those who do not know –
if there are any so far away from you
or from the power which now rules over the Italians –
so that these things may also be told to future generations,
as an example of another of those bizarre evils in life
1135 which the vain progress of time produces,
weaving an increasing amount of evil in with the good.
I am not speaking here of those who stand straight in the faith,
the noble offspring of my pains,
who, one could say, rushed to the one who was there
1140 because there was no one else of similar beliefs.
They used my sermons to help them in their hunger,
as those without water rush towards patches of moisture which appear,
or as those surrounded by darkness towards a tiny light.
But what can I say of those who were strangers to the faith
1145 when one remembers how much they enjoyed my sermons?

*Catalogue of heresies (1146–1189)*

Many are the paths deviating from
the straight and established road,
all of which lead to the depths of destruction.
Along these paths the destructive one has shattered God's image,
1150 so that he might thereby gain some means of entry,
confounding doctrines rather than tongues as God did long ago.[97]
This was the cause of all corrupt beliefs:
those[98] who acknowledge nothing divine but movement alone,

---

[97] Cf. Genesis 11: 7.
[98] In lines 1153–8 Gregory alludes to various forms of paganism.

ὑφ' ἧς γενέσθαι καὶ φέρεσθαι πᾶν τόδε·

1155 οἱ πλῆθος εἰσάγοντες ἀνθ' ἑνὸς θεῶν
καὶ τοῖς ἑαυτῶν προσπεσόντες πλάσμασιν·
οἱ τὴν πρόνοιαν μὴ διδόντες τοῖς κάτω
καὶ πάντα συντιθέντες ἀστέρων πλοκαῖς.
ὅσοι τε λαὸς ὄντες ἔκκριτος θεοῦ

1160 τὸν υἱὸν ἐσταύρωσαν εἰς τιμὴν πατρός·
ὅσοι τε μικροῖς εὐσεβεῖς ἐντάλμασιν,
οἵ τ' ἀγγέλους καὶ πνεῦμα καὶ ἀνάστασιν,
οἵ τε προφητῶν γράμματ' ἐξαρνούμενοι·
Χριστόν θ' ὅσοι σέβουσιν ἐν νόμου σκιαῖς.

1165 οἱ τὸν Βυθὸν Σιγήν τε προχρόνους φύσεις
τιμῶντες αἰῶνάς τε τοὺς θηλάρσενας,
Σίμωνος ἰὸς τοῦ Μάγου, ὧν φύματα
οἱ συντιθέντες τὴν θεότητ' ἐκ γραμμάτων·
οἱ τὴν Παλαιὰν καὶ Νέαν δύω θεοῖς

1170 νείμαντες, αὐστηρῷ τε κἀγαθωτάτῳ·
οἱ τρεῖς φύσεις τιθέντες οὐ κινουμένας,
τὴν πνεύματος χοός τε τὴν τ' ἀμφοῖν μέσην.
οἱ τῷ Μανοῦ χαίροντες ἀρχικῷ σκότῳ.
οἱ Μοντανοῦ τὸ πνεῦμα τιμῶντες κακῶς;
1175 οἱ τὴν Ναυάτου κενὴν ἔπαρσιν ὀφρύος.
οἱ τῆς ἀρεύστου τριάδος συναιρέται,
οἱ τῆς ἀτμήτου φύσεως διαιρέται·
αὖθις τε τούτων ὥσπερ ἐξ ὕδρας μιᾶς
πολλῶν φυέντων δυσσεβείας αὐχένων,

by which this universe comes into being and is set in
    motion;
1155 those who introduce numerous gods instead of just one
and prostrate themselves before their own creations;
those who reject providence for the world below
and attribute everything to the intricate movements of the
    stars;
all those[99] who comprise the chosen people of God
1160 and who crucified the Son so as to honour the Father.
Some are devout in their observance of minor rules,
and some deny the angels, the spirit and the resurrection,
together with the writings of the prophets;
some, again, reverence Christ, but in the shadows of the
    Law;
1165 then there are those[100] who honour 'the Deep' and 'Silence'
and the beings existing before time and the bisexual aeons:
they are the poison of Simon Magus, from which spring
these diseased growths which construct the Deity out of
    letters.
There are those who allot the Old and New Testaments
1170 to two gods, one harsh, the other benevolent,
others who posit three unmoving natures,
one of the spirit, one of dust, and one between the two;
some who rejoice in Mani's primitive darkness,[101]
while others perversely honour Montanus' spirit
1175 or the empty pride of Novatian.
some merge the Trinity, which cannot be made to coalesce,
or take apart the nature which cannot be divided.[102]
Again from these, like necks from the one hydra,
spring forth numerous forms of heresy –

---

[99] In lines 1159–64 Gregory refers to different forms of Judaism: Pharisees (1161), Saducees (1162–3), Samaritans (1163) and those Christians of Jewish race, known as Nazarenes, who continued to obey much of the Jewish law (1164).
[100] In lines 1165–72 Gregory is referring to Gnostic sects, such as the Valentinians.
[101] i.e. the Manichees.
[102] Gregory is alluding in lines 1176–7 to the Sabellians and the Arians.

## ΠΕΡΙ ΤΟΝ ΕΑΥΤΟΥ ΒΙΟΝ

1180 ὁ τῇ κτίσει τὸ πνεῦμα συντιθεὶς μόνον,
ὁ καὶ τὸν υἱὸν προστιθεὶς τῷ πνεύματι·
οἵ τ' εἰσάγοντες ἥλικα Καίσαρος θεόν·
οἱ τὴν δόκησιν εἰσάγοντες ἐκτόπως·
οἱ δεύτερον λέγοντες υἱὸν τὸν κάτω·

1185 οἱ μὴ τέλειον τὸν σεσωσμένον, ἀλλ' ἄνουν.
αὗται γάρ εἰσιν, ὡς τύπῳ φράσαι, τομαί
τῆς ὀρθότητος ἐκτόπων τε μητέρες.
Τούτων δὲ τίς ἦν οὕτως ἀκίνητος τότε,
ὡς μὴ τὸ οὖς γε τοῖς ἐμοῖς κλίνειν λόγοις;

1190 τοὺς μὲν γὰρ ᾕρει τὸ κράτος τῶν δογμάτων,
οἱ δ' ἡμεροῦντο τῷ τρόπῳ τῆς λέξεως.
οὐ γὰρ μετ' ἔχθρας οὐδὲ λοιδόρως πλέον
ἢ κηδεμονικῶς τοὺς λόγους προήγομεν,
ἀλγοῦντες, οὐ παίοντες οὐδ' ἐπηρμένοι
1195 καιρῷ ῥέοντι καὶ πλάνῳ καθώς τινες —
τίς γὰρ λόγῳ τε καὶ κράτει κοινωνία; —
οὐδὲ πρόβλημα τὸ θράσος ποιούμενοι
τῆς ἀλογίας — δεινῶς γὰρ ἔντεχνον τόδε
καὶ σηπιῶδες, τὸ μέλαν ἐκ βάθους ἐμεῖν,

1200 ὡς τοὺς ἐλέγχους ἐκδιδράσκειν τῷ ζόφῳ —,
ἀλλ' ἡμέρως τε τοῖς λόγοις καὶ προσφόρως
ἐντυγχάνοντες ὡς λόγου συνήγοροι
τοῦ συμπαθοῦς τε καὶ πράου καὶ μηδένα
πλήσσοντος· ἐξ οὗ καὶ τὸ νικᾶσθαι λόγος,

1180 that which attributes the Spirit alone to creation,[103]
that which adds the Son to the Spirit.[104]
There are those, too, who propose a god who is Caesar's contemporary,[105]
and some who misrepresent Christ as only apparently divine.[106]
Some say that the one on earth is a second son,
1185 or that the one who was saved is not perfect but lacks a soul.[107]
These, in summary form, are the divergences
from orthodoxy and the sources of all strange beliefs.
Who among the champions of these was so immovable then
that he did not at least incline his ear to my words?

*Gregory's guiding principles (1190–1259)*

1190 Some were captivated by the power of my teachings
while others succumbed to my way of speaking.
For I delivered my sermons without hatred or abuse
but rather in a spirit of solicitude,
full of pain, not hitting out or carried away, as some are,
1195 by the success of the moment, fleeting and deceptive as it is.
For what do power and the word have in common?
Neither did I hide my weakness behind a defensive
boldness – for that is fiendishly cunning behaviour,
like that of the cuttlefish, spewing forth black ink
1200 so that in the murk one might avoid counter-arguments.
No, I spoke gently in my speeches, addressing them
accommodatingly as an advocate of that Word
which is sympathetic and mild and which hurts
no one. On account of it submission is justified

---

[103] i.e. the followers of Macedonius.
[104] i.e. the Arians.
[105] i.e. the Photinians.
[106] i.e. the Docetists.
[107] i.e. the Apollinarians, to whom Gregory has already referred in lines 612ff.

1205 and victory is much more valuable

1205 καὶ τὸ κρατεῖν δὲ τιμιώτερον πολύ
πειθοῖ βιαίᾳ τῷ θεῷ προσκτώμενον.
τοιαῦτα πλαξὶ ταῖς ἐμαῖς ἐνεγράφη.
Ἄλλος τις οὗτος τῆς ἐμῆς παιδεύσεως
νόμος, σοφῶς τε καὶ καλῶς γεγραμμένος·
1210 μὴ μίαν ὁδὸν τῆς εὐσεβείας εἰδέναι
τὴν εὔκολόν τε καὶ κακὴν γλωσσαλγίαν,
μηδ' ἐν θεάτροις καὶ φόροις καὶ συμπόταις
ὁμοῦ γελῶντας, ᾄσμασιν χαυνουμένους,
πρὶν καὶ πλυθῆναι γλῶσσαν ἐξ αἰσχρῶν λόγων,

1215 μηδ' ἐν βεβήλοις ὠσὶ καὶ Χριστοῦ ξένοις
ῥίπτειν ἀφειδῶς τῶν λόγων τοὺς μυστικούς,
παίζοντας ἐν τοῖς καὶ πόνῳ θηρωμένοις·
ἀλλ' ἐντολαῖς μὲν ὡς μάλιστα εὐσεβεῖν
πτωχοτροφοῦντα, ξενοδοχοῦντα, ταῖς νόσοις

1220 ἀρκοῦντα, καρτεροῦντα, καὶ ψαλμῳδίαις,
εὐχαῖς, στεναγμοῖς, δάκρυσιν, χαμευνίαις,
γαστρὸς πιεσμοῖς, ἀγχόναις αἰσθήσεων,
θυμοῦ γέλωτος χειλέων εὐταξίᾳ
τὴν σάρκα κοιμίζοντα πνεύματος κράτει.

1225     Πολλαὶ γάρ εἰσιν αἱ σωτηρίας ὁδοί,
πᾶσαι φέρουσαι πρὸς θεοῦ κοινωνίαν·
ἃς χρή σ' ὁδεύειν, οὐ μόνην τὴν ἐν λόγῳ.
λόγος γὰρ ἀρκεῖ καὶ ψιλῆς τῆς πίστεως,
μεθ' ἧς ἀτεχνῶς τὸ πλέον σῴζει θεός.

1230 εἰ δ' εἰς σοφοὺς ἔπιπτεν ἡ πίστις μόνον,
θεοῦ παρ' ἡμῖν οὐδὲν ἦν πενέστερον.
ἀλλ' εἶ φιλόγλωσσός τις ἢ ζήλου πλέως
καὶ δεινόν, εἴ σοι μὴ ῥυήσεται λόγος
(ἀνθρώπινον γὰρ εὔχομαι κἀνταῦθά σοι)·

when someone is won over to God by the force of persuasion.
Such things I had inscribed on my tablets.[108]
Another principle of my instruction was this,
wisely and fittingly engraved:
1210 a facile and harmful prolixity
should not be regarded as the only road to piety;
nor should one carelessly proclaim the mysteries of doctrine
or joke about things which are attained only with great effort,
in theatres and public places or at drinking sessions
1215 among people laughing together and relaxing in song,
before the tongue is washed clean from foul language,
and not to ears which are uninitiated and strangers to Christ.
Instead one should do one's best to honour the commandments
to feed the poor, show hospitality to strangers, relieve
1220 illnesses, persevering in psalm singing,
prayers, sighs, tears, sleeping on the ground,
curbing the appetite and mortifying the senses,
controlling anger, laughter and chatter,
and putting the flesh to sleep through the power of the spirit.
1225 For many are the paths to salvation,
all leading to communion with God;
along these you must travel, not only along that based on eloquence.
For the language of simple faith is sufficient,
and by this means God effortlessly saves the majority.
1230 If the faith were accessible only to the educated,
nothing in this world would be poorer than God.
But if you are fond of talking or full of zeal
and find it terrible if your words will not flow
(for I wish for something human for you here, too),

---

[108] Cf. 2 Corinthians 3: 3.

1235 then talk, but with fear and not continuously;

1235 λάλει μέν, ἐν φόβῳ δὲ μηδὲ πάντοτε,
μὴ πάντα μηδ' ἐν πᾶσι μηδὲ πανταχοῦ,
ἀλλ' ἔστιν οἷς ὅσον τε καί που καί ποτε.
καιρὸς γὰρ παντός, ὡς ἀκούεις, πράγματος·
"μέτρον τ' ἄριστον" τῶν σοφῶν ἑνὸς λόγος.

1240     Χωρὶς τὰ Μυσῶν καὶ Φρυγῶν ὁρίσματα,
χωρὶς τὰ τῶν ἔξωθεν τῶν τ' ἐμῶν λόγων.
τῶν μὲν γάρ εἰσι πρὸς ἐπίδειξιν οἱ λόγοι
ἐν μειρακίσκων συλλόγοις καὶ πλάσμασιν,
ἐν οἷς μέγ' οὐδὲν ἢ ἀτυχεῖν ἢ τυγχάνειν

1245 σκιᾶς – σκιᾶς γὰρ οὐδὲν εὐσθενέστερα.
ἡμῖν δ' – ἀληθεύειν γάρ ἐστιν ὁ σκοπός –
οὕτως ἔχειν, ἢ μή, περιδεὲς τὸν λόγον.
ὁδὸς γὰρ ἀμφίκρημνος, ἧς ἔξω πεσεῖν
πεσεῖν προδήλως ἐστὶν εἰς Ἅιδου πύλας.

1250 ὅθεν μάλιστα τοὺς λόγους φυλακτέον,
τὰ μὲν λέγοντας, τῶν δ' ἀκούοντας σοφῶς,
ἔστιν δ' ὅτ' ἐκχωροῦντας ἀμφοῖν ἐξίσης
στάθμῃ δικαίᾳ τῷ φόβῳ κεχρημένους.
ἧττον γὰρ οὖς ἢ γλῶσσα κίνδυνον φέρει·

1255 ἧττον δ' ἀκοῆς τὸ καὶ φυγεῖν ἐκ τοῦ μέσου.
τί δεῖ σε νάρκης ἀψάμενον νεκροῦν φρένα
ἢ πλησιάζειν ἄσθματι λυσσῶντος κυνός;
        Οὕτω μαθόντες ἐκ γραφικῶν θεσπισμάτων,
οἷς ἐτράφημεν πρὶν συναχθῆναι φρένα,

1260 οὕτως ἄγοντες καὶ πολίτας καὶ ξένους,
ἤδη γεωργῶν ἦμεν ἐν τοῖς πλουσίοις,
εἰ καὶ συνακτὸν οὐχ ὁμοῦ τοὐμὸν θέρος.

do not say everything nor speak to all people nor
> everywhere,
but think to whom, how much, and where, and when.
There is a time for everything, as you have been told,[109]
and 'due measure is best' is a saying of one of the sages.[110]
1240 The borders of the Mysians and Phrygians are far apart[111]
and so too are my words and those of the pagans.
For their rhetoric aims at display
and is full of fictitious arguments which impress young
> boys.
To them it does not matter whether one hits or misses
1245 the shadow – for their fictions have no more substance
> than a shadow.
But as for me, my aim is to speak the truth
and I worry whether things are as I say they are, or not.
For my path leads along a precipice, and to fall from it
is undoubtedly to fall down to the gates of hell.
1250 That is why I have to watch my words particularly carefully,
wisely saying some things but listening to others;
there is also a time when it is right to refrain from both
> equally,
using fear as the correct yardstick.
For the ear is less dangerous than the tongue
1255 and less dangerous than listening is retreat from public life.
Why should you need to deaden the mind by taking drugs
or go close to the breath of a rabid dog?
This is what I learned from the divine sayings of the
> scriptures
which I was brought up on before my mind was formed.
1260 Thus did I lead the citizens and foreigners
and as a farmer I was already among the wealthy,
even if my crops had not yet all been gathered in.

---

[109] Cf. Ecclesiastes 3: 1.
[110] Cf. Gregory's *Oration* 43.60.
[111] Cf. *In suos versus* 102.

For some I had to clear away from the thorns,

τοὺς μὲν γὰρ ἄρτι τῶν ἀκανθῶν ἡμέρουν·
οἱ δ' ὠμαλίζονθ', οἷς δ' ἐβάλλετο σπόρος,

1265 οἱ δ' ἐν γάλακτι, τῶν δ' ὑπὲρ γῆς ἡ φυή,
οἱ δ' ἐχλόαζον, οἱ δ' ἐδεσμοῦντο στάχυς,
οἱ δ' ἡδρύνοντο, οἱ δὲ λευκοὶ πρὸς θέρος·
ἅλως τιν' εἶχε, τοὺς δὲ θημῶν τις φίλος·
οἱ δ' ἐκρίνοντο, οἱ δὲ σιτώνων ἔσω,

1270 οἱ δ' ἦσαν ἄρτος, τῆς γεωργίας πέρας –
ἄρτος γεωργὸν τὸν καμόντα μὴ τρέφων
νῦν, τοὺς δὲ μηδὲν ἐκχέαντας ἰκμάδος.

Ἐβουλόμην ἐνταῦθα στῆσαι τὸν λόγον
καὶ μηδὲν εἰπεῖν τῶν ἀναξίων λόγου.
1275 νῦν δ' οὐκ ἐᾷ με τὰ πρόσω τῶν πραγμάτων·
ὧν τὰ μὲν ἦλθε δεξιῶς, τὰ δ' ἀγνοῶ,
τί χρὴ λέγειν με καὶ τίνι μοίρᾳ προσνέμειν.
τίς ἦν,³ ἐπαινῶ. τοῦτον ἐχόντων τὸν τρόπον
ἡμῶν ἐφίστατ' ἀθρόως αὐτοκράτωρ

1280 ἐκ τῆς Μακεδνῆς βαρβάρων στήσας νέφος
πλήθει τε πολλῷ καὶ θράσει τεθηγμένων·
ἄνθρωπος οὐ κακὸς μὲν εἰς πίστιν θεοῦ
ὅσον κρατῆσαι τὰς ἁπλουστέρας φύσεις,
καὶ τῆς τριάδος ὑπερφυῶς ἡττώμενος

1285 (σπλάγχνων γὰρ οὗτος ἐστι καὶ πάντων λόγος,
στερρᾶς ἐφ' ἕδρας ἀσφαλῶς βεβηκότων)·

³ 1278 τινας δ' ἐπαινεῖν PG

while others were being levelled and on others the seed was
    cast,
1265 some had only just come forth while others grew up above
    ground,
some were turning green, some firming up into ears of
    corn;
some were ripening, some white and ready for harvest.
The threshing floor took some, our own corn pile others.
Some were selected, others went into the granaries,
1270 some were made into bread, farming's end product –
bread which is no longer used to feed the weary farmer
but others instead, who have not expended a drop of sweat.

## Installation in the church of the Apostles (1273–1395)

I wished at this point to put a stop to my account
and to say nothing of matters which are not worth telling
    here,
1275 but later events prevent me from doing this.
Some of them turned out successfully, while with regard to
    others
I don't know what to say nor to which side to assign them.
Whichever it is,[112] I accept it. This is how matters stood for
    me
when the emperor[113] suddenly arrived
1280 from Macedonia after checking the barbarian hordes
that had been roused to action by their great numbers and
    fearlessness.
The emperor was not a bad man with regard to faith in God,
as far as controlling the simpler natures goes;
he was exceptionally dedicated to the Trinity
1285 (this is the view of all those hearts
which are securely set on a firm foundation),

---

[112] Juncgk finds this manuscript reading hard to accept but does so with reservations in preference to the editorial conjecture found in *PG*.
[113] Theodosius.

and yet he was not of such enthusiasm of spirit

οὐ μὴν τοσοῦτος τῇ ζέσει τοῦ πνεύματος,
ὡς ἀντισῶσαι τοῖς παρελθοῦσιν τὰ νῦν
καιρῷ τὰ καιροῦ πταίσματ' ἐξιώμενος·
1290 ἢ τὴν ζέσιν μὲν ἴσος, οὐκ ἴσος δέ γε,
τί φῶ; τὸ θάρσος ἢ θράσος; διδάξατε.
ἴσως δ' ἄμεινον τὸ "προμήθειαν" καλεῖν.
οὐ γὰρ κατείργειν, ἀλλὰ πείθειν ἔννομον
εἶναι νομίζων, καὶ πρὸς ἡμῶν τι πλέον
1295 αὐτῶν τ' ἐκείνων, οὓς θεῷ προσάξομεν –
τὸ μὲν γὰρ ἀκούσιον κρατούμενον βίᾳ,
ὥσπερ βέλος νευρᾷ τε καὶ χερσὶν δεθέν
ἢ ῥεῦμ' ἐν ὁλκῷ πάντοθεν στενούμενον,
καιροῦ διδόντος τὴν βίαν περιφρονεῖ.

1300 τὸ δ' ἑκούσιον βέβαιον εἰς πάντα χρόνον
δεσμοῖς ἀλύτοις τῶν πόθων ἐσφιγμένον –
ταῦτ' ἐννοῶν ἔμοιγε τὸν φόβον δοκεῖ
τέως κατασχὼν πάντας ἕλκειν ἡμέρως
προθεὶς τὸ βούλεσθ' ἄγραφον πειθοῦς νόμον.
1305   Ὡς δ' οὖν ἐπέστη ἄσμενος τρισασμένοις –
ἃ μὲν τετίμηκέν με τῇ πρώτῃ θέᾳ,
οἷς τ' εἶπεν οἷς τ' ἤκουσεν εὐμενέστατα,
τί χρὴ λέγειν με καὶ γὰρ αἰσχύνης γέμον,
εἰ τηλίκος ὢν φρονεῖν δοκοίην τηλίκοις,

1310 ᾧ τίμιον τοῦτ' ἔστι καὶ μόνον, θεός.
τὸ δ' οὖν πέρας· "δίδωσι", φησί, "τὸν νεών
θεὸς δι' ἡμῶν σοί τε καὶ τοῖς σοῖς πόνοις" –
φωνὴν ἄπιστον πρὶν προελθεῖν εἰς τέλος.
οὕτως γὰρ ἦσαν ἡ πόλις κατὰ κράτος

1315 ἑστῶτες, ἡ πολλή τε καὶ δεινὴ ζέσις,
ὡς μηδ' ἄν, εἴ τι τῶν ἀηδῶν συμπέσοι,
εἴξοντες, ἀλλ' ἕξοντες, ὧνπερ ἐκράτουν·

as to treat the present like the past,
using present opportunities to correct past errors.
1290 Or rather his enthusiasm was adequate but not his –
what shall I call it? – heroism or hardihood? Tell me.
Perhaps it is better to call it foresight,
for he believed that persuasion, not repression, was right,
particularly with regard to my position
1295 and to those whom I try to lead to God;
for that which is forced to submit against its will,
like an arrow held back by bowstring and hands
or like a stream whose channel is dammed up on every
    side,
given the chance it defies the restraining force.
1300 But that which willingly submits stands firm for ever,
bound by the indissoluble ties of love.
Such being his views, I think he put a check on fear
for a while, until he could bring everyone over gently,
proposing free will as persuasion's unwritten law.
1305 Then full of joy he came to me in my great joy –
for he had treated me with respect from our first meeting,
both in the way he spoke and in listening most kindly –
what need I say? For I would be greatly ashamed
if at my age I should appear concerned about such childish
    matters.
1310 To me only one thing is valuable and that is God.
The upshot of it all was this: 'God hands the church,'[114] he
    said,
'through me to you and to your great efforts,'
words which were unbelievable until they were fulfilled.
For the city was rebelling with such violence –
1315 a strong and terrible outburst of passion it was –
that people refused to yield even if something unpleasant
was likely to occur, but held on tight to what they
    controlled.

---

[114] The Church of the Apostles, hitherto in the hands of the Arians.
If they were forced out they would let their violent anger

εἰ δ' ἐκβιάζοιντ', ἀλλὰ τὸν βαρὺν χόλον
ἡμῖν ἐπαφήσοντες, ὧν ῥᾷστον κρατεῖν.
1320 Ὁ μὲν τόδ' εἶπεν· ἐμὲ δὲ συμμιγὴς τρόμῳ
παλμός τις εἶχεν ἡδονῆς. ὦ Χριστέ μου,
ὃς οἷς πέπονθας εἰς τὸ πάσχειν ἐκκαλῇ,
σὺ καὶ τότ' ἦσθα τῶν ἐμῶν πόνων βραβεύς,
καὶ νῦν γενοῦ μοι τῶν κακῶν παρήγορος.

1325 Παρῆν ὁ καιρός. τὸν νεῶν δ' εἶχε στρατός
ξιφηφόρος, λαθραῖος ἐκτεταγμένος.
ὁ δ' ἀντεπῄει δῆμος οἰδαίνων ἅπας,
ψάμμος θαλασσῶν ἢ νιφὰς ἢ κυμάτων
κινήματ', ὀργῇ καὶ λιταῖς μεμιγμένος,
1330 ὀργῇ καθ' ἡμῶν, πρὸς δὲ τὸ κράτος λιταῖς.
πλήρεις ἀγοραί, δρόμοι, πλατεῖαι, πᾶς τόπος,
διώροφα, τριώροφα νευόντων κάτω
ἀνδρῶν, γυναικῶν, νηπίων, παλαιτάτων·
πόνος, στεναγμός, δάκρυα, βρυχήματα,

1335 εἰκὼν ἁλόντος ἄστεος κατὰ κράτος.
Ἐγὼ δ' ὁ γεννάδας τε καὶ στρατηλάτης,
καὶ ταῦτ' ἐν ἀρρωστοῦντι καὶ λελυμένῳ,
μικρὰ πνέοντι τῷδέ μου τῷ σαρκίῳ,
μέσος στρατηγοῦ καὶ στρατοῦ, βλέπων ἄνω,

1340 ᾖειν βοηθῷ χρώμενος τῇ ἐλπίδι,
ἕως κατέστην εἰς νεών, οὐκ οἶδ' ὅπως.
Κἀκεῖνο δ' εἰπεῖν ἄξιον· πολλοῖς τε γὰρ
ἔδοξεν εἶναι τῶν τότε κρεῖσσον λόγου,
οἷς οὐδὲν ἁπλοῦν ἐστι τῶν ὁρωμένων,
1345 ἐν ταῖς μεγίσταις τὸ πλέον καιρῶν ῥοπαῖς.
ἐγὼ δ' ἀπιστεῖν τοῖς λέγουσιν οὐκ ἔχω,
καίτοι προσάντης τοῖς ξένοις εἴπερ τις ὤν.
τοῦ γὰρ προχείρως πάντα πιστεύειν θέλειν
χεῖρον τὸ πᾶσιν ἀντιτείνειν ἐξ ἴσης.

1350 τὸ μὲν γάρ ἐστι κουφότης, τὸ δὲ θράσος.

loose on me who could easily be made to submit.
1320 That was what he said. A quiver of pleasure mingled with
a certain tremor of anticipation ran through me. O my Christ,
you who summon to suffering those for whom you suffered,
just as you were then the one leading me in my hardship,
be now my comforter in my sorrows.
1325 The moment had arrived. The church was in the hands of
armed soldiers who had secretly taken up positions there.
A seething mob of townspeople confronted them,
like the sand of the seas or a snowstorm or the waves'
ebb and flow, torn between anger and entreaties,
1330 anger directed at me, entreaties to those in power.
The market places were full, the colonnades, streets, every place,
two and three storey houses were full of people leaning out,
men, women, children, the very aged.
There were scuffles, sobbing, tears and cries,
1335 all giving the impression of a town taken by force.
I, the hero and the commander,
with this sick and broken body of mine
which could hardly breathe any more,
caught between the general and the army, my gaze directed upwards,
1340 moved on, supported by hope,
until I entered the church, I don't know how.
This, too, is worth telling: for to many
it seemed that these events were miraculous;
to such people nothing seen is without significance,
1345 especially at the most critical moments.
I for my part cannot disbelieve those who say this,
although if anyone is averse to strange things, it is I.
For worse than being ready to believe everything without thinking
is to resist all believing indiscriminately:
1350 the first is frivolousness, the second presumption.

τί οὖν τὸ θαῦμ'· ὦ βίβλε, κηρύσσοις βίῳ,
τοῦ μὴ λαθεῖν τοὺς ὕστερον τόσην χάριν.
Ἦν ὄρθρος, ἡ δ' ἐπεῖχε νὺξ ὅλην πόλιν
νέφους ὑποδραμόντος ἡλίου κύκλον,

1355 ἥκιστα καιρῷ πρᾶγμα τῷ τότε πρέπον·
φιλαίθριον γὰρ οὐδὲν ὡς πανήγυρις.
ὃ καὶ παρεῖχε τοῖς μὲν ἐχθροῖς ἡδονήν
ὡς δυσφοροῦντος τοῦ θεοῦ τοῖς δρωμένοις,
ἡμῖν δ' ἀνίαν ἐν φρεσὶν κεκρυμμένην.

1360 ἐπεὶ δ' ἐγώ τε καὶ τὸ πορφύρας κράτος
κιγκλίδος ἦμεν τῆς σεβασμίας ἔσω,
πάντων δ' ἐπήρθη συμμιγὴς αἶνος θεοῦ
καλουμένου βοῇ τε καὶ χειρῶν τάσει,
τοσοῦτον ἐξέλαμψεν ἡλίου σέλας

1365 νέφους ῥαγέντος τῷ θεοῦ προστάγματι,
ὡς πάντα μὲν τὸν οἶκον ἀστραπηφόρον
εὐθὺς γενέσθαι, τὸν πρὶν ἐστυγνασμένον,
καὶ τῆς παλαιᾶς εἰκόνα σκηνῆς λαβεῖν
ἅπαντας, ἣν ἔκρυπτε λαμπρότης θεοῦ,
1370 εἶδος δὲ πᾶσιν αἰθριᾶσαι καὶ φρένας·
κἀνταῦθα θάρσους συνδραμόντος τῇ θέᾳ
ἡμᾶς βοᾶσθαι πανσθενεὶ ζητουμένους,
ὡς τοῖς παροῦσι τοῦδε λείποντος μόνου,
πρῶτόν τε καὶ μέγιστον ἐκ πρώτου κράτους
1375 τοῦτ' ἂν γενέσθαι πρὸ θρόνων πόλει γέρας·
ἡμᾶς δοθῆναι τοῖς θρόνοις τοῦ ἄστεος.
ταῦτ' ἦν ἀπ' ἀνδρῶν ἐν τέλει καὶ τῶν κάτω,
πάντων ἀπ' ἴσου τοῦ πόθου ἰσουμένων,

Why then the amazement? You, my book, must proclaim it
   to the world,
lest such great grace escape the notice of future
   generations.
Daybreak came, but darkness still enveloped the whole city,
for a cloud was passing across the sun's disk –
1355 a most unpropitious thing to happen at that crucial
   moment:
a special occasion, more than anything else, demands a
   clear sky.
This brought pleasure to my enemies
as they thought God was angry at this turn of events;
but to me it brought pain which I concealed within me.
1360 Yet when I and the emperor in his purple majesty
came within those awesome gates,
God's praises rang out from all the people with one accord,
as they addressed him with loud voices and hands
   outstretched:
then the brightness of the sun blazed forth so strongly
1365 as the cloud split apart at God's command
that all at once a flash of light filled the whole building
which had before been horribly dark
and everyone had a vision of the tabernacle
of old, covered in the brightness of God.[115]
1370 The gloom cleared from everyone's face and spirits,
and as their confidence increased at this vision,
they cried out with all their strength, asking for me,
as if this were the one thing lacking to those present;
it would be the first and greatest honour for the city
1375 from the highest power, more precious than the bishop's
   throne itself,
if I were to be appointed to that city's throne.
This was demanded by the men in high position and the
   less important,
who were all made equal by the equality of their demand;

---

[115] Cf. Exodus 40: 38.

ταῦτ' ἐκ γυναικῶν ὑψόθεν βοώμενα
1380 πέρα σχεδόν τι τοῦ γυναιξὶ κοσμίου.
βροντή τις ἦν ἄπιστος ἀντικλωμένη,
ἕως ἐγώ τιν' ἐξαναστήσας θρόνων
σύνεδρον – οὐκ ἐμοὶ γὰρ ἦν φωνῆς τόνος
συνωσμένῳ τε καὶ δέει κεκμηκότι –

1385 γλώσσης τάδ' εἶπον ῥήματ' ἐξ ἀλλοτρίας·
"ἐπίσχεθ' οὗτοι, τὴν βοὴν ἐπίσχετε.
καιρὸς γάρ ἐστι παντός· εὐχαριστίας
ὁ νῦν· ὁ δ' εἰσέπειτα καὶ τῶν μειζόνων."
λαὸς δ' ἐπερρόθησαν, οἷς ἐφθεγξάμην –

1390 πᾶσιν γάρ ἐστι προσφιλὲς τὸ μέτριον –
αὐτός τ' ἀπῆλθεν αἰνέσας αὐτοκράτωρ.
οὕτω μὲν οὗτος σύλλογος καταστρέφει
τοσοῦτον ἡμᾶς ἐκφοβήσας καὶ μόνον,
ὅσον γυμνωθὲν ἓν ξίφος πάλιν ἔσω

1395 πεσεῖν, θράσος τε συντεμεῖν θερμοῦ λεώ.


Τὰ δ' ἔνθεν οὐκ οἶδ', ὡς προάξω τὸν λόγον
ἔχοντα καί τιν' ὄγκον ἐν τοῖς πράγμασιν.
τίς συγγραφεύς μοι τῷ λόγῳ δοίη πέρας;
αἰσχύνομαι γὰρ ταῖς ἐμαῖς εὐφημίαις,

1400 κἂν ἄλλος εὖ λέγῃ με. τοῦτ' ἐμὸς νόμος.
ὅμως δὲ λέξω μετριάζων ὡς σθένος.
Ἦν ἔνδον· ἡ πόλις δὲ τὸ φρύαγμα μέν
κάτω βεβλήκει τοῦ ναοῦ κρατουμένου·

this was demanded by the women shouting from the upper gallery,
1380 almost exceeding the bounds of decent behaviour for women.
There was an incredible thundering noise echoing off the walls
until I made someone sitting beside me stand up
from his chair – for my voice had no force,
crushed and worn out by fear as I was –
1385 and I spoke these words with another's tongue:
'Restrain yourselves, you people, stop your shouting.
There is a proper time for everything. Now is the time for thanksgiving.
Afterwards there will be time for more important issues.'
The congregation applauded what I had said –
1390 for everyone values moderation –
and the emperor himself gave his approval and departed.
And so this meeting reached its close:
it had only caused me terror inasmuch as
one sword had been drawn and then fallen back inside its sheath,
1395 intended to check the wild behaviour of the hot-headed mob.

*Gregory's work under the new arrangement (1396–1505)*

As to what follows, I don't know how to continue my account,
seeing there is a certain pride involved in these matters.
Is there some writer who could bring my account to its conclusion?
For I am ashamed to be acclaimed
1400 even if someone else speaks highly of me. This is my rule.
Yet I shall speak, while trying as far as I can to keep matters in proportion.
I was inside. The city had abandoned its insolent behaviour
now that we had taken control of the church.

ὅμως δ' ὑπεστέναζεν, ὡς γίγας, φασίν,

1405 βληθεὶς κεραυνῷ πρόσθεν Αἰτναίῳ πάγῳ
καπνόν τε καὶ πῦρ ἐκ βάθους ἠρεύγετο.
τί οὖν με ποιεῖν, πρὸς θεοῦ, δίκαιον ἦν;
διδάξαθ' ἡμᾶς, εἴπαθ', οἱ νῦν ἐντελεῖς,
ὁ μειρακίσκων σύλλογος τῶν ἀθλίων,
1410 οἷς τὸ πρᾶον μὲν ἀδρανὲς νομίζεται,
τὸ δ' ἐμμανές τε καὶ κάκιστον ἀνδρικόν.
ὠθεῖν, ἐλαύνειν, ἀγριοῦν, ἀναφλέγειν
καιρῷ τ' ἀπλήστως χρωμένους καὶ τῷ κράτει;
ἢ φαρμακεύειν φαρμάκοις σωτηρίας;

1415 δύω γὰρ οὕτω καλὰ κερδαίνειν παρῆν·
αὐτούς τε ποιεῖν μετρίους τῷ μετρίῳ
ἡμᾶς τε δόξαν καὶ τὸ φίλτρον λαμβάνειν.
τοῦτ' ἦν δίκαιον, τοῦτο καὶ φανήσομαι
ἀεί τε ποιῶν καὶ τόθ', ὡς μάλιστ' ἐνῆν.

1420 Πρῶτον μέν, ὡς δείξαιμι μὴ καιροῦ φορᾷ
νέμων τὸ πλεῖον ἢ κράτει τῷ τοῦ θεοῦ,
τί νουθετοῦμαι τῷ καλῷ παραινέτῃ,
λόγον δ' ἔχω σύμβουλον ἀσφαλέστατον;
πάντων σεβόντων τὴν ὀφρὺν τῶν ἐν τέλει —

1425 τούτων μάλιστα τοὺς ἔσω παραστάτας,
οἳ πάντ' ἄνανδροι τἆλλα, πλὴν εἰς χρήματα —
τί δ' ἄν τις εἴποι, πῶς τε καὶ τέχναις ὅσαις
αὐτοῖς πυλῶσι βασιλικοῖς προσκειμένων,
κατηγορούντων, λαμβανόντων ἐκτόπως,

1430 τῆς εὐσεβείας ἐμφορουμένων κακῶς,
ἀσχημονούντων, ὥς γε συντόμως φράσαι,

Yet it gave forth a deep groan, like the giant who, so they tell,
1405 was struck by a thunderbolt long ago[116] in Etna's rock
and spewed forth smoke and fire from deep within.
What, for God's sake, was it right for me to do?
Tell me, speak, you who are now in power,
you miserable crowd of young people,
1410 in whose eyes gentleness is weakness,
while to be wild and immoral is courageous.
It was a question of whether to push, drive, provoke, inflame
and greedily exploit both the opportunity and power,
or whether to heal with the medicine of salvation:
1415 for this would bring two advantages –
by means of moderation I could make others moderate,
while I myself would win glory and affection.
This was the just course, and this is the one I shall always
be seen to take – as I did even at that time, as far as I was able.
1420 First of all, to prove that I am not assigning more
to the force of events than to the power of God,
why am I urged on by that beautiful adviser
and why do I have the Word as my most reliable counsellor?
While everyone bowed down before the arrogance of those in office –
1425 particularly those who were close to the emperor,
who in all other matters are not men,[117] except when it comes to money –
what could one say to describe how, and with what scheming,
they besieged the very doors of the imperial bedchamber,
making accusations, accepting bribes in immoral fashion,
1430 wickedly exploiting their faith,
in short, behaving disgracefully?

---

[116] The name of the giant monster was Typhon.
[117] Gregory is alluding to the eunuchs in employment at the imperial court. Cf. Ammianus Marcellinus 16.7.7.

μόνος ποθεῖσθαι μᾶλλον ἢ μισεῖσθ' ἔγνων
καὶ τῷ σπανίῳ τὸ σεμνὸν ἠμπολησάμην
θεῷ τὰ πολλὰ καὶ καθάρσει προσνέμων,

1435 τῶν δὲ κρατούντων τὰς θύρας ἄλλοις διδούς.
Ἔπειτα τοὺς μὲν ἠπορημένους βλέπων,
ἐφ' οἷς συνῄδεσάν σφισιν ἠδικηκότες,
τοὺς δ' εὖ παθεῖν χρῄζοντας ὡς εἰκὸς πάλιν,
τοῖς μὲν ἀφῆκα τὸν φόβον, τοὺς δ' ὠφέλουν,

1440 ἄλλους κατ' ἄλλην χρείαν, ὡς ἦν μοι σθένος.
ἓν δ' ἐξ ἁπάντων δείγματος λέξω χάριν.
Ἔνδον ποθ' ἡσύχαζον ἐξ ἀρρωστίας —
ἦρκτο γάρ, ἦρκτο συνδραμοῦσα τοῖς πόνοις.
ταῦτ' ἐτρυφῶμεν, ὡς δοκεῖ τοῖς βασκάνοις.

1445 οὕτω δ' ἔχοντος ἀθρόως δήμου τινές
ἐπεισίασι, σὺν δὲ τοῖς νεανίας,
ὠχρός, κομήτης, πενθικῶς ἐσταλμένος.
ἐμοῦ δ' ἐπιστρέψαντος ἐκ κλίνης πόδας
οὕτω τι μικρόν, οἷα τὰ πτοουμένων,
1450 οἱ μὲν θεῷ τε καὶ βασιλεῖ, ἃς ἦν φίλον,
φωνὰς ἀφέντες εὐχαρίστους ἀφθόνως
ὡς τὴν παροῦσαν ἡμέραν δεδωκόσιν
ἡμᾶς τ' ἐπαινέσαντες ἔστιν οἷς λόγοις
ἀπῆλθον. ὃς δὲ τοῖς ἐμοῖς ἄφνω ποσίν
1455 προσφύς, ἱκέτης ἄφωνος, ἔκπληκτός τις ἦν.
ἐμοῦ δέ, "τίς τε καὶ πόθεν, χρῄζεις δ' ὅτου;"
λέγοντος, οὐδὲν πλεῖον ἢ μείζους βοαί.
ᾤμωξεν, ἐστέναξεν, ἡ σφίγξις χεροῖν
πλείων· ὑπεισῄει τι κἀμὲ δάκρυον.
1460 βίᾳ δ' ἀποσπασθέντος (οὐ γὰρ ἦν λόγῳ)
τῶν τις παρόντων· "οὗτος," εἶπεν, "ὁ σφαγεύς
σοῦ τοῦ τὸ φῶς βλέποντος ἐκ θεοῦ σκέπης.

I alone decided I would rather be missed than hated
and bought for myself respect by withdrawing;
I devoted the greatest part of my life to God and to
    purification,
1435 leaving to others the gates of the powerful.
As I saw that some people were embarrassed
when they realised that they had acted unjustly,
while others naturally wished for better circumstances
    again,
I allayed the fears of the one group and helped the other,
1440 each according to their different needs, as well as I was
    able.
As an example, I will describe one episode out of many.
At one point I was at home resting as a result of ill health
(for my health had declined as my difficulties increased)
or rather, pampering myself, which is how my enemies
    regarded it.
1445 This being the situation, some of the townspeople suddenly
    burst in, accompanied by a young man,
pale, long-haired, dressed in wretched clothes.
When I made a move to put my feet out of bed,
but only a slight move, like one panic-stricken,
1450 they uttered profuse cries of thanksgiving,
to God and to the emperor, as it pleased them,
for granting them the present day;
then they praised me in a few words
and departed. But the young man suddenly clung
1455 to my feet, a silent suppliant, completely terrified.
'Who are you and where are you from? What do you want?,'
I asked. In answer there came only louder cries.
He wailed, he groaned, he tightened his grip
all the more. The tears welled up in me.
1460 After he was torn away by force (it was impossible to
    reason with him),
one of the men present said, 'This man is your assassin –
it is only as a result of God's protection that you still see the
    light.

ἑκὼν πάρεστι, δέσμιος συνειδότος,
φονεὺς ἀγνώμων, εὐγενὴς κατήγορος,

1465 τὸ δάκρυον δίδωσι τιμὴν αἵματος."
ταῦτ' εἶπεν· ἐκλάσθην δὲ τοῖς λόγοις ἐγώ,
φωνὴν δ' ἀφῆκα τοῦ κακοῦ λυτήριον·
"θεός σε σῴζοι· τὸν σεσωσμένον δ' ἐμέ
χρηστὸν φανῆναι τῷ σφαγεῖ οὐδὲν μέγα.
1470 ἐμὸν πεποίηκέν σε τὸ θράσος· σκόπει,
ὅπως ἐμοί τε καὶ θεῷ γένῃ πρέπων."
ταῦτ' εἶπον· ἡ πόλις δὲ (οὐ γὰρ λανθάνει
τῶν καλῶν οὐδέν) εὐθὺς ἐκμαλάσσεται,
ὥσπερ σίδηρος ἐμπύροις κινήμασιν.
1475      Τὸ δ' ἐκ τοσούτων χρημάτων θρυλουμένων,
ὧν οἱ μέγιστοι τῆς ὅλης οἰκουμένης
ναῶν ἐθησαύριζον ἐκ παντὸς χρόνου,
κειμηλίων τε καὶ πόρων τῶν πάντοθεν
οὐδ' ὁντινοῦν λογισμὸν ἐν τοῖς γράμμασιν

1480 εὑρόντα τῶν πρὶν προστατῶν ἐκκλησίας,
οὔτ' ἐν ταμίαις νέοις, ἐν οἷς τὰ πράγματα,
στέρξαι, ξένον τε μηδ' ὅλως λαβεῖν τινα,
ὅ μοι παρῄνουν καὶ παρώξυνόν τινες,
τούτων λογιστὴν εἰς ὕβριν μυστηρίου,


1485 πόσον δοκεῖ σοι; ὧν γὰρ ἔσχε τις μόνων,
οὐχ ὧν λαβεῖν δίκαιον, ἔσθ' ὑπεύθυνος.
ταῦθ', ὅστις ἥττων χρημάτων, καὶ μέμφεται·
ὅστις δὲ κρείσσων, καὶ λίαν προσδέξεται.
πᾶσιν γὰρ οὔσης τῆς ἀπληστίας κακῆς

1490 ἄπληστον εἶναι χεῖρον ἐν τοῖς πνεύματος.
εἰ πάντες οὕτως ἐφρόνουν εἰς χρήματα,
οὐκ ἄν ποτ' οὐδὲν τοῖον ἦν ἐκκλησίαις
πλήρωμ' ἀνευρεῖν (οὐ φρενὸς γὰρ τῆς ἐμῆς),

He is here of his own free will, a prisoner of his own guilty
    conscience.
A reckless murderer, a noble accuser,
1465 he presents these tears as compensation for bloodshed.'
This is what he said. As for me I was stunned by his words,
but I managed to utter something to wash away his crime:
'May God save you. That I, who have been saved,
should appear kind to my assassin, is nothing special.
1470 Your recklessness has made you mine. Consider
how you might become a credit to me and to God.'
Thus I spoke. The city (for nothing good escapes its
notice) immediately grew malleable,
like iron stirred around in the fire.
1475 Another point: all were talking about the enormous wealth
which the principal churches in the world
had been storing up as treasure from the beginning –
treasures and revenue from all over the place –
and the fact that I could find no account of them in the
    records
1480 of my predecessors who had been in charge of that church,
nor in those of the new treasurers in whose hands these
    matters lay;
also the fact that I accepted this and refused to choose
    some outsider
(this some people were urging and advising me to do)
to audit these accounts, as if this were an outrage to the
    divine mystery:
1485 what do you think? A person is responsible only for the
    things
in his possession, not for those he could have got hold of.
He who is a slave to money will find fault with this attitude,
but he who is superior to money will readily accept it.
For although everyone agrees that greed is an evil,
1490 greed among those of the spirit is even worse.
If all people had this attitude to money,
it would not be possible to find so many others like this
in the church (for they have not the same view as I) –

λέγω δ' ὅσον λειτουργόν, ἐγγίζον θεῷ.
1495 Καὶ τοῦτο δ' ἦν θρύλημα τῶν ἐναντίων,
μηδ' ἂν πυλῶσι τὸν λεὼν ἐξαρκέσαι,
τὸν πρὶν μερισθένθ', ἡνίκ' ἦμεν ἐνδεεῖς.
τοσοῦτον ἦμεν πᾶσιν εὐτελισμένοι,
ὧν νῦν νεῴ τε καὶ νεὼν πληρώματα.

1500   Ταῦθ' ἡμῖν ἐσπουδάζεθ' ὡς ἂν μὴ λέγω
πτωχῶν, μοναστῶν, παρθένων, τῶν ἐν νόσοις,
ξένων, παροίκων, δεσμίων ἐπιστάτας,
ψαλμῳδιῶν τε δακρύων τε παννύχων,
ἀνδρῶν γυναικῶν σεμνότητ' ἀσκουμένων,
1505 ἄλλοις τε, οἷς ἀγάλλετ' εὐτάκτοις θεός.

  Ἀλλ' οὐ γὰρ ἡσύχαζεν ὁ φθορεὺς φθόνος,
ᾧ πάνθ' ἁλίσκετ' ἢ φανερῶς ἢ λαθρίως·
ἀρχὴν κακῶν μοι τὸ κρατεῖν ἐπεισάγει.
ὅσον γὰρ ἦν ἑῷον, Αἰγύπτου δίχα,
1510 λαῶν πρόεδρον, ἄχρι Ῥώμης δευτέρας,
γῆς καὶ θαλάσσης ἐκ μυχῶν ἐσωτάτων
κινηθέν, οὐκ οἶδ' οἵστισιν θεοῦ λόγοις,
συνέρχεθ' ὡς πήξοντες εὐσεβῆ θρόνον.
ὧν ἦν πρόεδρος ἀνὴρ εὐσεβέστατος,
1515 ἁπλοῦς, ἄτεχνος τὸν τρόπον, θεοῦ γέμων,
βλέπων γαλήνην, θάρσος αἰδοῖ σύγκρατον
βάλλων ὁρῶσι, πνεύματος γεώργιον.
τίς ἠγνόησε τοῦτον, ὃν δηλοῖ λόγος,
τῆς Ἀντιοχέων προστάτην ἐκκλησίας,

I am speaking of the servants who are close to God.
1495 And this too was the talk of my enemies:
that my congregation did not even reach to the church doors,
my congregation, formerly separated, while our numbers were small.
To such a degree did everyone disparage me,
I to whom the church and those who filled it now belonged.
1500 These problems kept me busy, not to mention
the beggars, monks, virgins, the sick,
the foreigners, newcomers and prisoners for whom I was responsible,
as well as the psalm-singing and tears and all-night vigils,
the men and women leading lives of holy dignity
1505 and other things which it pleases God to see well-ordered.

*The Council of Constantinople (1506–1918)*

But deadly envy did not rest, envy
which destroys all things, whether openly or in secret.
It was power that brought me the beginning of my troubles.
For all the church leaders of the East, apart from Egypt,
1510 were summoned – I do not know by what divine injunction –
from the furthest corners of land and sea
as far as the second Rome.[118]
They met together to set firm the seat of orthodoxy.
Their president was a most pious man,[119]
1515 with a simple, guileless manner, filled with God;
a man of serene countenance, striking those who saw him
with his blend of confidence and modesty, a field of the spirit.[120]
Who has failed to recognise this man whom my account reveals,
the leader of the church at Antioch,

---

[118] i.e. from all areas east of Constantinople.
[119] Meletius, bishop of Antioch 360–81.
[120] Cf. 1 Corinthians 3: 9.

1520 τὸν ὄνθ᾽ ὅπερ κέκλητο καὶ καλούμενον
ὃ ἦν; μέλιτος γὰρ καὶ τρόπος καὶ τοὔνομα.
ὃς πόλλ᾽ ἀνέτλη πνεύματος θείου χάριν
(εἰ καὶ ξένη τι μικρὸν ἐκλάπη χερί)
ἀγῶσι λαμπροῖς τὴν πλάνην ἀποξέων.

1525  Οὗτοι μ᾽ ἐνιδρύουσι τοῖς σεμνοῖς θρόνοις
βοῶντα καὶ στένοντα, πλὴν δι᾽ ἓν μόνον
οὐ σφόδρ᾽ ἄκοντα. τοῦτο μαρτύρει, λόγε.
τί τοῦτο; τἀληθὲς γὰρ οὐ κρύπτειν θέμις.
ᾤμην ματαίοις καρδίας φαντάσμασιν

1530 (τὸ γὰρ θέλειν πρόχειρον εἰς τὴν ἐλπίδα
καὶ πάντα ῥᾷστα τῇ ζέσει τοῦ πνεύματος,
κἀγώ τις ἄλλως εἰς τὰ τοιαῦθ᾽ ὑψίνους),
εἰ τὸ κράτος λάβοιμι τοῦδε τοῦ θρόνου –
πολλὴν ῥοπὴν γὰρ καὶ τὸ φαίνεσθ᾽ εἰσφέρει –,

1535 ὥσπερ χορευτὴς ἐν μέσῳ δυοῖν χοροῖν
ἄμφω πρὸς αὑτὸν συντιθεὶς τοὺς πλησίον,
τῇ μὲν τὸν ἔνθεν, τῇ δὲ τόν, χοροῦ νόμῳ
εἰς ἓν συνάξειν τοὺς διεστῶτας κακῶς.
πῶς δ᾽ οὐ κάκιστα καὶ δακρύων πλουσίων


1540 θρήνων τε πολλῶν καὶ σπαραγμῶν ἀξίως,
οἵων τις οὔπω τῶν πάλαι ἢ τῶν νέων
ἐπ᾽ οὐδενός ποτ᾽ ἀνιαρῶν ἐστήσατο,
πολλῶν κακῶν πολλοῖς τε συμπεπτωκότων,
οὐδ᾽ ἢν ἅπαντες ᾄδουσ᾽ Ἰσραὴλ σποράν,

1545 ὃν χριστοφόντης ἐξελίκμησεν χόλος.
  Οἱ γὰρ πρόεδροι καὶ λαοῦ διδάσκαλοι,

1520 who was what he was called and was called
what he was?[121] For 'of honey' was his name and nature.
Many things did he endure for the sake of the Holy Spirit
(even if he was somewhat deceived at the hands of strangers),
washing away his error by means of splendid struggles.
1525 These men set me upon the awesome throne,[122]
crying out and sighing; for one reason alone
was I not completely unwilling. Bear witness to this, my account.
What was it? – for it is not right to conceal the truth.
The vain illusions of my mind led me to think
1530 (for a wish is quick to hope
and all things are easy when the spirit is bubbling with eagerness;
I tend anyway to be over-optimistic in such matters)
that if I were to accept the power of the bishop's throne
(for outward appearances are also very influential)
1535 I might be like a chorus-leader between two choruses,
bringing both groups together at his side:
as in a dance I would be able to bring together,
some from one side, some from another, those who were dreadfully divided.
Was this division not most terrible, a cause for abundant tears,
1540 for many laments and agonies?
These were sufferings such as no one yet in days gone by
or recently has ever inflicted on anyone else,
although many evils have befallen many people,
not even at the time of the scattering of Israel of which all men sing,
1545 Israel which the Christ-slaying anger winnowed.
For the leaders and the teachers of the people,

---

[121] i.e. his nature reflected the meaning of his name.
[122] Here Gregory implies that he was properly installed as bishop of Constantinople only after the bishops had gathered for the Council, i.e. in the spring of 381.

οἱ πνεύματος δοτῆρες, ὧν σωτήριος
θρόνων ἀπ' ἄκρων ἐξερεύγεται λόγος,
οἱ πᾶσι κηρύσσοντες εἰρήνην ἀεί
1550 φωναῖς πλατείαις ἐν μέσαις ἐκκλησίαις
τοσοῦτον ἐπεμάνησαν ἀλλήλοις πικρῶς,
ὥστ' ἐκβοῶντες, συλλέγοντες συμμάχους,
κατηγοροῦντες καὶ κατηγορούμενοι,
διδόντες, ἐκδημοῦντες ἐν πηδήμασιν,

1555 διαρπάζοντες, οὓς τύχοι τις προφθάσας,
λύσσῃ φιλαρχίας τε καὶ μοναρχίας –
πῶς ἐκβοήσω ταῦτα καὶ τίσιν λόγοις; –
ἔρρηξαν ἤδη τὴν ὅλην οἰκουμένην,
ὃ πρόσθεν εἶπον, ἡνίκ' ἠρχόμην λόγου.
1560 λῆξις δ' ἑῴα καὶ δύσις λόγου πλέον
τομὴ νομίζετ' ἢ τόπων καὶ κλιμάτων.
τὰ μὲν γὰρ ἥνωτ', οὐκ ἄκροις, ἀλλ' οὖν μέσοις·
οἱ δ' οὐδέν ἐστιν, ᾧ δέοντ' ἐρρωγότες,
οὐκ εὐσέβειαν (τοῦτ' ἀνευρίσκει χόλος,

1565 ψεύστης ἕτοιμος), τὴν δ' ὑπὲρ θρόνων ἔριν.
τί τοῦτο φάσκω τοὺς σκοπούς; οὐ τοὺς σκοπούς
τοσοῦτον (ἄμφω καὶ γὰρ οἶδα μετρίους),
ὅσονπερ ἀμφοῖν τοὺς κακοὺς σπουδαρχίδας,[4]
αὔρας φυσώσας τὴν ἀνημμένην φλόγα,

1570 τὰ σφῶν τιθέντας εὖ καλῶς ἐν τοῖς φίλοις,
εἴπερ καλῶς τοῦτ' ἔστιν, οὐ λίαν κακῶς.
    Τούτων τι κἀγὼ τῶν κακῶν ἀπωνάμην.
ἐπεὶ γάρ, ὃν μὲν ἀρτίως ἐπῄνεσα,
τῆς Ἀντιοχέων προστάτην ἐκκλησίας

---

[4] 1568 I have corrected Jungck's σκουδαρχίδας which is a misprint.

the bestowers of the spirit, from whose high thrones
the word of salvation is poured forth,
they who always proclaim peace to all
1550 in ringing voices from the midst of their churches,
these men were raging against each other with great bitterness.
They shouted, gathered together their allies,
made accusations and were themselves accused,
handed things out and leaped about,
1555 grabbing whomever they could get to first,
in a frenzy of desire for power, for sole power.
How can I denounce these things? What words can I use?
They had already torn the whole world into shreds
as I have mentioned earlier, at the start of my account.
1560 It was as if the eastern and western parts of the empire were divided
by their beliefs more than by site or climate,
for in these respects they are united, not at the edges but at the centre.
But there is nothing to bind those people who had been torn apart,
not by orthodoxy (bitter anger invented this
1565 for it is an accomplished liar), but by the dispute over the bishop's throne.
Why do I say this of the bishops? It was not the bishops[123]
so much (for I knew that both of them were men of moderation),
as those wicked power-seekers on both sides,
winds fanning the flames which had blazed up,
1570 looking after their own interests nicely among friends,
if indeed that is nice, or rather, exceedingly immoral.
I, too, received my share of these troubles.
For when he (whom I was just now praising –
I mean the leader of the church at Antioch),

---

[123] Paulinus and Meletius, both bishops of Antioch simultaneously.

1575 πλήρης μετρητῶν τῶν τ' ἀμετρήτων ἐτῶν
πόλλ', ὡς ἀκούω, συμβατικὰ παραινέσας,
ἃ πρόσθεν ἐξηκούετ' ἐκλαλῶν φίλοις,
ἔνθεν μετῆλθε πρὸς χορὸν τῶν ἀγγέλων,
πομπῇ τε θείᾳ καὶ χύσει τοῦ ἄστεος

1580 τόθ' ὡς μάλιστα δειχθέντος, ὥσπερ λόγος,
πρὸς τὴν ἑαυτοῦ στέλλεται παροικίαν,
καλόν τι θησαύρισμα τοῖς ἐγνωκόσιν.
βουλὴ δὲ προύκειθ' ἡμῖν οὐ βουλευτέα,
ἣν οἱ στασιώδεις καὶ κακοὶ συνεκρότουν

1585 σπουδὴν ἔχοντες ἀνταναστῆσαί τινα
πρόεδρον ἄλλον τῷ τέως μονοθρόνῳ.
πολλοὶ δ' ἐκινήθησαν ἐξ ἀμφοῖν λόγοι,
εἰρηνικοί τε καὶ φέροντες εἰς κακόν·
τότ' εἶπον αὐτός, οὕσπερ ᾠόμην λόγους

1590 εἶναί τ' ἀρίστους καὶ κακῶν λυτηρίους·

"Οὔ μοι δοκεῖτε ταὐτὰ γινώσκειν, φίλοι,
ἅπαντες οὔθ', ὧν νῦν χάριν βουλευτέον,
ταῦθ' ἡμῖν ἥκειν ἀξιώσοντες λόγου,
πλείστῳ δὲ μέτρῳ τοῦ δέοντος ἁμαρτάνειν.

1595 ὑμῖν μέν ἐστιν ἄστεως ἑνὸς λόγος,
καὶ τοῦθ' ὅπως μάχοιτο νυνὶ καὶ πλέον —
ὁ γὰρ σκοπὸς τοῦτ' ἔστιν, ὃν σπουδάζετε —,

1575 a man full of measurable and immeasurable years,
    had given much advice, so I hear, which might lead to reconciliation,
    advice which he had been heard to give his friends on earlier occasions,
    he then passed on to the choir of the angels,
    and with a godlike procession, as the whole city poured out,
1580 showing itself more than ever before, so they said,
    he was escorted back to his own community,
    a wonderful treasure to those who recognised it.
    But a plan was put before me which did not merit discussion,
    a plan which the seditious and wicked were clamouring for
1585 in their eagerness to set up some
    other leader in opposition to the one who was sole bishop[124] at the time.
    Many speeches were made on both sides,
    some seeking peace and others leading to disaster.
    Then I myself spoke, saying what I considered
1590 to be best and what would deliver us from our troubles.

*Gregory's speech to the Council (1591–1679)*

'You do not all seem to me to hold the same opinion, my friends,
nor do I think you have any intention of resolving the issue
which we have met to decide upon;
in fact I think you are in the highest degree failing in your duty.
1595 The issue for you concerns one city,
and the fact that it is now more than ever engulfed in strife –
for this is the goal you are aiming at –

---

[124] Some bishops wished to see Flavian as Meletius' successor, rather than allowing Paulinus to remain as sole bishop.

χειρός τε δεῖσθε τῆς ἐμῆς συλλήπτορος·
ἐμοὶ δὲ μειζόνων τε καὶ πληρεστέρων.

1600 ὁρᾶτε τοῦτον τὸν μέγαν τῆς γῆς κύκλον,
ὃς ἐσφράγισται αἵματος τοῦ τιμίου
ῥοαῖς, θεοῦ παθόντος ἀνθρώπου τύπον
τιμήν θ' ἑαυτὸν ῥύσιον δεδωκότος,
ἄλλοις τε πολλοῖς θύμασιν καὶ δευτέροις.
1605 οὗτος δύω δονεῖται, θῶμεν, ἀγγέλοις —
ἀλλ' οὐδ' ἐκεῖνοι (φθέγξομ' ἀλγοῦντος λόγον)
τιμῆς τοσαύτης ἄξιοι. τοὐναντίον,
ὅσῳπέρ εἰσιν ἄγγελοι, τόσῳ πλέον
οὐκ ἄξιοι μάχης τε καὶ τῶν χειρόνων·
1610 εἴπερ τὸ κρεῖσσον ἄξιον καὶ κρεισσόνων.

Ἕως μὲν οὖν ἦν ἐν μέσῳ θεῖος σκοπός —
οὐδ' ἦν σαφές πω, πῶς ποθ' οἱ τῆς ἑσπέρας
τὸν ἄνδρα δέξοντ' ἠγριωμένοι τέως —,
συγγνωστὸν ἦν πως καὶ τὸ λυπεῖν μετρίως

1615 τούς, ὡς λέγουσι, "τῶν νόμων ἀμύντορας".
ἀνήρ τε γὰρ πρᾶός τις ὀργῆς φάρμακον,
τό τ' ἀγνοεῖν μέγιστον εἰς παρρησίαν.
νῦν δ' (οὐ γάρ ἐστιν οὐδὲ εἷς σάλος θεοῦ
δόντος γαλήνην τοῖς ἑαυτοῦ πράγμασιν)

1620 τί φημι χρῆναι; καὶ δέξασθέ μου λόγον,
λόγον προμηθῆ, τῶν νέων σοφώτερον.
οἱ γὰρ γέροντες τὸ ζέον γ' οὐ πείσομεν·
κενῆς γάρ ἐστιν ἧττον εὐκλείας ἀεί.
θρόνος κρατείσθω τῷ κρατοῦντί νιν τέως.

and now you need my hand as your accomplice.
But for me the issue concerns greater, more important matters.
1600 Look at this earth's great sphere
sealed with streams of precious blood,[125]
since God suffered in human form
and gave himself as compensation to save us,
sealed too by means of many other later sacrifices.
1605 This world, let us assume, is being agitated by two angels –
but not even these (I will say something that causes pain)
are worth such a price. On the contrary,
insofar as they are angels, all the more
are they undeserving of this strife and acrimony,
1610 if indeed what is superior deserves superior things.
As long as the godlike bishop[126] remained in our midst –
for it was not yet clear how the westerners,
who up to this point had been angry, would receive this man,
it was quite understandable that these 'guardians of the laws'
1615 as they call them, should feel somewhat aggrieved.
For a gentle person provides a kind of remedy for anger
and ignorance offers great encouragement to freedom of speech.
But now (for there is no longer a single wave
now that God has granted calm to his own affairs),
1620 what should I say needs to be done? Accept my advice,
advice based on careful thought, wiser than that of the young.
(We old people will not convince those who seethe with passion,
for they are ever a prey to popularity, which is without substance.)
Let the bishop's throne belong to the one who has occupied it hitherto.[127]

---

[125] Cf. Ephesians 1: 13 and 1 Peter 1: 19.
[126] i.e. Meletius.
[127] i.e. Paulinus.

1625 τί δεινόν, ἄν τι καὶ μικρὸν πλείω χρόνον
τὸν ἄνδρα πενθήσωμεν, ὡς πάλαι νόμος;
ἔπειτα δώσει τὴν λύσιν τοῦ πράγματος
τὸ γῆρας ἡ κοινή τε παντὸς τοῦ γένους
ἀναγκαία τε καὶ καλὴ προθεσμία.
1630 ὁ μὲν θανὼν οἰχήσεθ' οἷ ποθεῖ πάλαι,
δώσων θεῷ τὸ πνεῦμα τῷ δεδωκότι.
ἡμεῖς δὲ τηνικαῦτα ἐκ συμψυχίας
λαοῦ τε παντὸς καὶ σοφῶν ἐπισκόπων
θρόνῳ τιν' ἄλλον δώσομεν σὺν πνεύματι.
1635     Ἥδ' ἂν γένοιτο τῶν κακῶν λύσις μία,
ἢ γὰρ τὸ μεῖζον, προσλαβεῖν καὶ τὸ ξένον
(ξένον γάρ ἐστιν, ὡς ὁρῶ, νῦν ἡ δύσις),
ἢ δεύτερος πλους, συμφρονῆσαι τὴν πόλιν,
λαὸν τοσοῦτον καὶ χρόνῳ κεκμηκότα.
1640 στήτω ποτ' ὀψέ, κοσμικὸς στήτω σάλος.
οἶκτον λάβωμεν τῶν τε νῦν ἐσχισμένων
τῶν τ' ἐγγὺς ὄντων τοῦ πάθους τῶν θ' ὕστερον.
μή τις θελήσῃ, ποῖ προβήσεται, μαθεῖν,
εἰ ταῦτα νικήσειεν ἐν μακρῷ χρόνῳ.
1645 ἐπὶ ξυροῦ βέβηκεν, ἢ σῴζεσθ' ἔτι
τὸ σεμνὸν ἡμῶν δόγμα καὶ σεβάσμιον
ἢ μηκέτ' εἶναι τῇ στάσει διαρρυέν.
ὥσπερ γὰρ ἡ τῶν χρωμάτων μοχθηρία
τοῦ ζωγράφου νομίζετ', οὐκ ὀρθῷ λόγῳ,
1650 ἢ τῶν μαθητῶν ὁ τρόπος διδασκάλων,
οὕτως ὁ μύστης ὢν κακός — πόσῳ πλέον
ὁ μυσταγωγὸς ὕβρις εἰς μυστήριον.
μικρόν τι νικηθῶμεν, ὥστε προσλαβεῖν
νίκην τε μείζω καὶ τὸ σωθῆναι θεῷ,

1655 κόσμον τε σῶσαι τὸν κακῶς ὀλωλότα.
οὔτοι τὸ νικᾶν δόξαν ἐν πᾶσιν φέρει.

1625 Is it strange that we should mourn a little longer
the other man,[128] as was the custom long ago?
Then old age will provide a solution of the matter,
bringing the inevitable and beautiful moment,
fixed beforehand for each member of our human race.
1630 For he who dies goes to the place he has long desired,
giving his spirit back to God who gave it him.
Then, with the agreement of all the people
and the wise bishops, we shall with the help of the Spirit
appoint someone else to the bishop's throne.
1635 This would be the only solution to our problems,
either (this would be better) to win back what is alienated –
for as I see it, the west is alienated at the moment –
or (as a second best) to bring the city into agreement,
these people exhausted by the lengthy dispute.
1640 Then at last may the earthquake cease.
Let us have pity on those now separated,
both on those close to this trouble and on later generations.
Let no one desire to know how these things will turn out,
if this viewpoint gains the upper hand for a long period.
1645 We are on a knife-edge: either our holy and venerable
dogma can yet be saved,
or it will cease to exist, torn apart by strife.
For just as the ugliness of the colours
is considered the painter's fault, though not rightly so,
1650 or the behaviour of the pupils is held to be the teacher's
fault,
so an incompetent priest – and how much more so an
incompetent
bishop – is regarded as an outrage to the mystery.
Let us concede a little, so that we may gain
a greater victory and be saved by God,
1655 as well as saving the world which has been so dreadfully
devastated.
Victory certainly does not bring honour in every case.

---

[128] i.e. Meletius.

καλῶς στέρεσθαι κρεῖσσον ἢ κακῶς ἔχειν.
ταῦτ' οἶδεν ἡ τριάς τε καὶ τὸ σὺν λίθοις
κήρυγμα λαμπρὸν τῆς ἐμῆς παρρησίας,

1660 ὃ καί μ' ἔθηκε τοῖς κακοῖς ἐπίφθονον.
Εἴρηθ' ἁπλῶς τε καὶ δικαίως σήμερον,
ἅπερ συνοίσειν οἶδα τοῖς σκοπουμένοις.
εἰ δ' οἴεταί τις τῶν κακῶν ἢ πρὸς χάριν
λέγειν τάδ' ἡμᾶς αὐτὸς ἠγορασμένος

1665 (εἰσὶν γάρ, εἰσὶν ἔμποροι τῶν ἐκκρίτων
χρυσοῦ γέμοντες καὶ προθυμίας ἴσης)
ἤ τι σκοπεῖν οἰκεῖον, ὡς πολλοῖς νόμος,
αὐτὸς τεχνάζων λανθάνειν ἐν τοῖς κακοῖς
ἢ τὸ κρατεῖν ἐντεῦθεν αὐτῷ μνώμενος,

1670 δότω τὸ κρίνειν τῷ τελευταίῳ πυρί.
ἡμῖν δὲ συγχωρήσατ' ἄθρονον βίον,
τὸν ἀκλεῆ μέν, ἀλλ' ὅμως ἀκίνδυνον.
καθήσομ' ἐλθών, οἷ κακῶν ἐρημία.
κρεῖσσον γὰρ ἢ τοῖς πλείοσιν μεμιγμένον

1675 μήτ' ἄλλους ἕλκειν πρὸς τὸ βούλημ' ἰσχύειν
μήτ' αὐτὸν ἄλλοις συμφέρεσθ', οὗ μὴ λόγος.
δεῦρ', ὅστις οἶδε τὸν θρόνον, προσβαινέτω·
πολλοὺς ἀμείψει, ἀξίους τε καὶ κακούς.
πρὸς ταῦτα βουλεύεσθε. εἴρηται λόγος."


1680    Ταῦτ' εἶπον· οἱ δ' ἔκρωζον ἄλλος ἄλλοθεν,
δῆμος κολοιῶν εἰς ἓν ἐσκευασμένος,
τύρβη νέων τις, καινὸν ἐργαστήριον,
λαῖλαψ κόνιν σύρουσα πνευμάτων στάσει,

It is better to lose something honourably than to possess it
    dishonestly.
The Trinity knows this, as does my outspoken preaching
(which also caused the wicked to hate me)
1660 shining forth even amid stonings.
I have said plainly and justly today,
what I know will be of use in the matters under
    consideration.
But if some wicked person thinks that I say these things
to please someone, although it is he himself who has been
    corrupted,
1665 (for there are some, yes, some who trade in sacred offices,
weighed down equally by gold and greed)
or that I am aiming at some personal objective, as many do,
while he himself cunningly tries to escape notice in this
    crisis
or attempts to gain power out of it for himself,
1670 let him leave judgement to the final fire.
Grant me a life without a bishop's throne,
a life without fame, maybe, but at least without danger.
I will go and settle far from any troubles,
for this would be better than to be at the centre of a great
    crowd
1675 but to be unable to win others over to one's point of view
or to give one's support to others whose views are
    unreasonable.
Let someone who knows the bishop's throne come forward
    here.
He will get many people in exchange, both worthy and
    wicked.
With regard to all this, make your decision. My speech is
    finished.'
1680 This was what I said. But they screeched on every side,
a flock of jackdaws all intent on one thing,
a mob of wild young men, a new kind of gang,
a whirlwind causing the dust to swirl as the winds went
    out of control,

οἷς οὐδ' ἂν ἠξίωσε τῶν τις ἐντελῶν

1685 φόβῳ τε θείῳ καὶ χρόνῳ δοῦναι λόγον
ἄτακτα παφλάζουσιν ἢ σφηκῶν δίκην
ᾄττουσιν εὐθὺ τῶν προσώπων ἀθρόως·
τοῖς δ' ἠκολούθουν ἡ σεμνὴ γερουσία.
τοσοῦτ' ἀπεῖχον σωφρονίζειν τοὺς νέους.

1690 καὶ τὸν λογισμόν, ὡς ἐπαινετός, σκόπει.
δεῖν γὰρ συνάλλεσθ' ἡλίῳ τὰ πράγματα
ἐντεῦθεν ἀρχὴν λαμβάνονθ', ὅθεν θεός
ἔλαμψεν ἡμῖν σαρκικῷ προβλήματι.
τί οὖν; μάθωμεν μὴ σέβειν περιτροπάς,
1695 Χριστοῦ δὲ σάρκα παντὸς ἡμῶν τοῦ γένους
οἴεσθ' ἀπαρχήν. "ἡ δ' ἐντεῦθεν ἤρξατο",
εἴποι τάχ' ἄν τις, "ἔνθα πλεῖον τὸ θράσος,
ὡς ῥᾳδίως ἐνταῦθα καὶ θανούμενος,
ἐκ τοῦ δ' ἔγερσις, ἐκ δὲ τοῦ σωτηρία."

1700 τοὺς ταῦτα δοξάζοντας οὐκ εἴκειν ἐχρῆν
τοῖς, ὥσπερ εἶπον, εὐμαθῶς ἐγνωκόσιν;
ἐξ οὗ καὶ τἆλλα δῆλον ὡς ὑψίφρονες.


Κἀκεῖνο δ' οἷον· τὴν γλυκεῖαν καὶ καλὴν
πηγὴν παλαιᾶς πίστεως, ἢ τριάδος
1705 εἰς ἓν συνῆγε τὴν σεβάσμιον φύσιν,
ἧς ἦν ποθ' ἡ Νίκαια φροντιστήριον,
ταύτην ἑώρων ἁλμυραῖς ἐπιρροαῖς
τῶν ἀμφιδόξων ἀθλίως θολουμένην,
οἳ ταῦτα δοξάζουσιν, οἷς χαίρει κράτος,
1710 μέσοι μὲν ὄντες — ἀσμενιστὸν δ' εἰ μέσοι
καὶ μὴ προδήλως κλήσεως ἐναντίας,

men with whom not even a ruler with the authority of fear
    or age
1685 would think it proper to reason,
    buzzing around as they were in complete disorder,
    like a swarm of wasps suddenly flying into your face.
    Yet the respected council of elders, far from attempting to
        recall
    the young men to their senses, actually joined them!
1690 Just consider how admirable was their reasoning:[129]
    matters should move along the same course as the sun,
    taking as their starting point the place where God
    shone forth for us in human form.
    What? Let us learn not to honour the sun's circular course,
1695 but to believe that the incarnate Christ is the first fruit
    of our whole race. 'But he took this place as his starting
        point,'
    someone might perhaps say, 'where there was greater
        shamelessness,
    so that he might also easily be put to death there;
    thence comes the resurrection, thence also our salvation'.
1700 Should not those who think like this yield
    before those who, as I said, hold the correct views?
    It was clear from this how utterly arrogant they were.

## *Gregory withdraws from the Council (1703–1796)*

So much for that! The sweet and pure
spring of our ancient faith, which had merged
1705 the sacred nature of the Trinity into one
    (as had been worked out some time ago at Nicaea),
    this spring I saw being tragically polluted
    by the briny influx of those of dubious beliefs,
    those who believed whatever was approved by authority.
1710 They sat on the fence, and that was acceptable
    as long as they did not openly join the opposition.

[129] Gregory ridicules those who argued for the supremacy of the eastern church on the grounds that Christ had been born in the east.

ἐπίσκοποι νῦν μανθάνοντες τὸν θεόν,
διδάσκαλοι χθές, καὶ μαθηταὶ σήμερον,
τελειοποιοί, καὶ τέλειοι δεύτερον,
1715 λαὸν καταρτίζοντες, οἳ τὰ σφῶν κακά,
οὐκ οἶδ᾽ ὅπως μέν, ἐκλαλοῦσι δ᾽ οὖν ὅμως,
καὶ ταῦτα χωρὶς δακρύων· ὃ καὶ ξένον,
ἄδακρυς ἐκλάλησις ἀρρωστημάτων.
Οὗτοι μέν οὕτω. δοῦλα καιροῦ γάρ φασιν
1720 τὰ πάντα. τοῦ παίζειν δὲ τίς μείζων τρυφή;
ὃ μήτε μόχθῳ κτητόν, ὡς τὰ πόλλ᾽ ἔχει,
μήτ᾽ ἄλλοθεν ποριστόν, ἀλλ᾽ οὐδ᾽ ὤνιον —
ἡμεῖς δὲ πῶς ποθ᾽ οἱ φιλάνθρωποι λίαν;
προυθήκαμεν κήρυγμα πρόσθεν βημάτων·

1725 πᾶσιν βοῶμεν· " ὃς θέλει, δεῦρ᾽ εἰσίτω,
κἂν δίστροφός τις ἢ πολύστροφος τύχῃ.

1726a θέατρόν ἐστι πᾶσιν ἠνεῳγμένον,
πανήγυρις ἕστηκεν· ἀπίτω μηδὲ εἷς
ἀπραγμάτευτος. ἂν μεταστραφῇ κύβος
(καιροῦ γὰρ οὐδέν ἐστιν εὐστροφώτερον),
1730 ἔχεις τὸ τεχνύδριον· ἀνάδραμε τοὐμπαλιν.
οὐκ εὐμαθὲς τὸ πίστει προσκεῖσθαι μιᾷ,
βίων δὲ πολλὰς εἰδέναι διεξόδους."
Ἐξ οὗ τί γίνεθ᾽; ἡ πολύπλοκος πάλαι
εἰκὼν ἐν ὕπνοις· χρυσός, ἐξῆς ἄργυρος,
1735 χαλκός, σίδηρος, ὄστρακον τὰ πρὸς πόδας.
δέδοικα, μὴ τὰ πάντα λικμήσῃ λίθος.
καὶ Μωαβίταις κἀμμανίταις, οἷς οὐ πάλαι,
νῦν εἰσιτητόν ἐστιν εἰς ἐκκλησίαν.
"σὺ δ᾽ οὐκ ἐπῄνεις ταῦτα τὸ πρόσθεν; λέγε.
1740 τῶν συλλόγων δὲ τίς ποτ᾽ εἶχε τὸ κράτος;"
οἱ σύλλογοι μὲν ἦσαν, ὧν ἦσαν τότε

>       They were bishops who were still learning about God,
>       teachers yesterday and students today,
>       making you perfect[130] but themselves perfect only later,
> 1715  setting the people right, and yet they openly –
>       I don't know how – confess their own misdeeds,
>       and this without tears. This is indeed strange:
>       a tearless confession of their weaknesses!
>       So much for these men. For they say that all depends
> 1720  upon circumstances. What more enjoyable than to joke?
>       A joke cannot be obtained by hard work, as most things can,
>       nor can it be acquired in any other way, neither can it be
>           bought –
>       so how did I manage it then, I who tend to be too kind?
>       I made an announcement from in front of the pulpit,
> 1725  addressing them all in a loud voice, 'Whoever wishes, come
>           up here,
>       even if you have changed direction twice or many times.
> 1726a The theatre is open to all
>       and the banquet is ready. Let no one go away
>       without taking part. Should the die fall a different way
>       (for nothing is more changeable than circumstance),
> 1730  then you know the drill: change direction once again!
>       It is not really sensible to stick to one belief:
>       instead one should explore different paths through life.'
>       What was the result of this? That complex dream image
>       from of old: gold, then silver,
> 1735  bronze, iron, with feet of clay.[131]
>       I was afraid that a stone might destroy the whole thing.
>       And Moabites and Ammonites, formerly forbidden,
>       were now allowed to come into the church.[132]
>       'But tell us, did you not approve these things before?
> 1740  Who was in charge of the councils earlier?'
>       The councils were controlled by those who controlled them
>           at that time

[130] i.e. in baptism.
[131] Cf. Daniel 2: 31ff.
[132] Cf. Deuteronomy 23: 3.

(ὀκνῶ γὰρ εἰπεῖν αὖθις, οἷς αἰσχύνομαι),
ἦσαν δὲ πάντων, ἴσον εἰπεῖν οὐδενός·
ἀναρχία γάρ ἐστιν ἡ πλεισταρχία.

1745    Ἐμοῦ δὲ καλῶς ἡ νόσος προεστάτει,
ἥ μ' εἶργεν οἴκοι πολλὰ δὴ καὶ πολλάκις
πρὸς ἓν μόνον βλέποντα, τὴν ἐκδημίαν,
ἣ πάντων εἶχε τῶν κακῶν ἀπαλλαγήν.
ὃ δ' οὖν παρέστη, τοῦτο καὶ κείσθω νόμος.
1750 τινὲς μὲν ἦσαν, οἳ βίᾳ μὲν καὶ μόγις,
ἀλλ' οὖν συνῆλθον, οἷς τι μετῆν παρρησίας,
ὅσοις ἄγνοια τοῦ κακοῦ συνήγορος
τῇ διπλόῃ κλαπεῖσι τῶν διδαγμάτων
τό τ' ἐν μέσῳ κήρυγμα εὐσεβῶς ἔχον,

1755 τόκος τεκόντων παντελῶς ἀλλότριος.
τὸν συρφετὸν δὲ τὸν πολὺν χριστεμπόρων
τότε προσήσομ', ἡνίκ' ἂν καὶ βόρβορον
εὐωδίᾳ μίξῃ τις ἀχράντου μύρου.
ῥᾷον κακοῦ γὰρ ἢ καλοῦ μετουσία.
1760 τούτοις ὁ καινόδοξος οὐκ ἠρέσκετο
(οὕτω καλοῦσι τοὺς προμηθεῖς οἱ θρασεῖς),
ἀλλ' οὐδ' ἐκεῖνοι τῷ προμηθεῖ. γίνετ' οὖν
ὁ Λὼτ ἐκεῖνος ὁ πατριάρχης τ' Ἀβραάμ·
ὁ μὲν βαδίζει τήν, ὁ δὲ τὴν ἐναντίαν,

1765 ὡς μὴ στενοῦσθαι τῷ πλάτει τῆς κτήσεως.
    Τί δεῖ λέγειν, ὅσοις τε καὶ οἵοις λόγοις

(for I hesitate to repeat things of which I am ashamed);
they were controlled by everyone, which is the same as
    saying, by nobody,
for control by many is no control at all.[133]
1745 Fortunately illness came to my rescue,
which often kept me for the most part at home.
I was looking forward to one thing only, my departure,
which would bring release from all my troubles.
Whatever was decided, let that have the force of law.
1750 Some men there only took part under pressure and
    unwillingly,
yet did so nevertheless: they were quite open-minded,
but their ignorance of the problem was an excuse,
for they were deceived by the enigmatic nature of the
    teachings
and by the fact that the official line, being moderate,
    seemed orthodox,
1755 despite being an offspring completely unlike its parents.[134]
I will accept the great mob of Christ-traders
when someone is able to blend filth
with the fragrance of pure myrrh:
for it is easier to get mixed up in evil than in good.
1760 These people did not approve of one with new-fangled
    ideas[135]
(this is what the reckless say of those with foresight)
but neither did the one with foresight approve of them. So
    it happened
as with that man Lot and the patriarch Abraham:[136]
one went off in one direction, the other the opposite way,
1765 so that they would not be restricted as to the extent of their
    possessions.
Why should I relate the many different arguments used

---

[133] Cf. Homer, *Iliad* 2.204: 'mob rule is a bad thing'.
[134] Gregory refers here to the problem of expressing clearly the orthodox view of Trinitarian doctrine.
[135] i.e. Gregory himself.
[136] Cf. Genesis 13: 6–11.

ταύτην ἐπείρων τὴν πολιὰν οἱ φίλτατοι,
τὰ πρῶτα μὲν διδόντες, αἰτοῦντες δέ γε
τὸ γνήσιον, φεῦ, Γρηγόριον τὸν γνήσιον,

1770 οἱ γνήσιοι μέν, εἰς δὲ σύμπνοιαν κακῶν·
τὸ δ' ἐστίν, εἰς ἅπαντα συνεργοῦντ' ἔχειν.
πῶς εἰς ἅπαντα; τίς δ' ἐφαντάσθη τόσον,
ὡς πλῆθος ἄξει πρός τί μ', οὐ θεοῦ λόγος;
πρόσθεν ῥυήσετ' εἰς ἄνω πηγῶν φύσις

1775 καὶ πῦρ ὁδεύσει τὴν ἐναντίαν φοράν,
ἤ τι προδώσω τῆς ἐμῆς σωτηρίας.
 Ἐντεῦθεν ἐξέκλεπτον ἐκ μέσου πόδα.
δῆλον δέ· καὶ γὰρ οἶκον ἀντηλλαξάμην
ἕλκων ἐμαυτὸν ἐκ βυθῶν ἐκκλησίας

1780 πόρρω κακῶν τε καὶ λόγων καὶ συλλόγων.
πλὴν ὅσα κατεστέναζον οἱ προσκείμενοι —
λαοῦ μάλιστα, ὡς τὰ πάντων μὴ λέγω —
βοῶντες, ἱκετεύοντες, εἰς θεὸν χέρας
αἴροντες, ὁρκίζοντες, ὡς τεθνηκότα

1785 πενθοῦντες ἤδη — τοῦ πάθους, τῶν δακρύων.
πῶς ἦν ἐνεγκεῖν ταῦτα καὶ τίνος φρενός;
"ἡμᾶς ἀφήσεις τὸν σόν, ὡς ἠκούομεν,
στάχυν, στενόν ποτ', εὔκομον δὲ νῦν θέρος;
λαὸν δὲ τὸν προσήλυτον, τὸν μὲν θύραις

1790 ταῖς σαῖς προσεστῶθ', οἷς ἀνοῖξαι δεῖ μόνον,
τὸν δ' ἔνδον ἤδη, τὸν δὲ θηρευτὴν ξένων,
τίσιν προήσῃ; τίς σὸν ἐκθρέψει τόκον;

by my closest friends to try and win over this grey head of mine.
They conceded first place to me and yet they demanded
loyalty (alas!) from the loyal Gregory,
1770 they who were themselves loyal – loyal partners of the wicked!
What they wanted, was that I should work with them in everything.
How could I do so in everything? Who could have imagined this,
that I should be led to do anything by the majority, not by God's word?
Rather will streams change their nature and flow upwards
1775 and fire move in the opposite direction
before I betray any part of my salvation.
From that moment on, I began to creep from out of their midst.
It was obvious, for I moved house,
dragging myself out of the depths of the church,
1780 far from those difficult people, the arguments and meetings.
Of course, my supporters complained hugely –
particularly the ordinary people, for I will not mention them all –
crying out, pleading, raising their hands to God,
trying to make me take an oath, mourning for me
1785 as if I were already dead – what suffering! what tears!
How, in what state of mind, could I have endured all this?
'Will you abandon us, we who are regarded
as your crop, once a meagre one, but now an abundant harvest?
The people whom you have converted, some of whom stand
1790 before your doors, for whom you need only to open,
while some are already inside and others search for the outsiders –
whom will you hand them over to? Who will bring up your child?

τοὺς σοὺς πόνους τίμησον, οἷς προσερρύης·
δὸς τῆς πνοῆς τὸ λεῖπον ἡμῖν καὶ θεῷ.
1795 ναὸς γενέσθω σοῦ βίου πεμπτήριος.''
ταῦτ' ἦν κλάσις μέν, ἀλλ' ὅμως ἐκαρτέρουν.


Μικρόν τι, καὶ δίδωσι τὴν λύσιν θεός.
ἦλθον γάρ, ἦλθον ἐξαπίνης κεκλημένοι,
ὡς δή τι συνοίσοντες εἰρήνης σκοπῷ,
1800 Αἰγύπτιοί τε καὶ Μακεδόνες, ἐργάται
τῶν τοῦ θεοῦ νόμων τε καὶ μυστηρίων,
φυσῶντες ἡμῖν ἑσπέριόν τε καὶ τραχύ.
τοις δ' ἀντεπῇει δῆμος ἡλιοφρόνων.
κάπροι δ' ὅπως θήγοντες ἀγρίαν γένυν
1805 (ὡς ἂν μιμήσωμαί τι τῆς τραγῳδίας),
λοξὸν βλέποντες ἐμπύροις τοῖς ὄμμασιν
συνῆπτον. ἐν πολλοῖς δὲ τοῖς κινουμένοις
θυμοῦ τὸ πλεῖον ἢ λόγου κινήμασιν
καὶ τῶν ἐμῶν τι πικρότερον ἐπεσκόπουν,
1810 νόμους στρέφοντες τοὺς πάλαι τεθνηκότας,
ὧν πλεῖστον ἦμεν καὶ σαφῶς ἐλεύθεροι·
οὐ μὴν πρὸς ἔχθραν τὴν ἐμὴν οὐδὲ θρόνον
σπεύδοντες ἄλλῳ, οὐδαμῶς, ὅσον πόνῳ
τῶν ἐνθρονιστῶν τῶν ἐμῶν, ὡς γοῦν ἐμέ

Have respect for your hard work, which has worn you
    out.[137]
Grant to us and to God the breath you have left.
1795 Allow our church to send you on your way out of this life.'
At this point I nearly collapsed but managed to remain
    firm.

*Gregory's resignation (1797–1918)*

A short time passed and God granted a means of escape.
For they came, they came, hastily summoned
to contribute to the process of reconciliation,
1800 Egyptians and Macedonians, experts
in the laws and mysteries of God,
blowing upon us a harsh wind from the west.
They were confronted by all who thought in an eastern
    way.[138]
But just like wild boars sharpening their savage tusks
1805 (if I might use a quotation from tragedy),[139]
looking with suspicion at one another, their eyes ablaze,
they clashed together. Amidst all the cut and thrust,
driven more by passion than by reason,
they came to scrutinise a painful matter concerning me,
1810 turning up laws which had long been obsolete[140]
and which were clearly to a large extent irrelevant to me.
They did this not out of hatred for me nor from a desire
to gain the throne for someone else, no, but to create
    difficulties
for those who had placed me on the throne; at least, this
    they

---

[137] Jungck queries this reading as the usual sense of this word does not fit this context.
[138] i.e. those who were keen to push policies favouring the eastern half of the Empire.
[139] Euripides, *Phoenissae* 1380.
[140] Gregory alludes to the fifteenth canon of the Council of Nicaea (J. Stevenson (ed.), *Creeds, Councils and Controversies*, no. 91).

1815 σαφῶς ἔπειθον λαθρίοις δηλώμασιν.
οὐ γὰρ φορητὴν τὴν ὕβριν σφῶν εἰδέναι,
ὅση παλαιὰ καὶ νέοις ἐν πράγμασιν.
Ἐγὼ δὲ τέως μὲν ὥσπερ ἵππος δέσμιος,
καίπερ κακοῖς τε καὶ νόσῳ τετρυμένος,
1820 ἔνδον κροαίνων οὐκ ἐπαυσάμην πόδας
καὶ δοῦλον ἐχρεμέτιζον ἐκ δεσμῶν βίας
ποθῶν νομάς τε τήν τ' ἐμὴν ἐρημίαν.
ἐπεὶ δὲ κινεῖν, ἃ προεῖπον, ἠξίουν,
ἔρρηξα δεσμὰ τήν τ' ἀφορμὴν ἀσμένως

1825 (οὐκ ἂν πείσαιμι τοὺς φιλάρχους οὔποτε,
εὔδηλόν ἐστι, πλὴν ἀληθές) ἥρπασα.


καιρὸς γὰρ ἦν μοι· καὶ παρελθὼν εἰς μέσους
τάδ' εἶπον· "ἄνδρες, οὓς συνήγαγεν θεός,
ὡς ἄν τι βουλεύσησθε τῶν θεῷ φίλων,

1830 τὸ μὲν καθ' ἡμᾶς δευτέρου κείσθω λόγου·
μικρὸν γάρ, ὥς γε πρὸς τοσοῦτον σύλλογον,
ὅπως ποθ' ἕξει, κἂν μάτην αἱρώμεθα·
ὑμεῖς δὲ πρός τι μεῖζον ὑψοῦτε φρένα.
εἰς ἓν γένεσθε, συνδέθητε ὀψὲ γοῦν.


1835 ἕως τίνος γελώμεθ' ὡς ἀνήμεροι
καὶ τοῦτο μανθάνοντες ἕν, πνέειν μάχην;
δότε προθύμως δεξιὰς κοινωνίας.
ἐγὼ δ' Ἰωνᾶς ὁ προφήτης γίνομαι.
δίδωμ' ἐμαυτὸν τῆς νεὼς σωτηρίαν

1815  clearly informed me by means of secret communications:
they knew these people's outrageous behaviour was
    intolerable,
both that in the past and during recent events.
As for me, up till then, like a tethered horse,[141]
despite being worn down by misfortunes and illness,
1820  I had continued to stamp my hooves in my stable
and whinny at being held captive in such tight bonds,
longing for the meadows and for my independence.
But when they decided to bring up the matter I mentioned,
I tore loose from my bonds and gladly seized the
    opportunity
1825  for freedom. (I will never convince those eager for power,
that is clear, and yet this is true.)

*Gregory's resignation speech before the bishops (1827–1855)*

This was my chance and so I came forward into their midst
and made this speech: 'You men whom God has brought
    together
so that you might make a decision pleasing to God,
1830  let my affairs take second place,
for it is irrelevant, at least with regard to this important
    council,
how they should turn out, even if I have been raised up in
    vain.
You must raise your thoughts to something greater:
come together and unite, even at this late hour.
1835  How long shall we be laughed at as uncivilised beings
who only understand one thing, how to pant for battle?
Extend the hand of friendship cheerfully.
But I have become the prophet Jonah:
I give myself as a means of saving the ship,

---

[141] Cf. Homer *Iliad* 6.506ff. for this simile.

1840 καίπερ κλύδωνος τυγχάνων ἀναίτιος.
ἄραντες ἡμᾶς ῥίψατε κλήρου φορᾷ.
κῆτός με δέξετ' ἐκ βυθοῦ φιλόξενον.
ἐντεῦθεν ἄρξασθ' ὁμονοεῖν· ὁδεύετε
πρὸς πάντ' ἐφεξῆς. οὗτος εὐρυχωρίας
1845 τόπος καλείσθω. τοὐμὸν οὕτως εὐκλεές.
ἂν μέχρις ἡμῶν στῆτε, τοῦτ' ἀτιμία.
νόμον τίθημι μὴ θρόνων ὑπερμαχεῖν.
ἂν οὕτω φρονῆτ', οὐδὲν ἔσται δυσχερές.
οὔτ' ἐθρονίσθην ἄσμενος, καὶ νῦν ἑκὼν
1850 ἄπειμι· πείθει καὶ τὸ σῶμ' οὕτῶς ἔχον.
μίαν χρεωστῶ νεκρότητ'· ἔχει θεός.
ἀλλ', ὦ τριάς μου, σοῦ προκήδομαι μόνης·
γλῶσσαν τίν' ἕξεις εὐμαθῆ συνήγορον,
εἰ δ' οὖν ἐλευθέραν τε καὶ ζήλου πλέων;
1855 ἔρρωσθε καὶ μέμνησθε τῶν ἐμῶν πόνων.''
        Ταῦτ' εἶπον. οἱ δ' ὤκλαζον· ἐξῄειν δ' ἐγὼ
μέσος χαρᾶς τε καὶ τινος κατηφείας·
χαρᾶς τῷ παῦλαν τῶν πόνων λαβεῖν τινα,
λύπης τῷ λαὸν ἀγνοεῖν, οἷ κείσεται.

1860 τίς δ' οὐ σπαράσσετ' ὀρφανούμενος τέκνων;
ἐγὼ μὲν οὕτως· οἱ δ' ἴσασι καὶ θεός,
εἰ μή τι πλεῖον τοὐμμέσῳ τὸ λάθριον·
νεῶν ὄλεθρος καὶ σπιλάδες, λόχοι βάθους.
ἄλλοι λέγουσι ταῦτα, σιγήσω δ' ἐγώ.

1840 although I am not responsible for the storm.
Take me and throw me according to the casting of the lot.
A kindly whale from out of the deep will receive me.
From then on you can start to agree. Progress onwards
to all things in due order. Let this place be called
1845 the place of spaciousness:[142] this will be my fame.
If you were to stick with me, it would be a source of shame.
I lay down the law that there is to be no strife over bishops' thrones.
If you accept this, there will be no difficulty.
I was raised to the throne unwillingly and now I willingly
1850 depart. My present state of health also urges me to do so.
To death alone do I still owe a debt: that is in God's hands.
But you, my Trinity, for you alone I care.
What tongue will you have that is clever enough to defend you,
or is at least independent and full of zeal?
1855 Farewell and be mindful of my hard work.'
That is what I said. They were deeply shocked, but I walked out,
experiencing a mixture of joy and disappointment,
joy, because I was to get some respite from my struggles,
sorrow, because I did not know what lay in store for my congregation.
1860 Who is not torn apart when he is bereft of his children?
That was how I felt. They know, and so does God,
whether or not something more than what was seen lay hidden.
Reefs, lying in wait deep below, also cause destruction to ships.
Others may speak of these things, but I shall remain silent.

---

[142] See Genesis 26: 22: Gregory alludes to the fact that Isaac's herdsman quarrelled with the indigenous herdsman over the digging of wells at Gerar but did not quarrel over the third well they dug, so Isaac called this well Rehoboth, meaning 'spaciousness', because the Lord had made room for them in this land and there was at last peace between the different parties.

1865 οὐ γὰρ σχολή μοι πλεκτὰ γινώσκειν κακά
τὴν ἁπλότητα καρδίας ἀσκουμένῳ,
ἐξ ἧς τὸ σῴζεσθ', οὗ μόνου πᾶς μοι λόγος.
ὅμως τόδ' οἶδα· πλεῖον, ἢ καλῶς ἔχει,
ἄφνω τετίμημ' εὐκόλῳ συναινέσει.

1870 τοιαῦτα πατρὶς τοῖς φίλοις χαρίζεται.
       Οὕτως ἔχοντα ταῦτα. πῶς δὲ τὰ κράτους;
ἔκυψ'; ἐκλίνθην; ἡψάμην τῆς δεξιᾶς;
ἱκετηρίους προσήγαγόν τινας λόγους;
ἄλλους δὲ πρέσβεις ἐκ φίλων προυστησάμην,

1875 τῶν ἐν τέλει μάλιστα τούς μοι φιλτέρους,
χρυσὸν δ' ἔρευσα, τὸν δυνάστην τὸν μέγαν,
χρῄζων τοσούτου μὴ πεσεῖν ἔξω θρόνου;
ἄλλων τάδ' ἔστω τῶν λίαν πολυστρόφων.

    ἐγὼ δ', ὡς εἶχον, προσδραμὼν ἀλουργίδι,
1880 πολλῶν παρόντων καὶ τάδε σκοπουμένων,
"κἀγώ τιν'", εἶπον, "ὦ βασιλεῦ, αἰτῶ χάριν
τὴν σὴν μεγαλόδωρον τὰ πάντ' ἐξουσίαν.
οὐ χρυσὸν αἰτῶ σ', οὐ πλάκας πολυχρόους
οὐδὲ τραπέζης μυστικῆς σκεπάσματα,
1885 οὐ πρὸς γένους τιν' ὕψος ἀρχικὸν λαβεῖν
ἢ σοί γ', ἄριστε, πλησίον παραστατεῖν.
ταῦτ' ἐστὶν ἄλλων, οἷς μικρὰ σπουδάζεται.
ἐγὼ δ' ἐμαυτὸν ἀξιῶ καὶ μειζόνων.
ἕν μοι δοθήτω· μικρὸν εἶξαι τῷ φθόνῳ.

1890 θρόνους ποθῶ μέν, ἀλλὰ πόρρωθεν σέβειν.
κέκμηκα πᾶσι, καὶ φίλοις, μισούμενος

1865 I do not have the time to understand the complexities of evil,
I who practice simplicity of heart,
the source of salvation which alone is my whole concern.
Yet I know this: they immediately accorded me honour
with greater readiness and unanimity than was proper:
1870 thus does the city reward those it loves!
So much for that. How was it with the emperor?
Did I bow down? Did I fall down before him? Or clasp his right hand?
Did I address him with words of entreaty?
Did I send others from among my friends to represent my cause,
1875 especially those who were close to me among those in high office?
Did I pour forth gold, that mighty power,
in my desire to avoid falling from so high a throne?
Let this be the way of others who are ready to turn again and again.

*Gregory's resignation speech before the emperor (1881–1901)*

No, I hastened to the purple robe, just as I was,
1880 and in the presence of many who witnessed these events,
I said, 'I, too, my emperor, am asking a favour
of your powerful self who is generous in all things.
I am not asking you for gold, nor for colourful mosaics,
nor for rich cloths to cover the holy altar;
1885 nor that someone from my family might obtain a high position
or even just serve at your side, you greatest of men.
This is what others do who seek after trifles.
I consider myself deserving of greater things.
Let one thing be granted to me: to yield a little before envy.
1890 I wish to honour the bishop's throne, but from a distance.
I am tired of being hated by all, even by my friends,

τῷ μὴ δύνασθαι πρός τι πλὴν θεοῦ βλέπειν.
τούτους ἀπαίτει τὴν φίλην συμφωνίαν·
τὰ ὅπλα ῥιψάτωσαν, ἀλλὰ σὴν χάριν,

1895 εἰ μὴ φόβῳ θεοῦ τε καὶ τιμωρίας.
στῆσον τρόπαιον τῆς ἀναιμάκτου μάχης,
ὃς βαρβάρων ἔστησας ἄτρεπτον θράσος.
ταύτην δ' ἀπαίτει (τὴν πολιὰν δεικνὺς ἅμα
καὶ τοὺς ἱδρῶτας, οὓς ἐρεύσαμεν θεῷ)

1900 τὸ καρτερεῖν πάσχουσαν εἰς κόσμου χάριν.
οἶσθ', ὡς ἄκοντα καὶ θρόνῳ μ' ἐνίδρυσαν.''
　　　Ταῦτ' ἐκρότει μὲν ἐν μέσοις αὐτοκράτωρ,
κροτοῦσι δ' ἄλλοι, λαμβάνω τε τὴν χάριν,
μόγις μέν, ὡς λέγουσι, λαμβάνω δ' ὅμως.

1905 　　　Τί δεύτερόν μοι τῷ κακῷ φροντίζεται;
πείθειν ἅπαντας πρὸς τάδ' εὐφόρως ἔχειν
μηδ' ἐκτράχηλον μηδὲν ἐννοεῖν ὅλως
φίλτρῳ τε τὠμῷ καὶ χόλῳ μοχθηρίας.
ἔθαλπον, ἤνουν, τοῖς κακοῖς συνεκρότουν

1910 τὸ βῆμα, τοὺς ἔξωθε, τοὺς ποίμνης κτίλους,
ὅσον παλαιὸν καὶ ὅσον προσήλυτον,
τοῦ πατρὸς οὐ φέροντας τὴν ἐρημίαν,
ἐπισκόπων τε τοὺς λίαν πεπληγότας.
πολλοὶ γὰρ ὡς ᾔσθοντο τοῦ βουλεύματος,

1915 φεύγοντες ᾤχονθ' ὡς κεραυνίους βολάς,
βύσαντες ὦτα καὶ κροτήσαντες χέρας,
ὡς τήν γε ὄψιν μήποτ' εἰσιδεῖν τόδε,
ἄλλον τιν' ὑψωθέντα τοῖς ἐμοῖς θρόνοις.

just because I will not turn my attention to anything except
    God.
Demand of these people a loving harmony:
let them throw away their weapons, at least as a favour to
    you,
1895  if not through fear of God and punishment.
Set up a trophy to celebrate this bloodless battle,
you who have checked the inflexible daring of the
    barbarians.
Demand of these grey hairs,' (and I pointed to them,
together with the sweat I had poured out for God)
1900  'that they persevere in suffering for the sake of the world.
You know how unwilling I was when they set me on the
    throne.'
The emperor applauded my words in front of everyone,
others applauded, too, and I was granted this favour,
reluctantly, as they say, but at least I did obtain it.
1905  What was my next concern in this terrible situation?
To persuade everyone to accept this outcome gladly
and in no way to consider any kind of violence
out of love for me or out of anger at wicked behaviour.
I comforted and encouraged them and tried to reconcile to
    my enemies
1910  the priests, the outsiders, the leaders of the flock,
all who had long been members and those who had
    recently joined,
(for they could not accept that their father was
    withdrawing into solitude),
as well as those bishops who had suffered all too much.
For many of them, when they heard of my decision,
1915  ran away as if they were fleeing from a thunderstorm,
blocking their ears and clapping their hands in disapproval,
so that their eyes might never see this:
someone else being raised to my throne.

Πέρας λόγου· πάρειμι νεκρὸς ἔμπνοος.
1920 ἡττημένος — τοῦ θαύματος — στεφηφόρος,
ἔχων θεόν τε καὶ φίλους τοὺς ἐνθέους
ἀντὶ θρόνων τε καὶ κενοῦ φρυάγματος
ὑβρίζετ', εὐθυμεῖτε, πάλλεσθ', ὦ σοφοί·
ᾠδὴν τίθεσθε τὰς ἐμὰς δυσπραξίας
1925 ἐν συλλόγοις τε καὶ πότοις καὶ βήμασιν.
κοκκύζετ' ἀλεκτόρειον ὡς νικηφόροι
ἀγκῶσι πλευρὰς περικροτοῦντες, ὄρθιοι,
ὑψαυχενοῦντες ἐν μέσοις τοῖς ἄφροσιν.
ἑνὸς θέλοντος πάντες ἐκρατήσατε.
1930 "εἰ μὲν θέλοντος" — τοῦ φθόνου — καὶ τοῦδέ με
στερεῖτε κομπάζοντες ὡς ἀπωσμένου·
εἰ δ' οὐ θέλοντος, ἐντρέπεσθε τοῖς κακοῖς,
χθὲς ἐνθρονισταὶ καὶ διῶκται σήμερον
ταῦτ' ἐκφυγόντα. στήσομαι σὺν ἀγγέλοις.

1935 ἐμοῦ δ', ὅπως ἔχει τις, οὐ βλάψει βίον,
ἀλλ' οὐδε' ὀνήσει. συσταλήσομαι θεῷ.
γλῶσσαι δέ μοι ῥείτωσαν ὡς αὖραι κεναί.
καὶ τῶν κόρος μοι πολλὰ μὲν δυσφημίαις
βληθέντι, πολλὰ δ ἐξόχοις εὐφημίαις.

1940 ζητῶ τιν' οἰκεῖν ἐκ κακῶν ἐρημίαν,
οὗ μοι τὸ θεῖον νῷ μόνῳ ζητούμενον
ἐλπίς τε κούφη τῶν ἄνω γηροτρόφος.
ἐκκλησίαις δὲ τί δώσομεν τὸ δάκρυον.
εἰς τοῦτο γάρ με καὶ συνήγαγεν θεός

1945 πολλαῖς ἑλίσσων τὴν ἐμὴν ζωὴν στροφαῖς —
ἢ ποῖ προβήσετ'; εἰπέ μοι, θεοῦ λόγε·
εἰς τὴν ἄσειστον εὔχομαι κατοικίαν,
ἔνθα τριάς μου καὶ τὸ σύγκρατον σέλας,
ἧς νῦν ἀμυδρῶς ταῖς σκιαῖς ὑψούμεθα.

## Epilogue (1919–1949)

My account is at an end: here stand I, a living corpse,
1920   beaten and yet – amazingly – victorious,
for I have God and friends who are filled with God
instead of a throne and insubstantial acclaim.
Mock me, rejoice, leap with joy, you wise men.
Make my misfortunes into a song
1925   to sing at your gatherings, your parties and at the altar.
Crow like the cock in triumph,
beating your sides with your wings, strutting,
showing off to a crowd of fools.
All of you together have beaten one man who wished for it.
1930   'If he wished for it . . .' What spite! You wish to deprive me
of this also, when you boast as if you had driven me away.
But if I did not want it, then repent of your wrongful deeds,
you who yesterday set me on the throne and today chased
    me away
as I fled from all this. I shall stand with the angels.
1935   No one, whatever his views, will harm my life
but neither will he help. I shall live for God alone.
Let the chatter of tongues flow over me like an insubstantial
    breeze:
I have had enough of them, for I have been many times
assailed by their slanders and by their extravagant praises.
1940   I seek to live in some isolated place, far from the wicked,
where I can possess the divine which is to be sought by the
    intellect alone,
and hope of things above will bring relief, supporting my
    old age.
But what shall I give the churches? My tears.
For God has led me to this point,
1945   after letting my life roll through many vicissitudes;
where will it end? Tell me, Word of God.
I pray that it will end up in the unshakeable home
where lives the bright union of my Trinity,
by whose faint reflection we are now raised up.

# ΣΧΕΤΛΙΑΣΤΙΚΟΝ ΥΠΕΡ ΤΩΝ ΑΥΤΟΥ ΠΑΘΩΝ

Πολλάκι Χριστὸν ἄνακτα κακοῖς μογέων μεγάλοισιν
ὠνοσάμην· καὶ γάρ τις ἄναξ θεράποντος ἔνεικε
δούλιον ἐν στομάτεσσι λαλεύμενον ἠρέμα τρυσμὸν,
ὡς δὲ πατὴρ ἀγαθὸς καὶ ἄφρονος υἷος ἑοῖο
5 πολλάκις ἀμφαδίων ἐπέων θράσος ᾗχ' ὑπέδεκτο,
τοὔνεκα καὶ σὺ λόγοισιν ἐμοῖς, θεὸς, ἵλαος εἴης,
οὕς τοι ἀκηχεμένη κραδίη, ἀγανώτατε, πέμψει.
βαιὸν ἄκος παθέεσσιν ἐρευγομένη φρενὸς ὠδίς.
   Χριστὲ ἄναξ, τί τόσοις με κακοῖς διέπερσας ἄνωθεν,

10 ἐξότε μητρὸς ὄλισθον ἐμῆς ἐπὶ μητέρα γαῖαν;
εἰ μὴ καὶ λαγόνεσσιν ἐνὶ σκοτίῃσι πέδησας,
τίπτε τόσοις ἀχέεσσι, καὶ εἰν ἁλὶ, καὶ κατὰ γαῖαν,
ἐχθροῖσίν τε φίλοις τε καὶ ἡγεμόνεσσι κακίστοις,
ξείνοις, ἡμεδαποῖς τε καὶ ἀμφαδὸν, ἢ λοχόωσι,

15 μύθοις τ' ἀντιθέτοις, καὶ λαϊνέαις νιφάδεσσι
βέβλημαι; τίς ἅπαντα διακριδὸν ἐξαγορεύσει;
μοῦνος ἐγὼ πάντεσσιν ἀοίδιμος, οὐδ' ἐπὶ μύθοις,
οὔτ' ἐπὶ κάρτεϊ χειρὸς ἔχων περιώσιον ἄλλων,
ἄλγεα δὲ στοναχάς τε περισταδὸν, ὥστε λέοντα

# Complaint concerning his own calamities[1]

Often have I reproached Christ the king when I suffered
    great misfortunes:
for a king endures his servant's mutterings
if expressed in a restrained manner, just as a good father
often calmly accepts the outspoken words
5  his thoughtless son utters in public.
So may you, my God, receive with indulgence the words
my grieving heart addresses you, most gentle one.
To pour forth mental anguish provides some relief for
    sufferings.
Lord Christ, why have you inflicted such terrible
    misfortunes on me
10 from the moment I slipped from my mother onto mother
    earth?
If you did not keep me confined in the dark womb,
why was I assailed by such painful attacks, both by land
    and sea,
by enemies and friends alike and by most wicked leaders,
by foreigners and fellow countrymen, in public and in
    secret,
15 by means of invidious rumours and blizzards of stone?[2]
Who will give a detailed account of all the attacks?
I alone am known to all, not because of my superiority
over others either in words or in physical strength,
but because of the pain and despair besetting me on every
    side, like a lion

---

[1] *Poem* II.1.19. This poem is in hexameters.
[2] Gregory here, as often, alludes to the occasion on which he was stoned at Constantinople.

20 πάντοθεν ἀμφυλάουσι κακοὶ κύνες, οἰκτρὸν ἄεισμα,
ἀντολίῃ τε δύσει τε. τάχ' ἄν ποτε καὶ τὸ γένοιτο,
ἤ τις ἀνὴρ θαλίῃσι λύων φρένα, ἤ τις ὁδίτης,
ἤ τις ἐϋκρέκτῳ κιθάρῃ ἐπὶ δάκτυλα βάλλων,
φθόγγοις οὐ λαλέουσιν, ἐμῶν ἀχέων ὀαριστὴς,

25 Γρηγορίου μνήσαιτο, τὸν ἔτρεφε Καππαδόκεσσιν
ἡ Διοκαισαρέων ὀλίγη πτόλις. ἀλλ' ἐπίμοχθον
ἄλλοις πλοῦτον ὄπασσας ἀπείριτον· υἱέας ἄλλοις
ἐσθλούς· κάλλιμος ἄλλος, ὁ δ' ἄλκιμος, ὃς δ' ἀγορητής.
αὐτὰρ ἐμοὶ κλέος ἐστὶν ἐπ' ἄλγεσιν· εἰς δέ με πάντας

30 σῆς γλυκερῆς παλάμης πικροὺς ἐκένωσας ὀϊστούς.
ἄλλος 'Ἰὼβ νέος εἰμί· τὸ δ' αἴτιον οὐκέθ' ὁμοῖον.
οὐ γὰρ ἀεθλεύσοντά μ' ἄγεις, μάκαρ, ὥς τιν' ἄριστον
ἀντίον ἀθλητῆρος ἀπήνεος, ἀλκὶ πεποιθὼς,
ὥς κεν ἀριστεύσαντι γέρας καὶ κῦδος ὀπάσσῃς.

35 οὔπω τόσσος ἔγωγ', οὐδ' ἄλγεσι κῦδος ἔπεστι.
ποινὴν δ' ἀμπλακίης τίνω τάδε. τίς δέ θ' ἁμαρτὰς
δίζημ' ἐν πλεόνεσσιν, ὅ σοι πλέον ἄχθεται ἄλλων.
ἐξερέω πάντεσσιν, ὅ μοι νόος ἐντὸς ἔεργε·
ἢ τάχα κεν δρύψειεν ἁμαρτάδα μῦθος ἄναυδος.

40     Ὠϊόμην, ὅτε δή σε φίλον λάχος οἷον ἐδέγμην,
πάντ' ἄμυδις βιότοιο ἀφυσγετὸν εἰς ἅλα ῥίψας,
καὶ νόον ὑψιβιβάντα τεῇ θεότητι πελάζων,
σαρκὸς νόσφιν ἔθηκα, νόμος δὲ μοι ἡγεμόνευε·

20   surrounded on all sides by cruel dogs: I am a pitiable
      subject for song,
  in east and west alike. Perhaps this, too, might happen:
  a man relaxing amid festivities or a traveller
  or someone strumming with his fingers the fair-sounding
      lyre,
  when the music plays no more, will discuss my misfortunes,
25   remembering Gregory, whose hometown lay in Cappadocia,
  in the small town of Diocaesarea.[3] To some you have
      granted
  wearisome wealth without measure; to others, children
  who turned out well: one is handsome, another brave,
      another
  a good speaker. But my fame lies in my sufferings. Against
      me
30   you unleashed all the sharp arrows from your sweet hand.
  I am a second Job but for a different reason:
  you are not sending me to take part in a contest, blessed
      one,
  like some outstanding opponent of a tough athlete,
      confident of my strength,
  that you might grant the prize and glory to the winner.
35   I am not yet so great nor have my sufferings won glory.
  No, this is how I am paying the penalty for my sins. Which
      sin among so many,
  I ask, is it that grieves you more than the rest?
  I shall tell everyone what my mind conceals within,
  for if left unsaid it might tear off the scab covering my sin.
40   I thought – when I embraced you alone as my beloved
      destiny,
  casting everything, all the trivialities of life, to the waves
  and raising my mind up high, bringing it close to your
      divine nature,
  when I was distant from my body and reason was my
      guide –

---

[3] Diocaesarea seems to have been the Roman name for the town of Nazianzus.

πάντων μὲν κρατέειν, πάντων δ' ὕπερ αἰθέρα τέμνειν
45 χρυσείαις πτερύγεσσι· τό μοι φθόνον αἰνὸν ἄγειρε,
καί με κακοῖς ἐπέδησεν, ἀφυκτοτάτῃσί τ' ἀνίαις.
σὸν κλέος ὑψόσ' ἄειρε, κλέος δὲ σὸν ἐς χθόν' ἔθηκεν.
αἰὲν ἀγηνορίῃσιν, ἄναξ, κοτέεις μεγάλῃσι.
κεῖνό γε μὴν ἀΐοιτε, καὶ ἐσσομένοισι γράφοιτε,

50 λαοί θ' ἡγεμόνες τε, ἀπεχθέες, εὐμενέες τε,
πατρὸς ἐμοῦ μεγάλοιο φίλον θρόνον οὐκ ἀθέριξα·
οὐκ ἔστ', οὐδ' ἐπέοικε, θεοῦ θεσμοῖσι παλαίειν.
κείνῳ θεσμὸς ἔδωκεν· ἐγὼ δέ τε χειρὶ γεραιῇ
χεῖρα νέην ὑπέρεισα, πατρὸς δ' ὑπόειξα λιτῇσι,

55 πατρὸς ἐμοῦ, τὸν ἔτισε, καὶ ὅς μάλα τηλόθι μάνδρης
ἀζόμενος πολιήν τε καὶ ἥλικα πνεύματος αἴγλην.
αὐτὰρ ἐπεὶ ζωῆς σημάντορι καὶ τόδ' ἔαδεν
ἡμετέρης, ἄλλοις με Λόγον καὶ Πνεῦμ' ἀναφῆναι,
ξείνοις, τρηχαλέοισιν, ἀκανθοφόροισιν ἀρούραις,
60 βαιὴ μὲν ψεκάς εἰμι, πολὺν δέ τε λαὸν ἐπῆρσα.
καὶ τόδε γ' αὖθις ἔαδε παλίμπορον ἐνθάδε πέμψαι
νούσῳ τε στυγερῇ, καὶ ἀργαλέαις μελεδώναις
τηχθέντ' ἐξαπίνης. ἰὸς δέ τε ἀνδρὶ μέριμνα.
βαιὸν δὲ χρόνον ἔσκον ἐμοῖς μελέεσσιν ἀρηγών,

65 ποιμενικὴν σύριγγα, βοηθόον ἐσθλὸν ὀπάσσας,
μή τις ἐμοῖς μήλοισιν ἀσημάντοισιν ἐπελθὼν
ἐχθρὸς, ἐὴν πλήσειεν ἀναιδέα γαστέρα φορβῆς,.
Αὐτὰρ ἐπεὶ δονέοντο ἀγοί, δονέοντο δὲ λαοὶ
ἡγεμόνος τε ποθῇ, καὶ θήρεσιν οὐλομένοισιν,

I thought that I could overcome all things and cleave the air
45 high above all on golden wings. This aroused terrible envy of me,
entangling me in misfortunes and sufferings with no means of escape.
Your glory raised me on high, your glory made me fall to earth.
You are always angered, Lord, by great pride.
Listen to this, then, and record it for posterity,
50 you people and leaders, you who are hostile and you who wish me well:
I did not reject the beloved episcopal throne of my great father.
It is not possible, not right to struggle against the laws of God.
The law had given him the throne and on his aged hand
I layed my young hand; I yielded to my father's entreaties,
55 my father, who was revered also by one far from the fold,
who respected his grey hair and the radiance of spirit which goes with it.
But since the guide of my life decided
that I should reveal to others the Word and the Spirit,
to foreign, rugged and thorn-bearing lands,
60 I have brought relief to many despite being but a tiny drop.
And this is what he decided next, to send me back to this place,
although I was wasting away with a terrible disease
and agonising worries: for anxiety acts like poison on a man.
For a short while I was able to assist my members,
65 giving them an excellent helper, a shepherd's pipe,
to prevent any enemy attacking my shepherdless sheep
in the hope of filling his shameless belly with food.
But when the leaders are disturbed, so are the people,
by the leader's ambition and by the cruel beasts

70 οἳ θεὸν ἀνδρομέοισιν ἐνὶ σπλάγχνοισι παγέντα,
ἔκνοον ἦτορ ἔχουσι νόου δίχα μορφώσαντες,
πολλοὶ μὲν τρύζεσκον ἐμοῖς παθέεσσιν ἄπιστοι,
καὶ μ' ὑπεροπλίῃσι θεουδέα λαὸν ἀτίζειν,
ἢ φάσαν, ἢ νόος εἶχε. θεῷ γ' ἐμὸν ἄλγος ἔφαινον.

75 πολλοὶ δ' αὖ νυχίοισιν ἐμὲ κρίνεσκον ὀνείροις,
ζωγράφος ὧν πόθος ἦεν, ἀθύρματα πολλὰ χαράσσων·
ἢ θεὸς ἐξεκάλυπτεν, ἐμοὶ τέλος ἐσθλὸν ὀπάζων,
ὄφρα κε μὴ χαλεπῇσι σὺν ἐλπωρῇσι δαμείην,
ἐξοδίην κακότητα ἐφεσσάμενος βιότοιο.
80 τοὔνεκεν αὐχέν' ἔκαμψα, τεὴν δ' ὑπὸ χεῖρα κραταιὴν
δέσμιος ἔρχομ' ἔγωγε· δίκη δ' ἄλλοισι μεμήλοι.
οὐδὲν ὄνειαρ ἔμοιγε δικαζομένης βιότητος.
τῇ νῦν, Χριστὲ, φέροις με, ὅποι φίλον. ἄλγεσι κάμφθην.
κητείαις λαγόεσσι τετρυμένος εἰμὶ προφήτης.

85 σοὶ παρέχω ζωῆς τόδε λείψανον. ἀλλ' ἐλέαιρε
μικρὸν ἔτι πνείοντα. τί μ' ἄλγεσι τόσσον ἐλαύνεις;
οὔτ' ἀγαθοῖσι μόνοισι θάνες, θεός, εὖτ' ἐπὶ γαῖαν
ἤλυθες (ἢ μέγα θαῦμα, θεὸς βροτὸς αἵματι ῥαίνων
ψυχὰς ἡμετέρας καὶ σώματα), οὔτε κάκιστος

90 μοῦνος ἐγώ. πολλοῖσι χερείοσι κῦδος ὄπασσας.
τρεῖς βίβλοισι τεῇσι μεγακλέες εἰσὶ τελῶναι,
Ματθαῖός τε μέγας, νηῷ τ' ἔνι δάκρυα λείψας,
Ζακχαῖός τ' ἐπὶ τοῖσιν· ὁ τέτρατος αὐτὸς ἔοιμι.

70 who senselessly imagine that God, who took shape in a human womb,
has human form without a human soul.
Many muttered, not believing in my sufferings,
and either said or thought that in my pride I did not respect
the people made in God's image. To God I revealed my pain.
75 Many judged me on the basis of dreams they had at night,
designed by their own desire, the source of many illusions;
or God disclosed this, granting me a happy end
so that I would not be overcome by troublesome hopes
when he had organized the final act of misery in my life.
80 For this reason I bent my neck and beneath your strong hand
I walk captive. Let others be concerned about justice.
The fact that my life was put on trial brought me no benefit.
Now, Christ, take me where you want. I am worn out by suffering.
I am a prophet lying shattered in the whale's belly.[4]
85 To you I hand over what is left of my life; have pity on me
for a little, while I still live. Why do you persecute me with such sufferings?
Not only for good men did you die, my God, when you walked
the earth (a great miracle that the God-Man should sprinkle our souls
and bodies with his blood), nor am I the single
90 most wicked person. To many worse have you accorded glory.
There are three famous tax-collectors in your scriptures:
great Matthew,[5] and the one who shed tears in the temple,[6]
and in addition Zacchaeus:[7] may I be the fourth.

---

[4] Gregory compares himself several times to the prophet Jonah.
[5] Matthew 9: 9, Mark 2: 14, Luke 5: 27.
[6] Luke 18: 13.
[7] Luke 19: 2.

## ΣΧΕΤΛΙΑΣΤΙΚΟΝ ΥΠΕΡ ΤΩΝ ΑΥΤΟΥ ΠΑΘΩΝ

τρεῖς δ' ἄρα λυσιμελεῖς, ὅ τε λέκτριος, ὅς τ' ἐπὶ πηγῇ,
95 ἥν τε πνεῦμ' ἐπέδησεν· ὁ τέτρατος αὐτὸς ἔοιμι.
τρεῖς δέ σοι ἐκ νεκύων φάος ἔδρακον, ὡς γὰρ ἄνωγας·
ἄρχοντος θυγάτηρ, χήρης πάϊς, ἐκ δὲ τάφοιο
Λάζαρος ἡμιδάϊκτος· ὁ τέτρατος αὐτὸς ἔοιμι.
καὶ νῦν φάρμακ' ἔχοιμ' ὀδυνήφατα, καὶ μετέπειτα

100 ζωὴν ἄτροπον, ἐσθλὲ, τεῷ μέγα κύδεϊ γαίων.
ποίμνης ἡγεμόνευσα θεόφρονος. εἰ δὲ λυθείην,
ποιμένος οἵδε τύχοιεν ἀρείονος· εἰ δὲ ἄρ' ὁμοίου,
ἥσσονος ἐν παθέεσσι, μακάρτατε· οὐ γὰρ ἔοικε
τὸν νούσων ἐλατῆρα κακοῖς ἀχέεσσι παλαίειν.

There are three with palsy: one on the bed,[8] one by the
    pool,[9]
95 and then the woman bound by a spirit:[10] may I be the
    fourth.
Three saw the light after being corpses, as you commanded:
the daughter of the ruler,[11] the widow's son[12] and
    Lazarus,[13]
half-rotting from the tomb; may I be the fourth.
Now let me have remedies to still the pain and afterwards
100 eternal life, rejoicing greatly in your glory, excellent one.
I have led the pious flock: if I am released from this,
may they find a better shepherd, or if a similar one,
may he suffer less, most blessed one; for it is not right
that he who drives away disease should wrestle with
    terrible pains.

---

[8] Matthew 9:2–7; Mark 2:1–12; Luke 5: 17–25.
[9] John 5: 2.
[10] Luke 13: 11–13.
[11] Mark 5: 22–4, 35-42; Luke 8: 41–2, 49–55.
[12] Luke 7: 11–17.
[13] John 11: 1–44.

# ΕΙΣ ΤΗΝ ΕΝ ΤΑΙΣ ΝΗΣΤΕΙΑΙΣ ΣΙΩΠΗΝ

Ἴσχεο, γλῶσσα φίλη· σὺ δέ μοι, γραφὶς, ἔγγραφε σιγῆς
ῥήματα, καὶ φθέγγου ὄμμασι τὰ κραδίης.
ἡνίκα σάρκας ἔδησα, θεοῦ βροτέοις παθέεσσι
μύστιν ἄγων θυσίην, ὥς κε θάνω βιότῳ,
5  ἤμασι τεσσαράκοντα, νόμοις Χριστοῦ βασιλῆος,
εὖτε καθαιρομένοις σώμασιν ἕσπετ' ἄκος.
πρῶτα μὲν ἀτρεμίῃ νόον ἥδρασα, οἷος ἀπ' ἄλλων
ναιετάων, ἀχέων ἀχλὺν ἐφεσσάμενος,
εἴσω πας ἐαλεὶς, φρένας ἄκλοπος· αὐτὰρ ἔπειτα
10    ἀνδρῶν εὐαγέων δόγμασιν ἑσπόμενος,
χείλεσι θῆκα θύρετρα. τὸ δ' αἴτιον, ὥς κε μάθοιμι
μύθων μέτρα φέρειν, παντὸς ἐπικρατέων.
καὶ γάρ τις πλεόνεσσιν ἐπ' ἀνδράσι θοῦρον ἀείρων
ἔγχος, παυροτέρους ῥηϊδίως δαμάσει,

15 καὶ πτερόεντα βέλεμνα ὃς εὔσκοπα τηλόθε βάλλοι,
οὔποτε ῥοιζήσει ἄσκοπον ἀσσοτέρω.
νῆα δὲ ποντοπόρειαν, ἐπὴν μέγα λαῖτμα περήσῃ,
πέμπειν θαρσαλέον βαιῶν ὑπὲρ λιμένων.
ὃς μὲν γὰρ μικρῶν κρατέει, μεγάλων ἀΐδηλον

20    εἴ ποθ' ὑπερσχήσει, καὶ μάλα περ ποθέων·
ὃς δὲ μέγα προφέρει, τόδ' ἀριφραδὲς, ὡς ἄρα τυτθῶν
ἕξει ῥηϊδίως, εὖτε θέλῃσι, κράτος.
τοὔνεκα πάμπαν ἔδησα λόγου μένος. ἦ γὰρ ἔολπα

# On silence at the time of fasting[1]

Hold still, dear tongue. You, my pen, write down the words
   of silence and tell to the eyes the matters of my heart.
When I restrained the flesh, I was initiated into
   the human sufferings of God, so that I might die to this life,
5 for forty days, according to the laws of Christ the lord,
   since for bodies made pure the remedy follows.
First I sought stillness for my mind, living apart from others
   and alone, clad in a cloud of sorrows,
completely drawn into myself, my mind unshaken. But then
10    I followed the advice of holy men
and placed a door on my lips. The reason was that I should learn
   to set a limit on my words and be in control of everything.
For he who attacks many men with an aggressive
   spear, will easily subdue a smaller number,
15 and he who lets fly from afar a winged arrow with unerring aim,
   will never miss his mark when he stands closer;
once a ship which traverses the sea has crossed the mighty deep,
   one may confidently send it across small harbours.
But it is uncertain whether he who succeeds in small things
20    will prevail in important matters, even if he greatly desires it.
But he who excels in great events, it is clear, will easily
   gain control over little things, when he so wishes.

[1] *Poem* II.1.34. This poem is written in elegiac couplets.

ΕΙΣ ΤΗΝ ΕΝ ΤΑΙΣ ΝΗΣΤΕΙΑΙΣ ΣΙΩΠΗΝ

μηκέθ' ὑποβλύζειν μῦθον ἐμῶν στομάτων.

25 ὡς οὐδὲν γλώσσης ὀλοώτερόν ἐστι βροτοῖσιν·
ἵππος ἀεὶ προθέων, ὅπλον ἑτοιμότατον.
λεύσσει μὲν τίς ἅπαντα; τὰ δ' ἐν ποσὶ χεῖρες ἔχουσι
βαιὰ μάλ', οὐδὲ πόδες γαῖαν ἐπῆλθον ὅλην.
μόχθος ἀνδροφόνοις, μοιχοὶ δέ τε καὶ τρομέουσι

30 λύσσαν ἑὴν, κλέπταις ἦμαρ ἀπευκτότατον,
πλοῦτος δ' οὐ κἀμόγητος· ἔχω τὸ μὲν, ὤλεσα δ' ἄλλο,
τόσσα περισφίγγων, ὅσσα ῥόον παλάμη.
νήεσ', ὁδοιπορίη ληϊστορες· ἄλλος ἄπληστος,
ὄμματα πικρὰ φέρων ἀλλοτρίοις κτεάνοις.

35 τόσσα φιλοχρύσοισι προσαντέα πᾶσιν ἔπεστι,
μόχθος χειροτέροις, μόχθος ἀρειοτέροις.
γλῶσσαν δ' οὐδὲν ἔρυξεν ἐπειγομένην ἐπὶ μῦθον,
οὐ βροτὸς, οὐ νιφετὸς, οὐ ῥόος, οὐ σκόπελος.
ἐγγὺς ὁ τοξευτής· τόξῳ δ' ἔπι πικρὸς ὀϊστός
40 νευρὴ κύκλον ἄγει, δάκτυλον ἐν γλυφίσι.
νοῦς ἀφέηκε βέλεμνα· τὰ δ' ἔπτατο, πάντα δὲ βάλλει,
οὐρανίους, χθονίους, ζῶντας, ἐπεσσομένους,
ὅσσοι μιν δοκέουσι, καὶ οὐ δοκέοντας, ὁμοίως
ἐσθλοὺς ἠδὲ κακοὺς, δυσμενέας, φιλίους,

That is why I completely restricted the power of my tongue,
   hoping thus that the words would no longer flow from my lips.
25 For there is nothing more deadly to mankind than the tongue.
   It is like a horse, always rushing headlong, a most ready weapon.
Who can see everything? The hands can hold things near to them,
   but only a few, and the feet do not traverse the whole earth.
The tongue is a danger to murderers, and adulterers tremble
30   at their own madness, while daylight is terrifying to thieves.
Wealth is not trouble-free: some I hold on to, some I have lost,
   keeping a tight grip only on as much as flows through the hand.
Brigands threaten ships and travellers on foot. One man is greedy,
   casting his keen eyes on other people's property.
35 Such problems afflict all who love gold,
   bringing troubles to worse and better alike.
Nothing can restrain a tongue which is eager to speak,
   neither man nor snowstorm, neither flood nor cliffs.
The archer is close; on the bow the sharp arrow,
40   the bowstring forms an arc, one finger on the arrow's notched end;
   the mind shoots the darts: they fly forth and all hit their targets:
     heavenly beings, earthly ones, those living and those to come;
   both those who watch out for them and those who do not,
   good and bad alike, the hostile and the friendly,

## ΕΙΣ ΤΗΝ ΕΝ ΤΑΙΣ ΝΗΣΤΕΙΑΙΣ ΣΙΩΠΗΝ

45 τηλόθεν, ἐγγὺς ἐόντας· ἀπόσκοπον οὐδὲν ὀϊστῷ.
τὴν δέ τις αἰχμάζων, πρῶτα φέρει σοφίης.
πολλὰ μὲν αἰσχρὰ μάχλοισιν ἐρεύγεται, ὥς κε γελοῖος
αὐτὸς ἐών, ἄλλοις βράσμα γέλωτος ἄγῃ,
παλλόμενος, πάλλων τε, καὶ εἰκόνα θείαν ἀτίζων.

50     πολλὰ δὲ τῶν κρυπτῶν οὔασιν ἐξεμέει.
πολλάκι δ' αὖτε χόλοιο δυσαέος ἄγριον ἀφρὸν
ἐκτὸς ἀποσκεδάει, πᾶσαν ἐπεσβολίην.
πολλάκι δ' αὖ λοχόωντι φέρει χάριν ἔνδοθι θυμῷ,
καὶ κραδίης ἑτέρης χείλεσιν ἄλλα φέρει,
55 ψεύδεά θ', αἱμυλίους τε λόγους, ἀνδροκτασίας τε.
τίς κεν ἅπαντα λέγοι, τόνδ' ὅσα λυπρὰ πέλει;
ἐχθρὸν ἔθηκ' ἐθέλουσα δόμον δόμῳ, ἄστεϊ δ' ἄστυ
αὐτίκα, μηδὲν ὅλως γλῶσσα πονησαμένη,
δῆμον κοιρανέοντι, ἀνασσομένοισιν ἄνακτα,

60     ὡς σπινθὴρ καλάμης ὦκα ῥιπιζομένης.
σύμπλοον, υἷα, τοκῆα, κάσιν, φίλον, εὖνιν, ἀκοίτην,
πάντας ἐπ' ἀλλήλοις ὥπλισε ῥηϊδίως.
τὸν κακὸν, ἐσθλὸν ἔθηκε, τὸν ἔμπαλιν ὤλεσεν ἐσθλὸν,
τοῦτ' ἀνέζευξε πάλιν· τίς δύναθ' ὅσσα λόγος;

65 βαιὴ μὲν γλῶσσ' ἐστὶν, ἀτὰρ σθένος οὐδενὶ τόσσον·
αἴθ' ὄφελε θνήσκειν αὐτίκα τοῖσι κακοῖς!
πᾶσιν μὲν δὴ γλῶσσα πέλει κακὸν ἀφραδέεσσιν,
ἔξοχα δ' αὖ μύσταις οὐρανίης θυσίης.
ὄργανόν εἰμι θεοῖο, καὶ εὐκρέκτοις μελέεσσιν

70     ὕμνον ἄνακτι φέρω, τῷ πᾶν ὑποτρομέει.

45 far off and close: there is nothing the tongue's arrow cannot hit.
Anyone who subdues it wins the first prize for wisdom.
It shouts out many shameful things to the lustful, so that although
it is itself ridiculous, it keeps shaking with laughter at others,
shaking and making others shake, desecrating the divine image.
50 Many secrets it vomits forth to others' ears.
Often it sprays far and wide stormy anger's
fierce foam, every kind of abuse.
Often it offers kindness while inside anger is laying a trap,
and the lips say something different from the heart,
55 lies and wheedling words and those causing murder.
Who could recount all the offensive things the tongue produces?
If it wants, it can set one house or town against another,
in a moment, with little effort on its part,
or set the people against their leader, the king against his subjects,
60 like a spark setting fire to the stubble in a moment.
Comrade, son, parent, brother, friend, wife, husband,
all of them it easily arms against each other.
It regards the wicked as good and then destroys the good,
dismantling it again. Who could achieve as much as speech?
65 The tongue is a little thing but has more power than anything else.
Would that it could be destroyed straightaway for these wickednesses!
To be sure, the tongue is a danger to all fools,
especially to the priests of the heavenly sacrifice.
I am an instrument of God and with fair-sounding melodies
70 I present a hymn of praise to the King before whom all tremble.

ΕΙΣ ΤΗΝ ΕΝ ΤΑΙΣ ΝΗΣΤΕΙΑΙΣ ΣΙΩΠΗΝ

μέλπω δ' οὐ Τροίην, οὐκ εὔπλοον οἷά τις Ἀργώ,
οὐδὲ συὸς κεφαλὴν, οὐ πολὺν Ἡρακλέα,
οὐ γῆς εὐρέα κύκλα ὅπως πελάγεσσιν ἄρηρεν,
οὐκ αὐγὰς λιθάκων, οὐ δρόμον οὐρανίων·

75 οὐδὲ πόθων μέλπω μανίην, καὶ κάλλος ἐφήβων,
οἷσι λύρη μαλακὸν κρούετ' ἀπὸ προτέρων.
μέλπω δ' ὑψιμέδοντα θεὸν μέγαν, ἠδὲ φαεινῆς
εἰς ἓν ἀγειρομένης λάμψιν ἐμῆς Τριάδος,
ἀγγελικῶν τε χορῶν μεγάλους ἐριηχέας ὕμνους

80 πλησίον ἑσταότων, ἐξ ὀπὸς ἀντιθέτου
κόσμου θ' ἁρμονίην, καὶ κρείσσονα τῆς παρεούσης,
ἣν δοκέω, πάντων εἰς ἓν ἐπειγομένων
καὶ Χριστοῦ παθέων κλέος ἄφθιτον, οἷς μ' ἐθέωσεν,
ἀνδρομέην μορφὴν οὐρανίῃ κεράσας.

85 μέλπω μίξιν ἐμήν. οὐ γὰρ φατὸν ἔργον ἐτύχθην
ἔργον, ὅπως πλέχθην θνητὸς ἐπουρανίοις.
μέλπω δ' ἀνθρώποισι θεοῦ νόμον, ὅσσα τε κόσμου
ἔργματα, καὶ βουλὰς, καὶ τέλος ἀμφοτέρων·
ὄφρα τὰ μὲν κεύθῃς σῇσι φρεσὶ, τῶν δ' ἀπὸ τῆλε

90 φεύγῃς, καὶ τρομέῃς ἦμαρ ἐπερχόμενον.
τόσσων γλῶσσαν ἔχω, κιθάρην· φράζεσθ', ἱερῆες,
μή τι παρακρέξῃ ἔκτροπον ἁρμονίης.
γλῶσσαν καὶ θυέεσσιν ἁγνὴν ἁγνοῖσι φυλάξω,
οἷσιν Ἄνακτα μέγαν εἰς ἓν ἄγω χθονίοις.

I do not sing of Troy, nor, as some do, of the fair-sailing Argo,
   nor of the boar's head nor of mighty Heracles,
nor of how the wide globe of the earth was joined to the seas,
   nor of the brilliance of jewels nor the course of the heavenly bodies.
75 I do not sing of the madness of desire and the beauty of young men
   for whom the poets of old gently plucked their lyres.
I sing of the great God who rules on high and the splendour
   of my shining Trinity united into one;
of the great hymns of praise sounding forth from the angelic choirs
80   who stand close by; from their antiphonal voices derive
the cosmic harmony and that harmony greater than the present one
   for which I hope, when all are eagerly brought together.
I sing of the eternal glory of Christ's sufferings, by which he made me
   divine, combining human form with the heavenly.
85 I sing of this mixture of mine, for I was created in a mysterious manner,
   in such a way that I, a mortal being, was combined with the immortal.
I sing of God's law for men and all the works
   of the universe and the plans and outcome of both,
so that you may conceal some things in your heart and flee far
90   from others and tremble at the day which is to come.
To sing of these I have my tongue as my lyre. Beware, you priests,
   lest any discord should sound a false note.
My tongue I shall keep pure by means of pure sacrifices,
   so as to reconcile the great King to mortal creatures.

## ΕΙΣ ΤΗΝ ΕΝ ΤΑΙΣ ΝΗΣΤΕΙΑΙΣ ΣΙΩΠΗΝ

95 οὐ γὰρ ἀπ' ἀλλοτρίης γλώσσης, χραντοῦ τε νόοιο
πέμψω τῷ καθαρῷ ζωοφόρον θυσίην.
εἷς πόρος οὐ γλυκερόν τε ῥόον καὶ πικρὸν ἀνήσει,
εἵματι πορφυρέῳ βόρβορος ἀλλότριον.
καὶ πῦρ ξεῖνον ὄλεσσε θυηπόλου ἐν προτέροισι
100 παῖδας, μὴ καθαρῶς ἁπτομένους θυσίης.
τὴν δ' ἱερήν ποτ', ἄκουσα, θεοῦ μεγάλοιο κιβωτὸν,
ὡς καὶ κλινομένη κτεῖνε τὸν ἁψάμενον.
ταῦτ' αἰνῶς τρομέω, καὶ δείδια, μή τι πάθοιμι,
μὴ καθαρῶς καθαρῆς ἁπτόμενος Τριάδος.

105 αἴθε δὲ καὶ νόον ἦεν ἀτάσθαλον, ἀστατέοντα
τῇ καὶ τῇ, πολλοῖς οἴμασι μαψιδίοις
κάμπτειν τέρματος ἆσσον, ἐπὶ στρεπτῆρι χαλινῷ,
ἢ πάμπαν κατέχειν ἄκλοπον ἐν κραδίῃ
μᾶλλόν κε Χριστοῖο μεγακλέος ἆσσον ἐλαύνων,

110 λάμπετο μαρμαρυγαῖς τοῦ μεγάλοιο φάους!
νῦν δ' ὁ μὲν οὔτι τόσον τελέει κακὸν ἔνδοθι μίμνων,
κἂν ἀπὸ τῆλε θεοῦ τυτθὸν ὁδοιπλανέῃ.
οὐδὲ γὰρ εἰ πέτρῃσιν ἐεργομένη στεγανῇσιν,
ἔνδοθι καχλάζοι φλὸξ πυρός, ἠὲ ῥόος,

115 ἢ λόχμην πυκινὴν δηλήσατο, ἢ τιν' ἀλωήν·
ζώει δ' ἡμιθανὴς ἔνδοθι κευθομένη.
μῦθος δ' αὖ γλώσσης πολυηχέος εὖτ' ἀπορούσῃ,
ἄσχετα μαργαίνει μηκέτ' ἀνατροχάων.
ὡς δ' ὅτε τις λοξοῖο φυὴν πτόρθου παλάμῃσιν
120 ἦκα μετακλίνων ἔμπαλι γῦρον ἄγει,

95 For it is not from another's tongue and a mind defiled
   that I send this life-giving offering to the one who is pure.
   One stream will not send forth both sweet and briny water
   and mud is a stranger to the purple robe.
   Long ago a strange fire destroyed the priest's sons[2]
100   for not being pure when they undertook the sacrifice.
   Once, I hear, the holy ark of mighty God
   leaned over and killed the man who touched it.[3]
   I tremble dreadfully at these things and fear that I will suffer
   for not being pure when touching upon the pure Trinity.
105 I would that the wicked mind, wandering restlessly
   here and there, with much fruitless effort,
   could turn closer to the half-way post, with the reins pulled back,
   or could keep its thoughts completely safe within,
   driving ever closer to the glorious Christ
110   and shine out with flashes of that great light.
   But now, if it remains within, it cannot achieve so much evil
   even if it wanders a little way from God.
   For if it is hemmed in by enclosing rocks,
   then neither the fire's flame nor the stream can rush forth from inside,
115 damaging the dense undergrowth or some orchard:
   it lives on, barely existent, hidden within.
   But the tongue's loud speech rushes forth straightway,
   raging furiously and without restraint, never to return.[4]
   Just as when someone little by little bends with his hands
120   a curving branch, forcing it into a circle the opposite way:

---

[2] Two of the sons of Aaron were punished in this way: Leviticus 10: 1–2.
[3] Uzzah was killed in this way: 2 Samuel 6: 6–7.
[4] Cf. Horace, Epistle I.18.71, 'et semel emissum volat irrevocabile verbum'. On the many similarities noted between Gregory's poetry and that of Horace, see B. Wyss, 'Gregor von Nazianz', *Museum Helveticum* 6 (1949), Excurs II, 205–10.

ΕΙΣ ΤΗΝ ΕΝ ΤΑΙΣ ΝΗΣΤΕΙΑΙΣ ΣΙΩΠΗΝ

αὐτὰρ ὅγ' ὥς μιν ἔλειπε, βίῃ χερὸς ὄρθιος ἔστη,
    μηκέτ' ἐπὶ προτέρην κλινόμενος κακίην·
ὣς καὶ ἐγὼ μύθοιο μὲν εὐτροχάλοιο ἐρωὴν
    δερκόμενος στάθμης ἔκτοθι καὶ κανόνος

125 (καὶ γάρ μοι βίος ἦεν, ὅτ' ἦν λόγος), εὗρον ἄριστον
    φάρμακον· ἔσχον ὅλον ὑψινόῳ κραδίῃ,
ὥς κε μάθῃ τά τε φαντά, τά τ' οὐ φατὰ γλῶσσα φυλάσσειν·
    δέξαθ' ὅλην σιγὴν, δέξεται εὐεπίην.
τοῦ παντός μιν ἄμερσα· τὸ μέτριον οὐκέτ' ἀτίσει.

130     οὗτος ἀεὶ κείσθω τοῖς ἀμέτροισι νόμος.
ἦ μέγα καὶ τόδ' ὄνειαρ, ὅτ' ὠδίνοντα κατίσχῃς
    μῦθον, κρουομένης ἔκτοθι σῆς κραδίης.
μύθῳ δαμναμένῳ συνδάμναται οἶδμα χόλοιο·
    οὐ μὲν ῥηϊδίως, ἔμπα γε μὴν δαμάσεις.

135 ἢν γάρ σφ' οἰδαλέον τε καὶ ἄγρια μαργαίνοντα
    ἄγχῃς ἀσχαλόων, ὕβριν ἀποσκεδάσεις.
ἡγεμόνος φθιμένοιο, φάλαγξ παθέων ὑπόειξεν·
    ὧδ' ἂν ἀναπνεύσαις ἀργαλέοιο σάλου.
πάντα τάδ' ἡγεσίης Χριστοῦ μεγάλοιο ἄνακτος,

140     αὐτὰρ ἔπειτα νόου οἴακος ἡμετέρου.
εἰ γὰρ μὴ τὸν ἔχεις ἰθύντορα, οὔτε τι σιγῆς,
    οὔτε τε καρτερίης μείζονος ἔστ' ὄφελος·
καὶ λίμνης στόμα λεπτὸν, ἐπὴν παλάμῃσιν ἔρυξας,
    αὖθις ἀπορρήξεις, ἀθρόον ἐκπρορέσει.

when he lets go, the force of his hand makes it stand straight,
and it never bends back into the wrong shape it had before.
So I too, when I saw the force of hasty speech
exceeding measure and rule, (for there was a time
125 when speech was my life), found the perfect
remedy: I kept everything in my heart, its thoughts directed on high,
so my tongue might learn what it might say and what it should not:
it has learned complete silence and will learn to speak appropriately.
I deprived it of everything. Never again will it spurn moderation.
130 Let this law always hold for those who speak immoderately.
This is indeed most beneficial when you have within you words
which labour to come forth, while your heart is stirred from without.
When the words are restrained, so is the outburst of anger –
not easily, to be sure, but at any rate you will manage to restrain it.
135 For if you subdue the swelling and furious rage
when you are upset, you will dispel the violence:
once the leader is dead, the army of passions will give way.
In this way you can recover after a dangerous storm.
All this is achieved under the leadership of Christ, the great Lord,
140 but afterwards by means of the rudder of our mind.
For if you do not have this as your guide, neither silence
nor even greater endurance is of any benefit.
When with your hands you block up the narrow mouth of the pool
you will burst open again and flow forth in a great flood.

## ΕΙΣ ΤΗΝ ΕΝ ΤΑΙΣ ΝΗΣΤΕΙΑΙΣ ΣΙΩΠΗΝ

145 ἀλλὰ Λόγος κέλεταί σε φαάντατος, ἔνθεν, ἄριστε,
ἀρξάμενον, πάντων οἶδμα κακῶν κατέχειν.
ταῦτά τοι ἡμετέρης μελεδήματα, φίλτατε, σιγῆς·
ἐκ παλάμης λαλέω, νοῦν ὑποδεξαμένης.
οὗτος ἐμὸς πλόος ἐστί· σὺ δ' ἐς πλόον ἄλλον ἔπειγε.
150 ἄλλος ἀπ' ἀλλοίου πνεύματος ὅρμον ἔχοι.
εἰ δ' ἄγε, καὶ λόγον ἄλλον ἐμης ἀΐοιτε σιωπῆς,
ὅστις ἀπεχθαίρων, ὅς τε φίλα φρονέων.
ἦν ὅτε κάρτος ἔχεσκον ἐν ἠϊθέοισι μέγιστον,
καί με Χριστὸς ἄναξ ἦγεν ἐπ' ἀντιπάλῳ,

155 στερρροτέρην ἀδάμαντος ἐνὶ φρεσὶ πίστιν ἔχοντα,
τεύχεσί τε κρατεροῖς πάντοθε φραξάμενον.
θείοις μὲν λογίοισιν ἐμὸν νόον ἁγνὸν ἔτευξα,
γράμματος ἐξ ἱεροῦ Πνεῦμ' ἀναμαξάμενος,
οἷς βίβλων τοπάροιθε πικρὴν ἐξέπτυον ἅλμην,

160 κάλλος ἐπιπλάστοις χρώμασι λαμπόμενον.
σάρκα δ' ἐμὴν ζείουσαν, ἐπεὶ νεότητι τεθήλοι,
πολλοῖς καὶ πυκνοῖς ἔξεον ἐν καμάτοις.
γαστρὶ μὲν ὕβριν ἔπαυσα κόρου, καὶ γείτονα λύσσαν,
ὄμμα δ' ἐνὶ βλεφάροις πῆξα σαοφροσύνῃ.
165 βρύξα χόλῳ, καὶ δῆσα μέλη, καὶ κλαῦσα γέλωτα.
πάνθ' ὑπόειξε Λόγῳ· πάντ' ἔθανεν τὰ πάρος.
γαίη, κοῖτος ἐμοί· πλευρῶν ἄκος, εἵματα λυπρά·
φάρμακον ἀγρυπνίης, χῶρος ἐμῶν δακρύων.
ἤμασι νῶτον ἔκαμψα, καὶ ὕμνοις παννυχίοισι

170 στηλώθην, βροτέης ἔκνοος εὐπαθίης.

145 But that most shining Word orders you, best of men,
    to restrain the swollen tide of all evils issuing from here.
Such are the thoughts formed in my silence, dear friend.
    I chatter with my pen which is the spokeman of my thoughts.
This is my voyage; you can undertake a different voyage.
150     Let each person reach harbour driven by a different breeze.
Come on then, listen to another reason for my silence,
    both you who hate me and you who are kindly disposed:
there was a time when I had the greatest strength among the youth
    and Christ the Lord led me against my opponent;
155 I had in my heart a faith stronger than adamant,
    defended on all sides by powerful weapons.
With divine sayings I armed my pure mind,
    gaining some impression of the Spirit from holy scripture,
after I had spat out the unpleasant saltiness of those books[5]
160     whose beauty shone with meretricious colours.
My bodily desires, while they flourished in youth,
    I subdued by means of great and constant effort.
I checked the excesses of my appetite and its accompanying
    madness and by means of modesty I kept my gaze steady.
165 I controlled my anger, restrained my limbs, and wept at my laughter.
    Everything was ruled by the Word; all of my earlier life lay dead.
The earth was my bed; the remedy for my body was rough clothing;
    the cure for my insomnia was to make the ground wet with tears.
By day I bent my back, all night I spent standing, singing
170     hymns of praise, without experience of human pleasures.

---

[5] i.e. the works of pagan literature.

## ΕΙΣ ΤΗΝ ΕΝ ΤΑΙΣ ΝΗΣΤΕΙΑΙΣ ΣΙΩΠΗΝ

ταῦτα πάρος· σάρκες γὰρ ἐπέζεον, αἷσι μέμηλεν
οὐρανίης ἀνόδου φῶτα μέγαν κατέχειν.
καὶ κτεάνων βαρὺν ὄγκον ἀπέπτυσα, ὥς κεν ἀερθῶ
κοῦφος, ἀποσκεδάσας πρὸς θεὸν ἄχθος ἅπαν.

175 νῦν δ' ὅτε νοῦσος ἔχει με πικρή, καὶ γῆρας ἔκαμψεν,
ἦλθον ἐπ' ἀλλοίην τήνδε δυηπαθίην,
γλῶσσαν ἔχων ἀδάμαστον, εὔλαλον, ἥ με τόσοισι
πήμασι, τοῦ φθονεροῦ δῶκεν ἀεὶ παλάμαις.
οὔτε τινὸς θώκοισιν ἐπέδραμον· οὔτ' ἀπὸ γαίης

180   ἤλασα πατρῴης, οὐ δόλον ἐφρασάμην.
οὐ γλῶσσαν ἐφέηκα ἐπεσβόλον, οὔτε τι ῥέξα
ἡμετέρων θυέων ἔκνομον· οἶδε Λόγος.
οὐ σκοπὸν, οὐδὲ μὲν ἄλλον, ἐπεὶ καὶ πᾶσι νεμεσῶ,
λαῶν ἡγεμόσιν τοῖα κλεϊζομένοις·

185 ὧν νῦν πᾶσα θάλασσα, καὶ εὐρέα πείρατα γαίης
πέπληθε, δνοφερὸν πένθος ἐμῆς κραδίης.
ἀλλὰ λόγος μ' ἐχάλεψεν ἀτάσθαλος· οὐ μὲν ἔγωγε
πρόσθε τόδ' ὠϊόμην, ἀλλ' ἐχάλεψεν ὅμως
πᾶσι μ' ἔθηκε φίλοισιν ἐπίφθονον. ὦ φθόνε, καὶ σὺ

190   ἐξ ἐμέθεν τε λάβῃς. ἴσχεο, γλῶσσα φίλη·
βαιὸν δ' ἴσχεο, γλῶσσα· τόδ' ἐς τέλος οὔ τε πεδήσω.
οὐ τόσον ἐξ ἐμέθεν λήψεθ' ὁ μισολόγος.
πυνθάνομ' ὡς Σαμίων τις ἄναξ φθόνον ὡς ἀρέσαιτο,
δείσας εὐδρομίην, μήσατο τοῖον ἄχος.

This in years past: for the flesh was fervent in its
   determination
  to stop presumptuous man in his heavenly ascent.
 And I rejected the heavy burden of belongings that I might
   rise
  towards God after casting away everything weighing me
   down.
175 But now that a painful illness afflicts me and I am bent
   with old age,
  I have encountered this new misfortune:
 my tongue unrestrained and talkative has repeatedly
   betrayed me
  into the hands of the jealous, causing me great sufferings.
 I have not sought anyone's seat of office, nor have I driven
   anyone
180  from their homeland, nor did I plot any treachery.
 I did not attack anyone with a scurrilous tongue, nor did I
   offer
  anything unlawful in our sacrifices. The Word knows this.
 Neither a leader nor anyone else did I harm, although I am
   angry
  with all the leaders of the people who say such things.
185 The whole sea and the far-reaching boundaries of the earth
   are filled
  with them now, a source of dark grief to my heart.
 But cruel talk has crushed me. I did not
  think this before, but nevertheless it has crushed me
  and made me a prey to all men's jealousy. Envy, you too
190  will receive something from me. (Be still, dear tongue.
 Be still, tongue, for a while; not forever will I keep you
   fettered.
  Envy, the hater of words, will not receive so great a gift
   from me.)
 I hear that a king of Samos,[6] fearing his good fortune,
  contrived this means of suffering so as to placate jealousy:

---

[6] Polycrates of Samos.

## ΕΙΣ ΤΗΝ ΕΝ ΤΑΙΣ ΝΗΣΤΕΙΑΙΣ ΣΙΩΠΗΝ

195 πόρκην, ὃν φιλέεσκε, πατρῷϊον ἔμβαλε πόντῳ·
τὸν δ' ὑποδεξάμενον ἰχθὺν, ἔδησε λίνον·
ἰχθυβόλος μὲν ἄνακτι, ὁ δ' ὤπασεν ᾧ θεράποντι
τὴν ἁλίην· πόρκης δ' ἰχθύος ἐν λαγόσιν.
ἰχθὺν μὲν γαστὴρ ὑπεδέξατο, χεὶρ δέ τε πόρκην·

200 θαῦμα μέγ'· οὐδ' ἐθέλων εὕρατο κεῖνος ἄχος.
ὣς καὶ ἐγώ· μύθῳ γὰρ ἐμῷ φθόνος ἄγριον αἰεὶ
ὄμμα φέρει· σιγῆς βένθος ἐπεσπασάμην.
τόσσον ἐμοὶ Σαμίοιο· τόδ' αὔριον οὐ σάφα οἶδα,
εἰ κακὸν ἠὲ καλὸν ἀντιάσειε τέλος.

205 ἀλλὰ γε δὴ φθόνον ἴσχε, βροτῶν ἄκος, ἐκ δέ με πικρῶν
γλωσσῶν ἐξερύσας, σὴν ἐπὶ λάμψιν ἄγοις·
ἔνθα σε σὺν φαέεσσιν ἀειζώοισι γεραίρων,
μέλψομ' ἀπὸ στομάτων ἦχον ἐναρμόνιον.
δέχνυσο καὶ τάδε χειρὸς ἐναυδέα, ὡς μὲν ἔχοιτε

210 ἡμετέρης σιγῆς μνημόσυνον λαλέον.

195 he threw his father's ring, which was dear to him, into the sea;
he then caught in his net the fish which had swallowed it.
The fisherman presented the sea-creature to the king
and the king to his servant: the ring lay inside the fish.
The stomach received the fish and the hand received the ring.
200 A great miracle: not even when he wished to could he find misfortune!
So it is with me: to my words envy always directs
a malicious look; that is why I was drawn into a profound silence.
This is what the Samian taught me: I have no clear idea
whether tomorrow will end happily or in misfortune.
205 But put a stop to the envy, you remedy for mortals,[7] deliver me
from spiteful tongues, and bring me to your splendour.
There I will worship you with everlasting joys
and from my lips I will sing a song of harmony.
Accept these sounds from my hand that you may have
210 a speaking monument to my silence.

---

[7] i.e. Christ.

# ΕΠΙΤΑΦΙΟΣ ΚΑΙ ΣΥΝΤΟΜΗ ΤΟΥ ΑΥΤΟΥ ΒΙΟΥ

Χριστὲ ἄναξ, τί με σαρκὸς ἐν ἄρκυσι ταῖσδε ἐνέδησας;
τίπτε με τῷδε βίῳ θῆκας ὑπ' ἀντιπάλῳ;
πατρὸς μὲν γενόμην θεοειδέος, οὐκ ὀλίγης δὲ
μητέρος· ἐς δὲ φάος ἤλυθον εὐξαμένης.

5    ηὔξατο, καὶ μ' ἀνέθηκε θεῷ βρέφος· ἀφθορίης δὲ
θερμὸν ἔρωτα χέεν ὄψις ἐμοὶ νυχίη.
Χριστὸς μὲν δὴ τοῖα· τὰ δ' ὕστατα κύμασι βράσθην,
ἁρπαλέαις παλάμαις ἤρκεσα, σῶμα λύθην,
ποιμέσιν οὐ φιλίοισι συνέδραμον, ηὗρον ἄπιστα,

10    χηρώθην τεκέων, πήμασι χασσάμενος.
οὗτος Γρηγορίοιο βίος· τὰ δ' ἔπειτα μελήσει
Χριστῷ ζωοδότῃ. γράψατε ταῦτα λίθοις.

# Epitaph and synopsis of his life[1]

Lord Christ, why have you bound me in these toils of the flesh?
  Why have you subjected me to this painful life?
Of a godlike father I was born and of a mother who was not insignificant. As a result of her prayers I came into the light.
5 She prayed and dedicated me as a child to God.
  A nocturnal vision instilled in me a burning desire for purity.
Christ was responsible for all this, but later I was dashed by the waves,
  snatched by greedy hands, my body crushed.
I fell among uncaring shepherds and experienced treachery.
10  I was deprived of my children and overwhelmed by misfortune.
Such has been the life of Gregory: what remains will be the concern
  of Christ the giver of life. Inscribe these words on my tombstone.

---

[1] *Poem* II.1.92. This poem is composed in elegiac couplets.